More Praise for JAMES L. SWANSON

||||||||||||||||

For *The Deerfield Massacre*

"With his gifts of great storytelling and penetrating insight, James Swanson has given us a compelling account of an unjustly forgotten episode in American history. This is an immersive and memorable book."

—Jon Meacham, Pulitzer Prize–winning author of
And There Was Light: Abraham Lincoln and the American Struggle

"It is easy to forget that America's eastern frontiers were once just as savage as the more celebrated lands of the West. Call it the Wild East—the subject of James Swanson's engaging new book *The Deerfield Massacre*. From a single horrific event Swanson builds an epic, violent portrait of a world most of us have forgotten."

—S. C. Gwynne, author of *Empire of the Summer Moon*

"Acclaimed historian James Swanson's splendid *The Deerfield Massacre* plunges readers into the cauldron of faith, fear, and ferocity that was life in colonial New England. In this galloping work of narrative history, Swanson resurrects the long-forgotten massacre: the fate of the white captives as they fight to survive, and the plight of Native Americans as they struggle to preserve their ancestral lands. Swanson gives both sides their rightful place at the forefront of early American history."

—Peter Cozzens, author of the award-winning *The Earth Is Weeping:
The Epic Story of the Indian Wars for the American West*

"An epic thriller from one of America's most terrifying chapters—when the tomahawk and scalping knife ruled the New England wilderness. James Swanson's brilliant, action-packed story evokes a mysterious and dangerous land haunted by legends of supernatural witches, as well as the real threat of bloody Indian raids. By the end of *The Deerfield Massacre*, readers will think they hear the sounds of tomahawks chopping through their front door."

—Brad Meltzer, author of *The Lincoln Conspiracy* and *The Nazi Conspiracy*

"A wonderful read! James Swanson's eloquent and gripping account of Deerfield's bloody past transports readers across space and time, while critically assessing the town's multiple efforts to grapple with its history. He explores the persistence of colonial memories, and welcomes the inclusion of often-ignored Native American voices and perspectives. From a midnight vigil in a haunting colonial graveyard, a visit to the tomahawk-splintered Indian House door, or a stroll along an icy moonlit river on a cold February night, Swanson evokes disparate and unexpectedly poetic connections. He invites readers to walk with him into, through, and beyond this complicated past."

—Margaret M. Bruchac, professor emerita of anthropology,
University of Pennsylvania, and author of *Savage Kin:*
Indigenous Informants and American Anthropologists

"In this magnificent book, James Swanson brilliantly uncovers the long-forgotten Deerfield Massacre. His vibrant prose transports readers back to 1704, a distant and forgotten America, a period even the Founders would not recognize. In the dead of night, a barbaric attack engulfs a remote outpost on the Massachusetts frontier. At gunpoint, survivors of the slaughter are forced to march through a forbidding, frozen wilderness into captivity. Swanson's thriller-like narrative is an epic tale of survival that keeps readers on the edge of their seats. Highest recommendation!"

—Patrick K. O'Donnell, author of
The Indispensables and *Washington's Immortals*

"A great book! James Swanson hits the trifecta that all popular American historians seek: a gripping and important chapter in the story of our nation; rich and fascinating research; and a propulsive, vividly cinematic sweep that transfixes readers with the physical courage, terrible suffering, and profound hope of those fighting for their lives in early America. Swanson turns the bloodbath into a key flashpoint in early New England and tells an unforgettable story of endurance and survival for the ages, restoring Rev. John Williams to our pantheon of heroes. This is first-rate American history."

—Douglas Brinkley, professor of history, Rice University, and author of
Silent Spring Revolution: John F. Kennedy, Rachel Carson, Lyndon Johnson,
Richard Nixon and the Great Environmental Awakening

For *Manhunt: The 12-Day Chase for Lincoln's Killer*

"A terrific narrative of the hunt for Lincoln's killers that will mesmerize the reader from start to finish just as the actual manhunt mesmerized the entire nation. It is a triumphant book."

—Doris Kearns Goodwin

"Brilliant! Absolutely haunting . . . This historical book is almost impossible to put down."

—Patricia Cornwell

THE
DEERFIELD
MASSACRE

A Surprise Attack,
a Forced March, and the Fight
for Survival in Early America

JAMES L. SWANSON

SCRIBNER

New York   London   Toronto   Sydney   New Delhi

Scribner
An Imprint of Simon & Schuster, LLC
1230 Avenue of the Americas
New York, NY 10020

First Scribner hardcover edition February 2024

SCRIBNER and design are trademarks of Simon & Schuster, LLC

Simon & Schuster: Celebrating 100 Years of Publishing in 2024

For information about special discounts for bulk purchases, please contact Simon & Schuster Special Sales at 1-866-506-1949 or business@simonandschuster.com.

The Simon & Schuster Speakers Bureau can bring authors to your live event. For more information or to book an event, contact the Simon & Schuster Speakers Bureau at 1-866-248-3049 or visit our website at www.simonspeakers.com.

Interior design by Silverglass

Manufactured in the United States of America

1 3 5 7 9 10 8 6 4 2

Library of Congress Cataloging-in-Publication Data
Names: Swanson, James L., 1959– author.
Title: The Deerfield Massacre : a surprise attack, a forced march, and the fight for survival in early America / James L. Swanson.
Description: New York : Scribner, 2024. | Includes bibliographical references and index.
Identifiers: LCCN 2023043320 | ISBN 9781501108167 (hardcover) | ISBN 9781501108181 (ebook)
Subjects: LCSH: Deerfield Massacre, Deerfield, Mass., 1704. | Indian captivities--Canada. | Deerfield (Mass.)—History—Colonial period, ca. 1600–1775—Historiography.
Classification: LCC E197.S936 2024 | DDC 974.4/2202—dc23/eng/20231006
LC record available at https://lccn.loc.gov/2023043320

ISBN 978-1-5011-0816-7
ISBN 978-1-5011-0818-1 (ebook)

In memory of my parents, Lennart and Dianne Swanson, who set me on the path to Deerfield a long time ago.

In honor of John Hope Franklin, Arthur Mann, and Mark Kishlansky, with fond memories of University of Chicago days.

And in remembrance of Joseph Peter Spang III, passionate antiquarian, obsessive collector, and gentleman of the old school who embodied the spirit of Old Deerfield as deeply as John Williams.

One of the pillars of the land . . . he was redeemed from the flames, passed through the wilderness and sea of danger, and . . . reached a temple eternal in the heavens.

—*From an epitaph for the Reverend John Williams, spiritual leader of Deerfield, Massachusetts, 1686 to 1729*

It is no exaggeration to say that Deerfield is not so much a town as the ghost of a town . . . the most beautiful ghost of its kind, and with the deepest poetic and historic significance to be found in America.

—*from "Deerfield, A Beautiful Ghost," an essay written by Conrad Aiken for the Federal Writers' Project of the Works Progress Administration, 1937*

CONTENTS

||||||||||||||||

PART III:
Memory, Myth, and Legend 147

THE
DEERFIELD
MASSACRE

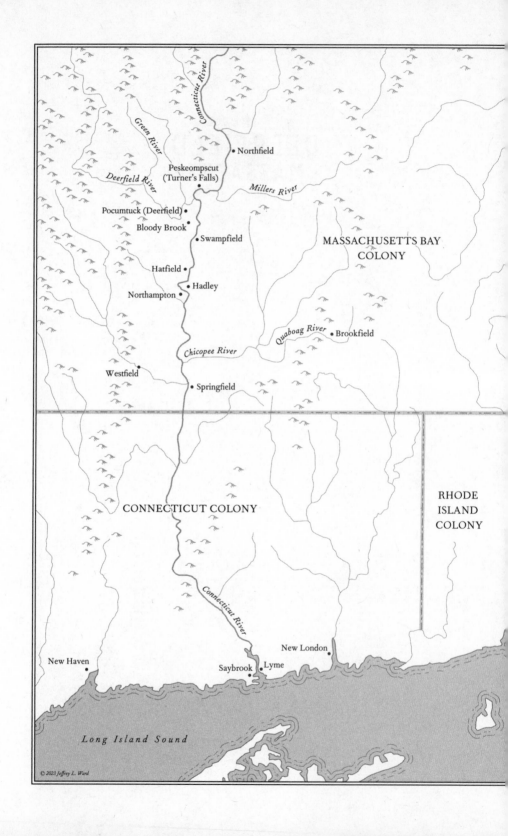

Connecticut River

Green River

Northfield

Peskeompscut
(Turner's Falls)

Deerfield River

Millers River

Pocumtuck (Deerfield)

Bloody Brook

Swampfield

MASSACHUSETTS BAY
COLONY

Hatfield

Hadley

Northampton

Quaboag River

Brookfield

Chicopee River

Westfield

Springfield

CONNECTICUT COLONY

RHODE
ISLAND
COLONY

Connecticut River

New London

New Haven

Saybrook

Lyme

Long Island Sound

© 2023 Jeffrey L. Ward

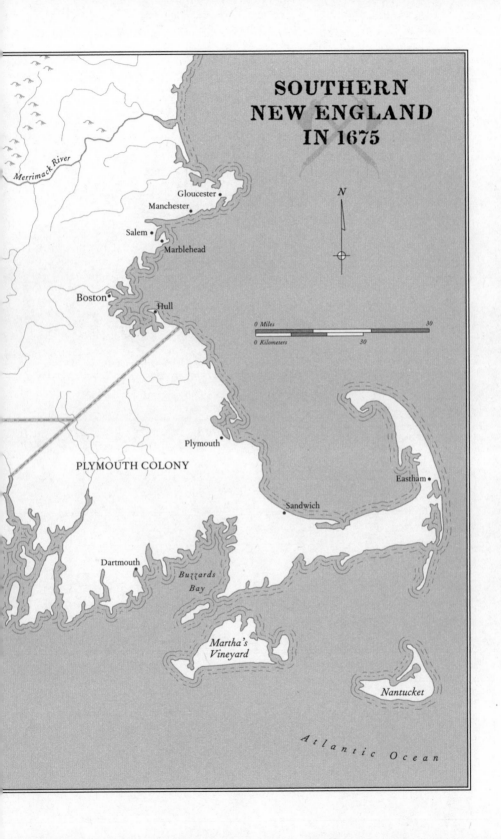

SOUTHERN NEW ENGLAND IN 1675

N

Merrimack River

Gloucester
Manchester
Salem
Marblehead
Boston
Hull

0 Miles 30
0 Kilometers 30

Plymouth

PLYMOUTH COLONY

Eastham

Sandwich

Dartmouth
Buzzards Bay

Martha's Vineyard

Nantucket

Atlantic Ocean

PROLOGUE

||||||||||||||||

Deerfield, Massachusetts, a remote village outpost of three hundred souls on the isolated, northwest New England frontier of a vast, early America. It is 4:00 a.m. on the ink-black predawn of leap year, February 29, 1704.

Outside the wind howls. It whistles around the eaves. Three feet of snow blanket the ground, muffling sounds in the night and drifting high against the tall palisade wall protecting the town. Life on the edge of the English empire is not easy. The town lies on the colony's northern-most outpost—Canada is closer than New York. The people are sur-rounded by a dark and dangerous wilderness, by wolves, and—some believe—by witches. Only recently, Salem discovered in its midst, and put to death, twenty witches for "entertaining" Satan. In faraway Bos-ton, Puritan preachers issue religious polemics. Here, in Deerfield, the people are more concerned with attacks by Indians. They have happened before, and the people live in dread of another one. Still, the snow is deep and the winter fierce. Who would risk an attack in such weather?

The sleeping inhabitants pull their blankets higher and huddle closer to stay warm.

The thud of a tomahawk smashing into his front door in the middle of this wintry, snowbound New England night startles Rev. John Williams awake.

This is the opening moment of the Deerfield Massacre, a forgotten tale of war and empire, life and death, endurance and survival, family and faith, and resurrection and redemption from a long-lost America when the destiny of a continent was at stake.

Deerfield, Massachusetts, lies between the Connecticut and Deerfield Rivers, in the Connecticut River Valley about ninety miles west of Boston. The picturesque town is now a popular tourist destination—a kind of miniature Williamsburg—which delights visitors with its Revolutionary War–era colonial houses stuffed with priceless antiques, a fine collection of early American silver, two museums, educational programs, harvest festivals, and a seasonal crowd of "leaf peepers" who throng to Deerfield to behold gorgeous autumn leaves. During the school year students from the prestigious Deerfield Academy buzz across its pastoral campus. If you go there today, there is little evidence of what made this town famous. That story lies buried below the surface.

Once, it was the most famous episode in early American history. Today, it has been forgotten. In an obscure one-hundred-fifty-year-old museum in this small village in western Massachusetts, there stands what was once the most revered relic from early America: a massive, tomahawk-scarred door that symbolized the notorious Deerfield Massacre. This impregnable barricade, venerated by early Americans as the "Old Indian Door"—constructed from double-thick panels of Massachusetts oak and studded with hand-wrought iron nails to repel the tomahawk and hatchet blades of Native warriors—is the sole surviving artifact from one of the most dramatic episodes in colonial American history: when hundreds of Natives and their French allies swept down from Canada to attack an isolated frontier outpost, burn the town, slaughter its inhabitants, and capture the rest. One hundred and twelve survivors, including Deerfield's fearless minister, Rev. John Williams, were captured and led on a three-hundred-mile forced march through the frozen wil-

derness to enemy territory in Canada. Any captive who faltered on
the way—including women and children—fell under the tomahawk
or war club, leaving signposts of blood in the snow all the way to
New France. The survivors willed themselves to live and endure the
sufferings of their captivity until a miraculous reversal of fortune
brought them home to Deerfield. They rebuilt their town, began
new lives, and told the incredible legend until their end of days. The
Old Indian Door is more than an iconic, antiquarian touchstone that
conjures ancient ghosts. It is a living portal that opens to reveal the
blurry line dividing past from present, and it resonates with hidden
meanings about the origins of the American experience.

The story unfolded in the vast, early America, long before there was
a United States. In 1704, the American Revolution was still seventy-
two years in the future. The idea that the English colonies might one
day rebel against the British Empire and form an independent nation
was unimaginable. George Washington, John Adams, and Thomas
Jefferson had not even been born. Three-quarters of a century later,
by 1776, the Deerfield Massacre was a long distant past in a place that
the Founders would have found unfamiliar, strange, and even alien to
them. This was a vanished New England possessed by fear, superstition, danger, and dread that would have been unrecognizable to the
Revolutionary generation.

Origins

Deerfield was not among the earliest settlements in New England.
Even in the mid-1600s the town did not yet exist. Pocumtuck Natives
and their ancestors had lived on these lands for several thousand years,
until 1664, when the Pocumtuck tribe was dispersed by Mohawks in
a revenge attack. Their village was destroyed, and the few survivors
scattered elsewhere. Long before the arrival of the white man, indigenous peoples had warred with one another in blood feuds over the
centuries. Violence on the land that became New England was nothing
new. To the white English colonists, the vast and fertile landscape of
what would soon become Deerfield appeared uninhabited. Connecti-

cut governor John Winthrop proclaimed New England a *vacuum domicilium*, or "empty dwelling," raw and unimproved for the taking. It was up to settlers to improve this "howling wilderness" by planting crops, building towns, and spreading Christian civilization.

Property rights and the sanctity of land ownership were fundamental to an English sense of justice, order, and identity. Thus, in 1663, the area that would include Deerfield became part an eight-thousand-acre land grant from the Massachusetts General Court to the distant town of Dedham. Much of this frontier was controlled (at least loosely) by Indian tribes. Colonists negotiated to obtain deeds to Native land that the English assumed would convey exclusive title and ownership. The Indians possessed a different understanding. To them, deeds might imply only a right to *shared* use of Native land. For many indigenous people, the meadows, forests, and river held significant memories and attachments. In the beginning, the Natives might have viewed the first white colonists who landed in Massachusetts as curiosities—weak, ignorant, and few in number. The settlers seemed to pose no direct threat to their way of life. Four hundred years ago it was impossible to predict that the European colonists would come to dominate the New World and in time seize it from the Natives, displacing them by disease, demographics, political intrigue, and warfare. Early on, an organized and decisive concerted effort by the Indians could have driven the colonists from their shores. However, by the early 1660s that window of opportunity was closing fast. Tribal feuds, rivalries, jealousies, greed, and shifting alliances between various tribes and the English colonists in New England and the French colonists to the north in Canada—New France—prevented the indigenous peoples of Atlantic North America from casting aside their grievances and forming a united front against their common enemy. If they did not act soon, the chance for that would be lost, perhaps forever.

Along the western frontier of Massachusetts, the English government established a series of small towns—in effect wilderness outposts—that defined the outer reaches of the known world, the borderline between civilization and what they defined as savagery. From the initial settlements in Plymouth, Massachusetts Bay, and Boston, English colonists pushed ever westward into the wilderness for new land and opportunity. Between 1620 and 1670, the government created new towns on the fringes of New England. Deerfield came late, and it was the northernmost. It would lie between the narrow band of English Puritan settlements to the east, the former Dutch colony of New Amsterdam on the Hudson River to the south, and French Canada to the west and the north. Deerfield was closer to French territory than to the English towns of Boston and Albany.

The first English settler in Deerfield—Samuel Hinsdale—arrived in 1669. Documents verify the fact: "Samuel Hinsdale of Hadley in the county of Hampshire having purchased some property in Pocumtuck [Deerfield] in the land granted and laid out to the inhabitants Dedham . . ."

Others followed after the land was surveyed in 1671. Forty-three home lots were laid out on either side of a mile-long, linear street—called to this day "The Street"—running north and south and surrounded by commons and open fields. By 1673 twenty families had settled in Deerfield, lured by the chance for land and prosperity. That year marked the birth of the town's first child—Mehuman Hinsdale. Deerfield applied to the General Court to become an independent town and the request was granted on one condition: "Provided that an able and orthodox minister within three years be settled among them."

The town was located in the midst of the wilderness, a strange, wild, dark, and uncharted place. Deerfield sprouted up on the frontier, on the very western edge of civilization in the Massachusetts colony. On three sides of its framed wood dwellings were open meadows, stretching two miles to the north and south of town, and one mile to the west. Beyond this was thick, unbroken forest. In this region of the colony, the English had spread out across a handful of towns on the northwestern frontier. Paths for horses, carts, and foot traffic were all there was, plus trails and crossroads traveled by

Native Indians, and waters they plied with canoes. While in bitter winter temperatures the streams, rivers, and lakes froze over and created more travel options, communication between distant towns remained difficult. The government in Boston was too small and far away to help much anyway, so everything depended on individual or community effort. In early America, warfare, famine, and disease defined daily existence. This hard life was not for everyone: In the 1630s and 1640s, about one in every six prospective settlers returned home to England in disappointment after failing to thrive in the paradise they had been promised. Conflict was an unavoidable part of life in this era, not just between colonists and Indians, but also between the great English and French powers, whose frequent European wars often crossed the sea to the colonies.

Many New England settlers who had survived into adulthood had lived through at least one such conflict. These experiences shaped their lives, and those of their families and children. Living under a state of siege and a lingering fear of surprise ambush heightened everyday anxiety. No one went anywhere without carrying a musket, even if it was to visit a neighbor. Toiling in the fields was more dangerous. Raiders could spring out from anywhere to seize an unwilling captive.

As a seventeenth-century governor of Massachusetts explained, fighting in America was "very different from the wars in Europe." There were no rules of conduct or gentlemanly behavior on the battlefield. "We have to do," the governor pointed out, "with very numerous barbarous savages within our borders that decline to come to any fair open battle but . . . [are] continually infesting us . . . lying skulking under the covert of horrid thickets, woods, and bushes where it is impractical to pursue them."

Despite the challenges and risks, however, the first residents of Deerfield chose to make this place their home. If the Spanish had come to the New World for gold, God, and glory, the French had come for trade, furs, and the Catholic faith. Why had the English come? They came for religious freedom, but the very name they christened this land—"New England"—reveals that the Puritans wanted to replicate in the New World the culture and way of life of farming villages of rural England. These were ordinary people, not explorers, soldiers, mercenaries, or adventurers. They coveted Deerfield's open land, fertile alluvial soil, and nearby river. The town possessed some of the finest and richest agricultural soil in all of New England. Most people in the town worked with their hands and their muscles and were not ashamed of it. They were not rich, and the promise of cheap land and the opportunity to improve their lives attracted them. They were farmers, not wealthy noblemen. Some practiced trades such as weaving, shoemaking, or barrel-making.

In 1634 William Wood published his influential book *New England's Prospect*, to entice settlers to emigrate from England to North America. Wood praised the quality of the land: "It is for certain the best ground and sweetest climate in all those parts bearing the name of New England." He extolled the richness of the soil and the crops it yielded, the opportunity to own land, and the chance to build a home. As for the Native population, he glossed over them "in a more light and facetious style" because "their carriage and behavior hath afforded more matter of mirth, and laughter, than gravity and wisdom." The seal of the Massachusetts Bay Colony, in a misguided act of historical ventriloquism, depicted a woodcut of an Indian who implored the white man to "Come Over and Help Us." To Wood, who returned to England in 1635, the Indians of New England were literally a laughing matter. If Wood had only stayed a year longer, he would have seen how wrong he was. In 1636, the bloody Pequot War ravaged New England. When the Natives unleashed their bottled-up fury and violence, no one laughed.

Deerfield's first residents had not emigrated straight off the boat, direct from England. Many were second-generation Americans born in New England. Most were not from the other colonies, or even from distant points in Massachusetts. Instead, most hailed from other towns in the vicinity. They knew the area well, "and knew the risks of living on the frontier," but were looking for a new start. Many had experienced legal troubles or other disputes and had been cast out from other towns. Deerfield was populated by a mix of the old families, including original landowners with extended marriage and kinship networks; married couples with young children, who owned their houses and farms; and unmarried single men who worked as laborers.

A second reason to settle in New England—and one more widely known—was to escape religious persecution. It is impossible to understand the story of early America without comprehending the paramount importance of faith and religion to the people of seventeenth-century New England. We live in a more secular age, where God, however defined or identified, may be a distant, abstract figure. But to the English settlers, He was something different. Their God was active in the world and in human affairs on earth. He intervened directly in daily life. Success was a sign of his approval, while misfortune of any kind—sickness, failure, accidents, death, and yes, even witchcraft—was a sign of his displeasure. As the famous Puritan clergyman Increase Mather asked, "Why should we suppose that God is not offended with us when his displeasure is written, in such visible and bloody characters?" In Puritan theology, the only way to heaven was through sustained faith; succumbing to temptation and indifference led to hell. Despite all their sufferings, Puritans believed that a better world awaited them. Their earthly ordeal and fidelity sanctified them, not unlike the story of Moses. Here, the reward was not a journey to a new, promised land, but a return to their old one. Their reward was a community restored and healed.

The French to the north and the English to the south differed over their chosen religion. Thanks to Henry VIII and his Reformation, the English were generally of the Protestant faith. The French, having stayed allied to the Church of Rome, practiced Catholicism. Missionary efforts by the French to convert their Indian allies and English enemies they captured added an additional layer of anxiety and jeopardy to daily life. Natives wanted to possess the physical bodies of those they captured, but the French wanted to possess their souls by converting them to Catholicism.

Daily Life

Life in Deerfield during the 1600s was—as the seventeenth-century philosopher Thomas Hobbes put it—"poor, nasty, brutish, and short." By our standards, most of the residents of Deerfield were poor. They owned their land but little else. Their labor provided enough food for their families to eat, but not much more. Their lives revolved around the never-ending cycle of planting, tending crops, and harvesting enough food to survive.

The first houses were built along The Street. It had once been a trail used by Pocumtuck people to link with other communities, located at a crossroads with an east-west route used by Mohawks and Mohicans. Forty-three neatly surveyed home lots of two to four acres were plotted along the road. Owners had rights to strips of land to farm wheat and corn in the meadows north and south of town, where they also grew hay to feed livestock. They also enjoyed rights to wood lots in the east for firewood and building materials. The first houses were small, single-story dwellings, positioned where the sun could warm them during cold New England winters. They were made of rough-hewn wood with the gaps daubed with clay to keep out wind and weather. These first dwellings gave way to finer frame houses, sided with clapboards and topped with a shingled roof. Windows were rare, given the expense, scarcity, and fragility of glass, and the need for protection—even a thin wall was safer than a window. Most houses were built of pine or oak.

In cold weather these homes would have been dark and damp, thus the need for a constant fire that was also used for cooking. Fires were built to keep burning, with big, foundational logs topped by kindling, sticks, and split logs. If a fire did go out, someone would have to run to a neighbor for hot coals or a lit candle inside a lantern. Or a tinderbox could be used, whereby a musket lock was fired and the sparks from the flint ignited cotton wadding. There were no carpets to keep the floors tidy and warm. Instead, fine white sand might be sprinkled across the threshold to capture dust and dirt and then, once soiled, to be swept out the door. Sometimes the sand would be brushed into beautiful patterns with birch brooms or twigs.

Homes in Deerfield were plain inside and out. Exterior walls, doors, and trim were unpainted—colorful paint was an expensive luxury good then and would not be seen in Deerfield for a generation. Furniture was sparse. Most people boasted a large, carved chest with a lid, in which they could store their few possessions, and a few stools and chairs to sit on. But there was little time during the day to sit and chat. Every home had beds, sometimes shared by several people. Early mattresses—"ticks"—were filled with straw or pine needles. Wealthier families had feather beds, filled with plucked goose or duck down. Box cradles protected infants from cold drafts and rocked them to sleep. Mothers swaddled their babies in tight wrappings and placed them in the long, narrow cradles, where they could not roll on their sides or bend their legs. It was believed that this would make babies develop good posture and encourage them to walk sooner.

A few tradesmen had set up shop in Deerfield, including a weaver, a cooper (who made barrels), and two cordwainers (who made shoes). There were three carpenters and a malster (who brewed and sold beer). More specialized professionals included the schoolteacher, millwright (who managed the corn mill), and one man who was studying medicine. Six men started a business to use local pine trees to make resin and turpentine, used for shipbuilding.

But farming and working the land remained at the heart of Deerfield's existence. Most people owned at least some farm tools—such as plows, sickles, hoes, shovels, rakes, scythes, and harrows—all employed for planting and harvesting, and they shared these implements with one another as needed. Animals were an important part of daily life on the frontier. Oxen and horses were used for farming and transport, and most families owned one or two cows, which provided milk for butter and cheese (and, if they died, meat and leather). Sheep and pigs were kept for wool and meat, respectively.

Every home boasted some cooking and eating tools. A family might own a few heavy iron cooking pots, like a bake kettle, some fire-tending tools, and ceramic dairy pans for milk, cheese, and butter. A bake kettle could be hung over the fire on an iron arm, or set on a bed of coals and covered with more. People ate from wood dishes called "trenchers" rather than formal place settings, although some people had earthenware or pewter plates. It was not until much later that individual forks, knives, and spoons came into common use, let alone rare silver and pewter mugs, tankards, plates, or candlesticks.

"Indian corn," a type of corn native to North America, was the basis of most diets. It was not eaten on the cob, but dried kernels were pounded or milled into flour or meal (cornmeal), which was often used to make "hasty pudding," a porridge made from a mix of cornmeal with milk or water. Protecting this crop—and guarding against widespread starvation—was so important that Deerfield adopted an "insurance policy" against predatory birds that might ruin corn in the fields: "That every householder shall kill 12 Black Birds apiece." If they killed fewer, they were fined. If they killed more, they were paid one pence for each dead blackbird, and four pence for each dead crow.

Wheat was also a popular crop, especially for making bread, while bean porridge was another common meal. Deerfield residents ate little meat, unless they hunted it themselves. Some families ate pork from pigs they raised, but eating beef was almost nonexistent. The town's food supply depended on good harvests. Cold and wet weather could ruin crops, and one year, caterpillars ravaged the corn crop, leaving serious food shortages. Hunger was a part of life in Deerfield.

Puritan families loved their children and, contrary to modern tropes, understood childhood as a separate sphere from adulthood and treated their little ones as individuals. As Anne Bradstreet, the Puritan poet, wrote in the mid-seventeenth century, "Diverse children have their different natures: some are flesh which nothing but salt will keep from putrefaction; some again like tender fruits are best preserved with sugar; those parents are wise that can fit their nurture according to their nature." In frontier farm towns like Deerfield, there was scant time for rest or leisure. But toys were not unknown. Northfield resident Clarissa Field was born blind and in the 1700s was given a special doll with uniquely long fingers that indicated the importance of touch in her sightless world. "Bangwell Putt," as the doll was named, was dressed in fine fashion, including a simple homespun dress and miniature corset. This doll still exists and is thought to be the oldest surviving rag doll in North America.

Like Bangwell Putt, seventeenth-century New Englanders did not own many pieces of clothing. Today the wardrobe of an average American—in quantity and variety—would have astounded anyone in Deerfield. Most people wore the same clothes every day. Women spun wool into thread, and weavers then made it into sturdy cloth for everyday wear. Wool clothing provided warmth and insulation from fierce New England winters.

About one-third of Deerfield residents owned at least one book—most often the Bible. And of course, every family possessed guns and ammunition. A flintlock musket was the de rigueur modern weapon of the day in the late 1600s and early 1700s, along with a supply of lead musket balls and black powder. These weapons were not just for protection against enemies. They were also for hunting game for meat and to kill wild animals, such as wolves, which roamed the thick woods. These predators were so dangerous that the Massachusetts governor offered to pay a one-pound bounty for every wolf killed—in one year Deerfield residents killed eleven of them.

There was almost no specie—or hard cash—in Deerfield and no local bank to hold it. Most people bartered for what they needed. Residents paid their taxes in crops, just as they paid their minister on occasion. Almost everyone in town owed others small debts. More important were the close bonds of support and friendship that developed as this small community worked together for survival.

And what sustained their survival was faith. The real center of the town's life was its church and its religion. Many families had descended from people who had escaped religious persecution in England. They valued their faith and the right to practice it freely. The law required them to attend church on Sunday, when there were two meetings divided by a lunchtime meal. Compared to other New England towns Deerfield was not overly religious. Yet the minister was

the most important person in town and led by example and inspiration. The people paid his salary and also helped work his fields,
harvest his crops, and chop his firewood.

A snapshot of life in Deerfield in the late 1600s could be described
by a memorable phrase that Abraham Lincoln once coined almost two
centuries later to characterize his own humble, colonial ancestry: "the
short and simple annals of the poor."

Part I

A HISTORY OF SUPERSTITION, VIOLENCE, AND MASSACRE

The only two known photographs of "the Old Indian House" (the Sheldon House) before its destruction. Daguerreotypes by William North in 1847 (top) and by Benjamin Popkins in 1847–1848.

1

"DEAR AND DEADLY GRAPES"

||||||||||||

The violence of the Pequot War had preceded the founding of Deerfield by decades. Not until the 1670s did Deerfield find itself immersed in a major conflict. In King Philip's War of 1675, a terrifying and bloody uprising against English colonists throughout New England, Indians from several tribes attacked and destroyed towns up and down the frontier, and ambushed, killed, or captured farmers working in their fields. Children who wandered into deep, dark forests vanished without a trace. It was dangerous and foolish to ever venture outside alone during this era. The theme of "the forest primeval" (in Longfellow's memorable phrase), the metaphor that divides civilization and savagery, has possessed the American mind from the beginning. William Bradford, a Puritan Pilgrim passenger aboard the *Mayflower*, signer of the Mayflower Compact, and longtime governor of Plymouth Colony, reflected upon his journey to the New World in his American literary masterpiece, *Of Plimoth Plantation*. Bradford described a bleak and foreboding wilderness that would come to haunt the colonial mind for generations: "Being thus passed the vast ocean, and a sea of troubles before . . . they had now no freinds to wellcome them, nor inns to entertaine or refresh their weatherbeaten bodys, no houses or much less townes to repaire too, to seek for succoure. . . savage barbarians . . . were readier to fill their sides full of arrows then other wise. And for the season it was winter . . . sharp and violent, and subjecte to cruell and feirce stormes, deangerous to travill to known places, much more to serch an unknown coast. Besides, what could they see but a hidious and desolate wildernes, full of wild beasts and willd men? . . . For summer being done . . . the whole countrie, full of woods and thickets, represented a wilde and savage heiw. If they looked behind them, there was the mighty ocean which they had passed, and was now as a maine barr and goulfe to separate them from all the civill parts of the world."

More than two centuries later, Abraham Lincoln was haunted by a family legend that he had been told as a child, of his grandfather, also named Abraham, whom Indians had ambushed and killed in 1786 while he planted corn with his sons Josiah, Mordecai, and Thomas (the future president's father). The latter two boys ran to their cabin, grabbed a rifle, and Mordecai shot and killed the Indian who was about to scalp his father. In December 1859, five months before he won the Republican nomination for the presidency, Lincoln penned a brief autobiography for Jesse Fell, a political ally who got it incorporated into a February 11, 1860, article in a Pennsylvania newspaper. "My paternal grandfather, Abraham Lincoln, emigrated from Rockingham County, Virginia, to Kentucky . . . where he was killed [in May 1786] by Indians, not in battle, but by stealth, when he was laboring to open a farm in the forest. . . . My father, upon the death of his father, was but six years of age. . . . He removed from Kentucky to . . . Indiana, in my eighth year. . . . It was a wild region, with many bears and other wild animals. There I grew up."

In an earlier letter that Abraham wrote to his cousin Jesse Lincoln on April 1, 1854, he related that the story of his grandfather's "death by the Indians, and of uncle Mordecai, then fourteen years old, killing one of the Indians, is the legend more strongly than all others imprinted upon my mind and memory."

Images like these terrified man, woman, and child and imprinted on the American imagination a generations-long nightmare of the wilderness, the forest, the darkness: the realm of Indians.

Natives could strike by surprise anytime and anyplace without warning. "Fear and distress pervaded the household," an observer wrote, "danger and death lurked in every by-way about the field." This was the way of life in early New England. But the colonists feared one thing even more than Indians and the perils of the wilderness: the supernatural, invisible world of the witches and devils who they believed surrounded them. Through the late seventeenth and early eighteenth centuries, the danger of Indian attacks near Deerfield proved more real and dangerous than hexes, spells, or witches riding broomsticks in the night. But make no mistake. In the late 1600s and early 1700s in New England and Massachusetts a belief in witchcraft was not harmless folklore. Witches were understood to be *real* and *deadly* and could be put to death for their pact with the devil.

The first inhabitants of Deerfield lived in peace with the neighboring Indians until King Philip's War, when the Wampanoag chief Metacom (the English gave him the name King Philip) led a fourteen-month-long rampage against the colonists along the New England frontier. The war shocked the English not only for its savagery, but because Philip's father, Massasoit, had attended the "First Thanksgiving" in Plymouth in 1621. To the English, it felt like a betrayal. To Philip it was payback. The war was the last serious attempt by the Indians to push back the ever-encroaching English off Native lands.

On August 25, 1675, a group of sixty Indians killed James Eggleston, a garrison soldier from Deerfield who was out alone in the fields "looking for his horse." Musket fire gave an alarm, and the townspeople fled to the safety of their fort. On September 1, Natives attacked Deerfield itself. Of about 125 inhabitants present that day, the majority were women and children, with the adult men numbering perhaps thirty. Led by Nipmuck leaders Sagamore Sam and One-Eyed John, a small Indian force killed eight men and burned seventeen outlying houses and barns. A relief force led by a Captain Beers, bearing food and supplies, was sent out, but they were ambushed and slaughtered. By September 6, a second force, commanded by a Major Treat, relieved Deerfield's isolated settlers. Treat also decided to abandon the Northfield garrison and evacuated the hundred-some colonists in a midnight retreat.

Yet Deerfield remained the northernmost outpost in Massachusetts and vulnerable to further attack. Its location in a fertile valley was exposed: Native scouts could survey the town from the heights of the surrounding hills to the east or west. All movements in or out of the fort were under surveillance. On September 12, emboldened Indian forces attacked again, this time during Sunday worship. They had laid an ambush for twenty-some garrison soldiers as they returned to the fort, but the soldiers repulsed them. Outnumbered by the Natives, the townspeople could only watch from inside the safety of their palisade as the enemy burned houses, stole horses, and looted valuable foodstuffs like grain and meat, all in full view of the stranded residents. Two days later, after a storm, rescue forces finally arrived.

But these predations were nothing compared to what would happen next.

By now so many soldiers had concentrated in the Connecticut River Valley that they strained the region's food supply. They needed to be fed. Orders went out to stockpile grain at a central location. Harvests had been poor that year, and food and grain were at a premium. Deerfield was a key supplier of wheat, and the equivalent of three thousand bushels of it languished in the fields there waiting to be harvested. The Natives had not burned the crop, possibly because they planned to collect it for their own use. Major John Pynchon, commander of the colonial troops in the Connecticut Valley, ordered men to go to Deerfield to collect and bag the wheat, and then transport it to Hadley, a temporary military headquarters about twenty miles away.

To transport the food Captain Thomas Lathrop and his company of soldiers traveled from Hadley to Deerfield. Their job was to rendezvous with an ox train of seventeen teams, carts, and drivers. Early on the morning of September 18, Lathrop's men marched down The Street in Deerfield. They loaded the waiting carts with heavy bags of wheat and some household goods—including feather beds—belonging to townspeople who wanted to flee to a safer location. As the caravan left town, the soldiers walked ahead, leading the ox train. The first leg of the route was not long, just two miles through the south meadows and up a rise known as Bars Long Hill. The terrain leveled out to a heavily wooded but flat plain, easing the burden on the oxen, who were already straining from their heavy loads. The weather was good and the sky clear. The road ahead looked safe as far as a man could see, which was not far because a dense forest and underbrush flanked both sides of the path.

After a mile and a half, the caravan approached a narrow spot of marshy swampland through which passed a meandering brook. There was no way that the heavy oxcarts could cross here without getting stuck in the soft muck. Captain Lathrop sought firmer ground. He ordered the wagon train to proceed parallel to the marsh and follow the gurgling brook for one mile, until it reached a spot where the water changed course, turned, and crossed directly in front of them. At this spot Lathrop and his men crossed the brook on foot and paused for the slow-moving carts to catch up.

As they waited, the soldiers looked up and spotted a huge canopy of grapevines hanging above their path. Tempted by the succulent fruit ripening under the sun, they laid down their heavy muskets to pick the fresh grapes.

Distracted, the soldiers failed to notice something hidden in the underbrush and lying low in the thicket, flanking them on both sides of the path, skulking just a few yards from where they stood: Indians. Lots of them. Native scouts had alerted them in advance that the colonists were on the way, allowing plenty of time to plan an ambush. Lathrop had failed to send out his own scouts ahead of the main column, which might have flushed out evidence of a war party massing. The hapless English, oblivious to the trap, stumbled right into it.

A large, combined force from several tribes—estimates vary between six hundred and one thousand warriors—waited for a signal to launch the surprise attack. The Nipmucks were led by Mattamuck, Sagamore Sam, Matoonas, and One-Eyed John; the Wampanoags by Anawan, Penchason, and Tatason; and the Pocumtucks by Sangumachu. The first sign of the attack *was* the attack. The Indians rose up from their hiding places, whooped the war cry, and discharged their muskets at the startled colonists, killing or wounding many with the first volley, before they even had a chance to pick up their own muskets and return fire. The English lucky enough to survive the first volley reached for their arms to return fire. But the Indians moved too fast. Many did not even bother to reload their muzzle-loading firearms. It was quicker to charge a man and kill him with a lightning-fast strike of a tomahawk than perform the methodical procedure to reload, aim, and fire. It might take half a minute—sometimes more—to withdraw the ramrod, ram a black powder cartridge and a ball down the barrel, and prime the firing pan with more gunpowder.

From all sides now, Indians descended upon the unprepared soldiers and teamsters, clubbing them with musket butts, slicing them open with tomahawks, stabbing them with knives, or fracturing their skulls with tremendous blows from ball-headed war clubs. These clubs were fashioned from a single piece of solid wood, some two feet long, with the weighted ball shaped around the natural burl from a tree. Elegantly carved, they were a perfect combination of deadly weapon and work of art. A blow from one was like being struck in the head with a modern baseball bat with the full power of a two-handed swing by a champion batter. These warriors relished close-in, hand-to-hand combat with their enemies. It enhanced their status and reputation for bravery. Without an intervening miracle, the outnumbered and outmatched colonists were, to a man, doomed to die.

Earlier that morning, just a few hours before, some of the colonists had bid goodbye to their wives, their children, and their friends in Deerfield. They assumed that this would be an easy, low-risk mission to deliver food and supplies. Up to the moment before the ambush, they were still thinking about feasting on grapes, not battling Indians. Now they were fighting for their lives. The combined noise of high-pitched war whoops, panicked cursing, booms of musketry, the shouts of hundreds of men, and the agonized cries of the wounded and dying made it almost impossible to hear. Underarmed, with muskets that took too long to reload, they were no match for the fearsome, close-combat weapons that the Natives wielded. At some point the English recognized their fate. They had two options: run or die. Henry Bodwell, from Newbury, was shot in his left arm, so with his right hand he swung his heavy musket as a club to fight his way past several Indians to cover, from which he made his escape to Hatfield. John Toppan, also from Newbury, was shot in the shoulder. Unable to fight, he hid in the woods beside the brook and escaped notice. Another man, Robert Dutch from Ipswich, was shot in the belly but survived because he had been left for dead.

The thunder of so much musket fire traveled far enough to alert Major Mosely and his company of sixty men who had also departed Deerfield, heading in another direction. On the New England frontier, that sound could mean only one thing. Somewhere, not far away, fellow colonists were under attack by the Natives. In the code of the frontier, any man who heard it was honor-bound to march toward the sound of the guns. "Hearing the report which the guns gave to this battel," Mosely wrote, "I came up with a handful of men, though too late."

By the time Mosely and his troops arrived, around ten o'clock in the morning, the crack of musketry had subsided, the shouts and cries had died down, and it was almost over. The bloodied corpses of sixty English colonists lay where they had fallen. Many Natives still tarried on the scene, thieving from the carts hitched to bellowing oxen teams and ransacking the still-warm corpses of the dead. They sliced open the sacks of wheat and spilled the precious content on the ground, where it mingled with the mud. They ripped apart the feather beds and the downy tufts floated like a cloud of winter-white snowflakes until they drifted to earth and stuck to the sticky, blood-drenched bodies of the slain. The rescuers discovered Robert Dutch "sorely wounded by a bullet that razed to his Skull and then mauled by Indian Hatchets, [who] was left for dead by the Savages, and stripped by them of all but skin." Dutch's stomach wound healed with the bullet—and part of his bandolier—still inside his body until three years later, when a surgeon removed them.

Mosely's timely arrival had taken several hundred Indians in the vicinity by surprise in the open. In an instant, he had to make one of two choices for himself and his men: flee the battleground and run for their lives—but risk being chased down and killed off one by one in a running battle with the Natives, a second massacre in one morning—or stand their ground and fight. Some of the Indians recognized Mosely. Confident in their superior numbers, they taunted him in English. "Come, Mosely! Come!" one of them shouted. "You seek Indians; here's enough Indians for you!"

Although the English were outnumbered almost as badly as Lathrop's now-slaughtered command, Mosely ordered his men to attack. They closed ranks into a tight formation and charged. Over the next five or six hours they stood fast and fought back with intense musketry volleys, resisting every attempt to break their ranks and cut them to pieces. Every trooper knew that failure to stay in formation invited a complete massacre. By midafternoon it became obvious that while Mosely's men had fought the Indians to a standstill, they could not drive them from the field. The colonists had fought well and inflicted many casualties, but by now they were exhausted and could not continue the battle much longer. Would New England lose another sixty men, one hundred and twenty in total, in the space of several hours? It looked like Mosely's men, just like Lathrop's, might be annihilated.

Then, another well-timed miracle: A relief force under the command of Major Treat arrived on the field. He had been on the way to Northfield to establish a new military headquarters there for Connecticut forces. His unit of one hundred Connecticut soldiers plus sixty loyal Mohegans under the command of Attawamhod, the second son of Uncas, joined the battle and helped Mosely's men push the enemy back until dark, and the Indians melted into the night, ending the marathon day of combat.

Exhausted and bloodied, the survivors retired to Deerfield, abandoning the dead where they lay. It was too dangerous to wander the ground at night searching for corpses and risk another fatal ambush. The next day, on the morning of September 19, a burial party from Deerfield went back to the place that would forever be remembered and enshrined in New England lore as "Bloody Brook." Here they dug a mass grave in which they laid sixty-four bodies close to the spot where they had fallen, including the "choice company of young men, the very flower of the county of Essex" plus the dead from Deerfield. Nearly three hundred and fifty years later, with their bones resting under a white memorial obelisk carved with each of their names, they lie there still.

Only one resident from the town is known to have survived: John Stebbins, who was "under the command of Captain Lathrop and with him when he and his company were destroyed." Of the seventeen teamsters, sixteen had been killed. In Deerfield alone, eight women had been widowed, and twenty-six children made orphans.

Increase Mather, from the legendary family of influential Puritan divines, rebuked, and even mocked, the victims in his scornful book, *A Brief History of the Warr with the Indians in New England*: "Many of the soldiers having been so foolish and secure as to put up their arms in the carts, and step aside to gather grapes, which proved dear and deadly grapes to them." To the people of Deerfield, the legend of Bloody Brook remained a warning of what might one day befall them.

But the danger was not over. A party of Indians returned to Deerfield and made another assault against the settlement. They traveled north from the scene of the Bloody Brook Massacre until they reached the town. The garrison rebuffed them and stopped them from breaking into the fort. Only some twenty men were in Deerfield at the time, far too few to fight off a larger Native force. The captain in command played a clever trick. When the Indians approached, he sounded a trumpet alarm, as if signaling for help from colonial reinforcements nearby. The ruse worked, and the Indians withdrew, but not before terrorizing the inhabitants with painful reminders of Bloody Brook. The Indians "most insolently braving the garrison of Deerfield . . . hanging up the garments of the English in sight of the soldiers, yet on the other side of the river." These were likely bloodied clothes stripped from the bodies of the dead at Bloody Brook. Perhaps some of the women sequestered in the fort recognized in this ghoulish display some of the bloodstained shirts, pants, and coats worn by their slain loved ones.

King Philip's War raged on. One of the most spellbinding events in the entire conflict happened in February 1676. Natives attacked Lancaster, Massachusetts, just fifty miles east of Deerfield. Mary Rowlandson, wife of the town's minister, was taken captive with her three children, along with twenty-four others. She was carried west to the Connecticut River, then north into present-day New Hampshire. Three months later, after poor treatment and the death of one of her children, her husband ransomed her back for a payment of twenty English pounds. She published an account of her experiences in a book printed in Boston, *The Sovereignty and Goodness of God*. The account became so famous that no complete copy of the first edition survives, just eight pages that had been used as recycled paper in the binding of another book. Examples of the first edition were literally read to death. In writing her memoirs, Mary Rowlandson contributed a pioneering and unique genre to American literature, the so-called "Indian Captivity Narrative." Other such accounts would follow in the future, including, almost thirty years later, one of the most celebrated narratives of them all.

By August 1676, King Philip was dead. Colonel Benjamin Church had led a manhunt for the fugitive warrior that tracked him to Wampanoag lands at Misery Swamp near Mount Hope, where he was shot to death near his hiding place, killed not gloriously in battle, an ending he might have preferred, but by stealth. In a great irony, Philip was killed not by Church, but by an Indian loyal to the English. So the chief who had triggered an uprising that terrorized the colonists, killed many of them, and threatened to drive the white man out of New England met his end not at the hands of a white man, but those of a Native American.

Whites desecrated King Philip's body. They quartered his corpse, decapitated him, and paraded his severed head as a trophy that, to them, symbolized the triumph of white civilization against Indian savagery, and the inevitable conquest of a dark and dangerous wilderness. Philip's head was impaled on a pole in Plymouth, a noxious and rotting symbol of victory. The colonists continued to hunt down many Indians who had fought against them, and took pleasure in putting to death a number of the most prominent Native leaders, many of whom had been tricked into surrendering. But this victory celebration would turn out to be short-lived.

New England lay desolated by the war, which continued with less organized raids and attacks. Twenty-five towns including Deerfield had been destroyed, more than half the English settlement. For the people of Deerfield, recent events proved too much to bear. In the aftermath of

Bloody Brook, it was decided that the town was too difficult to defend. Deerfield was too isolated, and the proximity of Indians too dangerous. Attacked, abandoned, and burned to the ground by Native tribes, Deerfield lay in ruins for several years. But with time, bad memories of the past receded and people recalled what was good about the town. The river still ran its course, the rich soil could still yield fine crops, and while there was a risk perhaps, the colonists hoped that the end of King Philip's War had pacified the Native tribes. Cautious settlers returned to the town in 1682. They included male survivors and widows from the conflict. This had once been their home. They had worked hard to till the soil and establish new lives for themselves, commitments not easy to abandon. John Plympton, who had lost a son at Bloody Brook, returned. So did John Root, with his new wife Mehitable, the widow of John Hinsdale, who had died there too. Benoni Stebbins arrived with his new wife Mary, whose husband had also been killed during King Philip's War.

The end of King Philip's War did not end all bloodshed on the frontier. On September 19, 1677, the Indians returned and ambushed the men at the end of a working day. Root was killed, and others taken captive and merged with another band of captives taken from Hatfield. They were marched to French Canada, where Plympton was burned at the stake, but others, including four-year old Sarah Coleman, were returned.

King Philip might be dead, but that did not end the risk of more raids, killings, captivity, and more. Deerfield still lived in the shadow of violence and death. Despite the danger, John Williams arrived in Deerfield in 1686 as its new minister.

John Williams

He was born on December 16, 1664, in Roxbury, one of the six original towns of the Massachusetts Bay Colony. He was the sixth of thirteen children of Samuel Williams and his wife Theda. His father had come to America from Norwich, England, around 1637 and as an adult worked as a shoemaker and served as a church deacon. As a child young John was tutored by his maternal grandfather, and then graduated from Harvard in 1683 at age nineteen. He decided to follow in his father's footsteps and became a minister just three years later in 1686. He was only twenty-one years old.

It took courage to choose the ministry in Deerfield. This was still a town in a remote part of western Massachusetts, not a bustling village with pretty streets and famous apple orchards like those he'd enjoyed in Roxbury. No, this was the northernmost outpost on an exposed frontier. For good reasons two other candidates had turned down the job before Williams. Deerfield was not a place where most people wanted to live.

By moving to the edge of the frontier, Williams accepted the risk of living on blood-soaked ground. He knew that during King Philip's War the region had seen much violence and desperate battles. He knew that Deerfield had been ravaged before. He knew all about the Bloody Brook Massacre.

Yet this was the place where John Williams decided to settle. Before he arrived, the townspeople had written a postwar description of Deerfield: "We find it hard to live in this iron age, and to come to the year's end with comfort; to tell you that our houses have been rifled and burnt, our flocks and herds consumed, the ablest of our inhabitants killed; that our plantation has become a wilderness, a dwelling for owl and a pasture for flocks." Deerfield's first minister, Rev. Samuel Mather, had quit the town in 1680, leaving the people without a permanent religious leader until Williams accepted the position. In September 1686 the inhabitants offered him a contract. Per the custom of the day, they offered housing, a salary, and other perks:

"That they will give him 16 cowcommons of meadow land with a home that lies on Meetinhouse Hill.

"They will build him a house, 42 foot long, 20 foot long, with a lean-to of the back side of the house and finish said house; to fence his home lot, and within 2 years after this agreement, to build him a barn, and to break up his plowing land.

"For yearly salary to give him 60 pounds year for the first, and 4 of 5 years after this agreement, to add to his salary and make it 80 pounds."

Deerfield's congregation hoped that these incentives would make it hard for him to ever leave town. In addition to the personal danger that he risked from Indian raids, Williams knew that this was not the safest place to start a family. But he married Eunice Mather—cousin to the famous Puritan minister Cotton Mather—a year after he came to Deerfield. Over the next eighteen years they would have ten children (eight of whom would survive their childhood). Although the townspeople built him a fine house shaded by a sycamore tree and enhanced by a spacious barn, John Williams was not rich. The taxpayers paid his salary, but not always in cash, despite what the contract stipulated. Instead, they provided it in wheat, corn, pork, and another essential good—chopped firewood, vital for cooking year-round and lifesaving heat through the freezing winter months. All told, Reverend Williams probably burned several thousand logs annually.

The salary the town owed Williams was often in arrears, but he empathized with their poverty:

> I was moved by certain knowledge of their poverty and distress to abate them of my salary for several years together, though they never asked it of me, and now their children must suffer for want of clothing, or the country consider them, and I abate them what they are to pay me. I never found the people unwilling to do when they had the ability; yea, they have often done above their ability.

Although many in Deerfield subsisted at or below the poverty line, the town tried to improve itself. New roads connected Deerfield to other places. By the 1690s the people had built a sawmill, a cornmill, and a school. An impressive meetinghouse was voted on in 1694 and built the following year. In a competitive fashion, the townspeople decided to match the "bigness" of the nearby Hatfield meetinghouse. Prior to 1698 children were educated in private homes by female teachers like Hannah Beaman. Now the people hired a male headmaster to teach lessons to all children between ages six through ten. Parents had to pay for lessons beyond age ten because that was considered enough schooling for most people.

King William's War

In 1688 another political upheaval across the ocean reached New England. In the home country, the autocratic and Catholic King James II was overthrown by his daughter Mary and her Dutch husband, Prince William III of Orange, in what became known as the Glorious Revolution of 1688–89. This so-called "Bloodless Revolution" gave more power to Parliament and caused political confusion in the colonies, where unresolved issues from King Philip's War created unrest. In February 1690, two hundred or so French and Native allies (Algonquin and Mohawk) destroyed Schenectady, New York, killed sixty people (including eleven enslaved Africans), and took twenty-seven captives (including five Africans) to French Canada. The news provoked a panic when it reached Deerfield. Paranoia about a possible attack was so widespread that the town voted for "a good sufficient fortification made upon the meetinghouse hill," with every resident required to assist in constructing it within ten days' time. Any family whose house was located outside the palisade would be provided with safe lodgings inside the wall. The Indians did not attack as expected, but Deerfield fell victim to another enemy—pestilent sickness. A letter to Governor Bradstreet reported:

> The righteous Lord is sorely visiting these frontier towns at
> present, with sickness by agues and fever, of which many are
> sick and weak and many are carried to their grave. The arrows
> of mortality and death, are flying thick from town to town, and
> from family to family. A hundred persons [are] sick at Deerfield.

Anxiety in Deerfield rose as the war continued. Rumors of an imminent raid were constant, but the assault did not come. By 1693 the people had become desperate and demoralized. The witchcraft hysteria trials in Salem, just over one hundred miles away, had spread the paranoia to Boston. Few dared to plant extensive crops, and harvests were meager and dispiriting. Even worse, a plague of caterpillars had devoured the Indian corn, leaving little behind for hungry humans. It was as though

Deerfield had been cursed by a series of Old Testament plagues. The biblical errand into the wilderness had become a descent into hell.

Seven years after John Williams arrived in town, he learned what a dangerous place Pocumtuck (later renamed Deerfield) could be. On June 6, 1693, Indians caught four women in the fields, out in the open. They were not interested in capturing them alive. Instead, the Indians chased down the widow Hepzibah Wells and her three daughters, struck them in the head with wooden war clubs, knocked them off their feet, and scalped them. Only one woman survived her bloody maiming and recovered. Scalping was not a clean, clinical procedure. It involved cutting a horizontal slice across the victim's forehead below the hairline, grabbing the hair and flap of skin above the cut, and in one violent motion ripping the scalp and its attached hair back and off the victim's head. On the New England frontier, the custom was practiced by Indians and English settlers alike.

On the same day, Thomas Broughton, his pregnant wife, and their three children were ambushed and killed, making the day's total eight dead and one beaten and disfigured. Conflicting reports argued later over who was actually wounded versus killed, but that distinction mattered little. News of the attack terrified the people of Deerfield. It was as though King Philip's War and its cycle of violence had never ended. From this moment on, just like the phases of the moon or the seasons on the calendar, a pattern of periodic violence was woven into life in Deerfield.

A year later, on September 16, 1694, a combined force of Indians and French attacked the fort at Deerfield again. Led by a Frenchman, Monsier Casteen, the war party failed to take the town but wounded two men in the fort, and when they caught a boy, Daniel Severance, alone in the meadows, they killed him. At the schoolhouse, located outside the fort, schoolmistress Hannah Beaman saw the Indians coming. She and her students fled and from the outlying house ran as fast as they could toward the nearest open gate at the fort. The raiders chased, flanked, and shot at them all the way, but the heroic Beaman shepherded her young scholars into the fort safely—and not a moment too soon. Musket balls thudded into the stockade as the gate swung shut. Although musket fire from the fort repulsed the attack, the pattern of violence continued throughout the next several years. There were seven raids or attacks in the 1690s alone.

Almost a year later, on August 18, 1695, Joseph Barnard and a group of men were returning to Pocumtuck from nearby Hatfield. About two miles south of Deerfield, they approached a bridge leading to the south meadows. They had crossed this familiar bridge a hundred times. This day was no different, and everything seemed in order. They did not know it, but several Indians lurked under the bridge, waiting to ambush them. They leaped out from their hiding place, shot and killed Barnard's horse, and wounded him in his hands and body. His friends rescued him and all of them escaped to the safety of the fort, but a few weeks later, on September 6, Barnard died from his wounds.

On September 30, John Pynchon wrote to the governor of Massachusetts to give him "some account of the discouraged state of the Inhabitants." Pynchon warned that the townspeople had seen "many straggling Indians" lurking in the vicinity "since the sudden surprise when Joseph Barnard received his death wound." Pynchon said that he had received a report that six hundred Indians planned to attack Albany, New York, and then Deerfield. The people in Pocumtuck were so afraid of a sudden attack that they were "shy of leaving their fort, or gathering in their corn" because they were not strong enough to defend themselves.

The fear of Indians became so overwhelming that the colonists could no longer tell the difference between a friendly and a hostile one. Thus, the General Court took no chances and announced that any Indian who got too close would be treated as an enemy. It issued a harsh decree: All Indians found within five miles east or twenty miles west of the Connecticut River should be treated as enemies who may be killed on sight. It offered a bounty for Indians taken captive, or for the scalps of those killed: fifty dollars for men and twenty-five dollars for women. For children there was a special bounty: twenty-five dollars for a captured child or twenty-five dollars for the scalp of a dead one.

But gruesome bounties did not deter future attacks. September 16, 1696, saw one of the most violent episodes in Deerfield's history. John

Smead and John Gillett ventured into the woods to hunt for bees, track them to their honeycombs, and collect their sweet nectar. A party of nineteen French Mohawks surprised them and took Gillett prisoner. Smead ran away. The raiders, fearing that he might warn the town, ran as fast as they could to attack Pocumtuck before he could.

It was a "lecture day," a weekday in which residents assembled to hear sermons. On their way there, the Indians came upon the house of Daniel Beldings, within gunshot sound of the fort. Beldings had just returned home from the fields, with his cart still filled with corn. He entered his house, leaving his children outside. The raiders rushed them and took Beldings, his twenty-two-year-old son Nathaniel, and his thirteen-year-old daughter Esther prisoner. Daughter Abigail Beldings was shot in the arm (possibly wounded by someone firing at the Indians) but escaped toward the fort, while her sister Sarah "hid herself among some Tobacco in the chamber and so escaped." Then the raiders killed Beldings's wife and sons Daniel and John, and another daughter, Thankful.

> One of the Mohawks grabbed another son, Samuel, from the cart, but the boy fought back and put up an immense struggle, so that the Indian set him down and planted the edge of his hatchet into the side of his head; he twitched twice or thrice to pull it out and so left him for dead . . . and as he came to himself he looked up and saw [Samuel] running from him. [Samuel] bled considerably and brains came out at the wound and he went into [an amazed] condition toward the fort, til he came to the little bridge where [he] fell off and was carried to Mr. Williams and was so bad as left for dead, but it pleased God his life was spared and his wound would be healed.

This might have been the first time that John Williams had seen a tomahawk wound up close. He could not have foreseen that in a few years he would see many more of them.

The Indians held back, not wanting to come within musket range of the fort, but then decided to rush it anyway. One of them was shot in the thigh, and after firing their muskets and wounding one colonist, they fell back. The colonists came out to pursue them, but after both sides fired ineffective volleys at each other without killing or wounding anyone, the Indians withdrew with their captives, Daniel, Nathaniel, and Esther Beldings, plus John Gillett. John Smead emerged from hiding and returned to the safety of the fort.

In 1698, the people vowed that they would be better prepared the next time the Indians came. That year Ensign John Sheldon built a formidable house near the center of town. Surviving details of its construction—thick walls, spacious rooms, hiding places, a double-thick front door studded with iron nails, and a second floor overhanging the front wall of the large house—all suggest that it was built for defense. The interior was big enough to house several families in an emergency and was meant to be impregnable against an Indian attack. Next door, Benoni Stebbins constructed a large house in similar style. Different from the smaller, typical single-family homes in town, these were more than houses—they were more like single-family, private forts, symbols of civilization in a hostile land.

But for a moment in 1698, Deerfield turned its attentions away from Indian raids and inward to a scandalous, local crime that threatened the harmony and spiritual health of the community.

Martin Smith had settled in Deerfield in 1674, the year before the Bloody Brook Massacre. Smith was a rowdy bachelor, and in May 1674 he was fined twenty pounds for "trying to kiss the wife of Jedediah Strong, on the street." In 1693, the now forty-two-year-old Smith, a widower, married a new and much younger wife, Sarah, and brought her from New Jersey to Deerfield. They did not have much time to establish a life together. That October Martin was captured by Indians and taken to French Canada. Sarah continued to live in their home "ten rods south of the south gate of the fort," without a husband to protect her. A guard was appointed to look after her while he kept an eye on the south end of the fort.

But an unaccompanied young woman living alone in the midst of a remote frontier town surrounded by the wilderness was a tempting target for male attention. On August 4, 1694, Sarah lodged a complaint: Five days earlier, she said, John Evans of Deerfield had been guilty of "attempting to force an unclean act upon her." By many accounts, it was an act of rape. He had been caught during a changing of the guard. This was a Puritan town, and Williams was strict about unclean acts, sexual promiscuity, and out-of-wedlock pregnancies. But Evans escaped the consequences. He was neither arrested for legal punishment nor excommunicated for religious penance. He was not even admonished with a trivial slap on the wrist. This might have been because Sarah was a young woman living alone who had no family and whose husband might never return from Indian captivity. Evans, on the other hand, was a respected member of the community, served on the watch that kept a keen eye out for Indian raids, and had a wife and children.

Sarah moved out of her house and into one occupied by the Wells family. Then her life took a tragic turn. Her absent husband had still not returned from captivity. In 1697, after an affair with a soldier from the garrison, she became pregnant. Some reports claim she tried to induce a miscarriage. In January she gave birth to a baby, "one female bastard child," said the report. The child was found dead, and court documents stated the case against her:

> Being led by the instigation of the devil, between the hours of one and seven o'clock afternoon of the same day, withholding her natural affection, [Sarah] neglected and refused all necessary help to preserve the life of said child, and with intent to conceal her lewdness [Sarah Smith] the said child did strangle and smother.

Smith was arrested in Deerfield and taken to Springfield, where she was imprisoned to await her trial for murder, which was delayed so that her husband, who had recently been freed from Indian captivity, could attend the proceedings. At her trial she pleaded not guilty, but a jury of twelve men found her guilty in one day, sentenced her to death, and ordered her to be hanged the next day. Martin Smith had returned to an unhappy reunion, just in time to see his wife convicted and executed. In Puritan society, a sin or an evil that touched one person necessarily touched the whole community. On the evening of her execution, John Williams delivered a merciless *four-hour* sermon in her presence that condemned Sarah's lustful promiscuity and called her a whore. Proud of his effort, he published the sermon the following year, in 1699. It was over sixty pages long. Not only did he castigate Sarah, he blamed the people of Deerfield "for hiding and concealing the uncleanness of which this poor condemned one was guilty, before she became guilty of murder." Williams's strict theology explained that:

> The wrath of God distresses a land where such iniquities
> abound; wars, impoverishing dispensations, to many families
> and towns, are the effects of God's anger, stirred up or kindled
> by such provocations. Why should you rebel against the
> Lord, and so provoke God to be wroth [*sic*] with the whole
> congregation.

Williams's sermon foreshadowed Hawthorne's *The Scarlet Letter*.

He addressed Sarah as "your soul's well-wisher," hoped that "such a sad example [would] deter others from like abominations." He admonished her to accept the painful punishment of her body (slow death by strangulation) as a prelude to her soul's eternal reward if she agreed to repent and receive God's forgiveness. Williams urged her to "hasten" to Christ. No punishment was meted out to the man who had impregnated her. Sarah did not name him, and if any townspeople knew his identity, none revealed it at the trial. When Williams spoke, Sarah seemed insensible to the proceedings and "the most unconcerned of any" in the audience as "she slept both at the prayer and sermon." The behavior of her newly returned husband Martin, who had to sit there in silence and hear it all, is lost to history. It would not be long before he suffered another tragedy—his own death at the hands of the Indians, who would return to take him again.

Today, John Williams's words sound harsh—even heartless—but his principal concern was not the fate of Sarah Smith, but the safety and spiritual health of the whole community. He believed that sin triggered God's anger, which He displayed in the form of hunger, sickness, misfortune, death, Indian raids, or captivity. Sarah Smith's conduct thus threatened the well-being of every soul in Deerfield; her sins could bring down divine wrath upon them all. As Williams saw it, she *had* to hang to purge the community of evil. His sermon sought to save his flock from earthly dangers as well as eternal damnation.

The hanging of Sarah Smith excited intense public attention, published commentary—and widespread approval. John Williams savored his prominent role in her fate. He could not have foreseen that, four years later, he himself would have great urgency to beg God for the mercy that Deerfield had denied Sarah Smith. But would he—and Deerfield—deserve or receive it?

The Sarah Smith scandal did not diminish Reverend Willams's stature. Since his arrival in 1686, his larger-than-life presence had reassured the people in times of Indian ambushes, raids, scalpings, killings, and the kidnapping of townspeople into captivity. Come what may, he was with them in times of trouble. His steadfast loyalty to the town was one of the reasons that many people stayed in Deerfield. In 1699, Rev. Cotton Mather wrote that the people had exhibited "an extraordinary instance of courage" and that John Williams "deserves the thanks of all this province for encouraging them all the ways imaginable to stand their ground."

One evil that Deerfield did tolerate during this era was slavery. In the 1690s, John Williams owned a "negro servant" named Robert Tigo, who died in 1695. Later, in 1703, Williams would purchase two more enslaved Black people—Frank and Parthena—a couple he would marry himself in June 1703. At least one more person of color—a man named Primus—also lived in Deerfield, either as a slave or a free man. Surviving records provide no further details. African slaves may have been present in the Massachusetts colony as early as 1624, but by the

1670s Boston sailing captains and slave traders had created lines of business to transport enslaved African people to other American colonies. Williams might have purchased Robert, Frank, and Parthena in Boston and then brought them to Deerfield to serve him.

Deerfield in Queen Anne's War

Another European conflict, Queen Anne's War, a squabble about the right of succession to the Spanish throne, broke out in 1702. Known in Europe as the War of the Spanish Succession, it was an argument between France and Spain about who had the right to be the next king of Spain. This war would soon come to New England.

King Louis XIV of France, the "Sun King," wanted to seat his grandson on the Spanish throne and to bring its global empire under French control. The last thing England wanted to see was a more powerful France across the Channel. To prevent this, England allied with Spain against its old enemy. The war skipped a pebble across the sea that made landfall in New England and bounced all the way to Deerfield. New England, where the conflict was called Queen Anne's War (after the English monarch at the time), became a battleground between France and England where the two great powers vied over control of the North American continent. Here the French undertook offensive action to protect their lightly populated and therefore vulnerable territory in New France (Canada and Acadia, today's Nova Scotia). The French riled up their Native Indian allies to war against the English south of the border. They launched raids into New England, hoping to delay or forestall any English sea-based attack on Acadia or Quebec, a real threat because the English navy was much stronger than France's.

The war came to Massachusetts on August 18, 1703, when "His Excellency Joseph Dudley, Captain General and Governour in Chief, in and over Her Majesties Province of the Massachusetts-Bay and New Hampshire in New-England in America, and Vice Admiral of the same," issued a "DECLARATION Against the Pennicooke and Eastern Indians." Dudley accused the Indians of "perfidy and ingratitude" by having "treacherously combined with her Majesties enemies the French." A large, printed broadside stated that the Indians had "appeared in open, actual hostilities, and had Committed sundry Outrages, cruel and inhumane Barbarities, Murders, Rapines and Spoils upon her Majesties good Subjects, and their Estates, surprised and taken away many of them Captive." Dudley proclaimed the Indians "to be Rebels and Enemies against Our Sovereign Lady Queen ANNE, Her Crown and Dignity." He warned that the Indians were now without her protection, and he gave the English carte blanche "to do and execute all Acts of Hostility" upon the enemy.

As early as May 1703, the governor of New York, Lord Cornbury, had sent a letter to Massachusetts governor John Dudley, warning him that Cornbury's Indian spies had informed him that the French planned to send an expedition against Deerfield.

But the French had targeted Maine, not Massachusetts. It would be a war of ambushes and raids. On August 10, French and Indian forces attacked English towns near the coast, mostly in Maine—not the western frontier. That month a force of some five hundred natives and twenty French leaders assaulted the town of Wells, killing twenty-two and capturing seventeen. To the southwest, in Massachusetts, the government took the danger so seriously that it posted a new twenty-pound bounty for every Indian scalp taken. A letter from one official justified the policy, arguing that the Indians behaved like animals: "They act like wolves, and are to be dealt withal as wolves." Given that there was already a bounty for killing wolves, it seemed only natural to extend the policy from killing animals to killing men.

Deerfield's strategic location made it coveted ground during the epic struggle between the two great European rivals. Given the violence that had already happened in Maine, Deerfield might be next. Town leaders insisted that the "fort shall forthwith be righted up," meaning that they voted to rebuild a ten-foot-high palisade fence that had fallen into disrepair surrounding Deerfield's town common. As early as July 1702, the town council had affirmed: "A considerable part of the line of fortification about [Deerfield's] plantation is decayed and fallen down . . . they are apprehensive of some evil designs forming by the Indians, an unwanted intercourse of Indians from other plantations being observed." The stockade was rebuilt. It had several gates to allow for the passage of traffic: people, carts, and a variety of animals. Inside the walls of the fortification were some ten permanent houses and the meetinghouse, which were surrounded with sharpened sticks (not unlike the notorious punji sticks employed by the Viet Cong and North Vietnamese Army during the Vietnam War). The walls of some houses were reinforced with bricks for insulation yet which also prevented penetration by musket balls. The town constructed temporary housing inside the stockade to house those whose homes stood outside.

The threat of another war evoked bloodcurdling memories of the notorious Bloody Brook Massacre that the town had suffered twenty-nine years earlier, during King Philip's War, and of the violence that followed it. Philip was not ancient history. In Deerfield, his terrifying war lived on in the memory of all the people who endured it and survived.

By 1702 the stockade had been rebuilt with a ten-foot-high palisade wall of tall, felled trees, with main gates at the north and south ends of town. The two best-built houses, the John Sheldon and Asa Stebbins houses, constructed like mini-forts with near-indestructible front doors, stood within the palisade. By 1703 some dozen buildings had been erected inside the perimeter, which, all told, could shelter three hundred townspeople and soldiers during an attack. Through the summer of that year rumors reached Deerfield that the French-Canadian government and their Indian allies were getting up an expedition to march south and attack Deerfield. In August 1703 Samuel Partridge, the militia commander of western Massachusetts, wrote to Fitz-John Winthrop, the governor of neighboring Connecticut, that Mohawk spies had told him that "300 of Indians with some French are come out from Quebec in order to come upon New England." Partridge warned that "we are in daily and hourly fear of the enemy's approach, especially at Deerfield." Partridge asked the governor for reinforcements of at least fifty men to defend the Connecticut Valley and its settlers, reminding him that "although we have not seen the enemy in our border yet, there [is] usually little or no time between the discovery of the enemy and their striking their blow."

But why attack Deerfield? It was not a large town, military outpost, or supply depot. It possessed no riches to plunder. The fifty families living there were mostly farmers struggling for subsistence. The answer was simple—location. For the French, raiding Deerfield would be part of an offensive move designed to stop English expansion into the territory of New France, an early volley in a larger war. The French preferred offense, not defense, and wanted to strike the first blow. An attack would also provide French leaders with military opportunities to distinguish themselves, in hope of ennobling their families and receiving praise and patronage.

The governor general of New France, Philippe de Rigaud de Vaudreuil, worried that if he failed to send his Native allies against the English, then the English would instigate attacks on the French by their own Native allies. Keeping Indian allies happy with the support of New France was all-important, and Vaudreuil was willing to go far to ensure their loyalty. Some Native tribes hoped to remain neutral in the forthcoming conflict, although any who lived in the lands between Boston and Montreal soon realized that this was impossible. Other tribes were eager to take sides.

Warring against the English allowed Natives to affirm their allegiance to France, and enjoy its patronage. For the Abenaki and Pennacooks, it was also an opportunity to get revenge against the English for displacing them from their lands in the Connecticut Valley. For others, like the Hurons and Mohawks, a raid was an opportunity to take captives as part of their tradition of a "mourning war." Such wars took place when a tribe needed to replenish itself after a family member had died, or was killed in battle, and the grief of the loss was acute and could not be assuaged. Women of the family could demand the male warriors initiate a raid and take captives to occupy the dead person's place in the community. A captive could also serve another purpose: assuaging the loss by being subjected to ritual torture and death.

Captives were valuable commodities. They could work as servants or slaves. They could be sold to the French as hostages for prisoner exchanges, or even conscripted into the French military. Or they could be ransomed to the English, who were always desperate to rescue their people from Native hands. Taking captives on the New England frontier provided opportunities for valuable political negotiation and hard-cash income. Last, the Indians prized captive girls and young women as eligible brides who could intermarry into the tribe.

Deerfield was the perfect target. It was an isolated, vulnerable outpost. The Connecticut River offered easy access to English territory. From Montreal, a war party could head to Lake Champlain, hike across the Green Mountains, head to Deerfield, and land smack in the middle of town. Deerfield was part of the Massachusetts colony, which was good news for the French and Mohawks because it saved them from attacking the more dangerous New York settlements that were allied with the powerful and ferocious Iroquois League. As the governor general of New France wrote: "Neutrality continues to last with the Iroquois . . . and I will not be the one to break it. . . . I am making no war that could turn them against us, sparing on their behalf the lands of Albany. The lands of Boston are a different story."

The town worried and waited, but the French and the Indians never arrived. Summer came and went without any evidence of danger, and with the approach of fall the townspeople relaxed into the familiar habits and rhythms of their daily lives. John Williams preached his sermons. Tree leaves turned their autumn crimson, yellow, and brown. People began to lay in firewood and supplies to carry them through the coming winter.

Then, in October, the first sign of trouble: A small, surprise raiding party attacked two Deerfield men, Zebediah Williams and John Nims, in the meadows outside the fort while they looked after their cows. The two men fired their muskets to defend themselves, but their bullets missed the Indians, so to avoid being shot to death in return, they surrendered to the Natives, who took them captive. People in town heard the gunfire and raced to the sound. But in the short time it took to get there, Nims and Williams were already gone. They had vanished without a trace, to a fate unknown. Their captivity might have saved their lives, given the fate that awaited Deerfield.

The abduction of Zebediah Williams and John Nims alarmed Rev.

Samuel Stoddard in nearby Northampton, and he proposed a novel plan to Governor Dudley: "The town of Deerfield has suffered much . . . from the Indians: of late two of their young men are carried into Captivity." Stoddard complained that incidents like this demoralized the people. His solution? "Hunt the Indians with dogs." But Stoddard was not suggesting commonplace guard dogs to bark a harmless warning at the enemy's approach. No, he suggested that savage hounds be trained to hunt and kill Indians the way they had already been trained to hunt bears. Bear-baiting had been a popular blood sport in Shakespeare's London, and he had written about it. "The dogs," Stoddard suggested, "would be an extreme terrour to the Indians" who, he lamented, are "not much afraid of us, they know they can take us—and leave us, if they can . . . get out of gun-shot range." Dogs would make it safer for people to live in their houses, work in the fields, or move through the woods. The hounds would also make it easier to track Indians to their hiding places and flush out ambushes. Stoddard conceded that hunting men with dogs might appear, at first, uncivilized. But then he revealed his unvarnished opinion: "If the Indians were as other people are, and did manage their war fairly after the manner of other nations, it might be looked upon as inhuman to pursue them in such a manner. But they are to be looked upon as thieves and murderers, and they do acts of hostility, without proclaiming war, they don't appear openly in the field to bid us battle, they use those cruelly that fall into their hands, they act like wolves, and are to be dealt with as wolves."

Stoddard was angry that the Indians did not fight wars in the conventional way that white European armies did—with massed formations of men in disciplined lines advancing toward each other in open fields and when they got within range—less than one hundred yards—firing volleys of musketry at each other. The Indians had developed and refined their own culture of warfare when fighting each other before whites had ever arrived in New England. That warfare prized stealth, concealment, ambush, and individual combat over the formal European style. In Europe the rules of war were changing, and it would soon be considered ungentlemanly to massacre women and children (although both sides committed such atrocities). Stoddard, and all the New England colonists, judged the Indians guilty of violating their imported rules and norms of civilized warfare. Of course, that did not inhibit the whites from taking the scalps of Indian men, women, and children, or slaughtering them, whenever it suited them.

Stoddard recommended that Dudley set aside money "for purchasing suitable dogs" as soon as possible. He knew what a huge, vicious hound could do to a man. Indeed, it was not unheard-of for a condemned prisoner to be sentenced to a horrific, gruesome death of being torn apart by savage dogs. There is no record that killer attack dogs were bought and sent to Deerfield that fall.

That season Deerfield received multiple warnings that the French and Indians would attack soon. On October 21, 1703, John Williams wrote to Governor Dudley warning him how vulnerable Deerfield was: "I would lay open our case . . . as it is. We have been driven from our houses and home lots into the fort (there are but ten house lots in the fort). Some a mile or two miles [away from town] where we have suffered much loss, we have in the alarms [of ambushes and raids] have been wholly taken off from any business, the whole town kept in, our children of 12 or 13 years and under we have been afraid to improve in the field for fear of the enemy, (our town plat and meadows all lay exposed to the view of the enemy . . .). We have been crowded together into houses to the preventing of indoor affairs being carried on to any advantage . . . and must . . . expend at least 50 pounds to make any comfortable provision of housing if we stay together in cold weather."

Williams complained that the cost of packing almost everyone in town into the limited number of houses and temporary shelters within the palisade would be more than what the town would have to pay in taxes. Deerfield was a poor place and every pound counted.

He lamented that "strangers tell us they would not live where we do for twenty times as much as we do, the enemy having such an advantage of the river to come down on us." Several of Williams's neighbors confided to him that "they would freely leave all they have and go away were it not that it would be disobedience to authority and discouraging of their brethren."

The town petitioned the General Court for support and got a tax break. Normally each Massachusetts town was levied about two hundred pounds to administer the colony. But in 1703 the court exempted Deerfield from the tax—it paid nothing. It was the only town in the colony to enjoy this dispensation. Williams reminded Dudley that the government had abated the taxes in the past, and revealed that he was so moved by the "poverty and distress" of the people that he had abated his salary. Deerfield was so poor, he reported, that its children "must suffer for want of clothing."

He urged Dudley to do all he could for the town because it would not be good "if this place is deserted."

The reverend preached a fatalistic, prophetic sermon exhorting his congregation: "I set apart a day of prayer, to ask God, either to spare, and save us from the hands of our enemies, or prepare us to sanctify and honor him in what way soever he should come forth towards us."

Williams was like an Old Testament prophet who foretold the coming of evil days. Yes, there had been Indian attacks before—King Philip's War, Bloody Brook—and over the years surprise ambushes, killings, scalpings, kidnappings, mysterious disappearances, and more. And arson, slaughtered livestock, theft, and plunder. It was altogether a catalog of blood and destruction from 1675 to 1704.

By the time the cold season of snow and ice arrived, the people had let down their guard again, confident that they were safe. After all, who could possibly imagine raiding Deerfield in the middle of winter? Canada was three hundred miles away. Ice-clogged rivers, frozen ground, deep snows, and bitter cold were natural protections against a winter expedition. Even the savvy Indian fighter John Pynchon concluded that "the approaching winter gives hope of some respite . . . and ease . . . winter will give some security, for in reason no attempt can be made from Canada now at this season." By custom, towns should have been free from attack between November and late March or maybe even early April. By that reckoning, Deerfield should have been safe for another month, from late winter until early spring. To reach the town, the enemy would have to trek across the frozen Sorel River to Lake Champlain, then follow the east side of the lake to the Winooski River, and finally hike through the upper Connecticut Valley. And then, after an attack, they would have to turn around and do it all over again to return home safe to Canada. Furthermore, they would have to tote provisions to feed several hundred warriors on the journey to Deerfield and back, and then extra food for the colonists they hoped to capture. Even with the help of dogsleds and snowshoes it would be a hard expedition. Yes, it was the worst possible time for a French and Indian raid. Which meant it was also the best.

As early as the fall of 1703, Native forces began gathering with their French allies at Chambly in New France to plan an expedition to march south under the command of Lieutenant Jean-Baptiste Hertel de Rouville. De Rouville was a top choice to lead the expedition. His father, Joseph-François, had been a legendary figure in earlier battles against the English and the Iroquois. In fact, he and his eldest son had once been taken captive by the tribe, allowing them to gain firsthand knowledge of Native languages, customs, and methods of warfare. This knowledge, passed down through the family, helped them interact successfully with their current Native allies. Jean-Baptiste had lived near the Abenaki village of Odanak in New France. His experience made him a formidable leader, and his position was even stronger because three or four of his brothers and two of his nephews would join the expedition.

The people of Deerfield did not know it, but forces far away and beyond their awareness or control had set in motion a ticking clock.

On December 3 John Sheldon, Jr. (also known as Ensign Sheldon, an honorary rank), son of John Sheldon, married Hannah Chapin. They rode on horseback—Hannah seated pillion-style behind John—from Springfield to Deerfield, where they took up residence in Ensign Sheldon's large, formidable house located on the town common, inside the palisade.

By late January 1704, a force of well-equipped and well-armed French officers, soldiers, Canadian militiamen (the force included ten colonial regulars of the *troupes de la marine* and about forty Canadian-born militiaman), and 250 to 300 warriors from several Native tribes—Abenakis from Odanak, Hurons of Lorette, Mohawks of Kahnawake, Pennacooks, and Iroquois of the Mountain—departed Canada on snowshoes on an arduous mission to sack Deerfield. Day by day, undetected by English spies, they drew closer. By the night of Wednesday, February 27, the enemy was only twenty-five miles from Deerfield.

And they had not been discovered.

They were too close to town to fire their muskets and hunt wild game, no matter how hungry they were. Unless a few Natives carried bows and arrows—an outdated technology during the reign of the flintlock musket—they did not hunt. Unlikely as it was that the sound of gunfire could travel as far as Deerfield, one shot might ruin the element of surprise on which the success of their mission depended. Soon enough the French and Indians would fire their muskets with abandon, as often as they wanted.

The clock was winding down. It would happen soon, when the greatest saga of terror and death, faith and family, love and loyalty, and survival and redemption in the history of early America would begin.

2

BLOOD IN THE SNOW:
FEBRUARY 29, 1704

||||||||||||

While the French and Indians gave no warning of their approach, eerie, supernatural signs seemed to foretell the raid. "For two or three evenings previous to February 29, 1704," wrote the Rev. Solomon Stoddard, "ominous sounds had been heard in the night," and according to him, "the people were strangely amazed by a trampling noise around the fort, as if it were beset by Indians." The older men recalled similar omens before the outbreak of Philip's War, when "from the clear sky came the sound of trampling horses, the roar of artillery, the rattle of small arms, and the beating of drums to the charge." The people "cowered with undefinable dread" under the shadow of impending disaster; and "asked each other with fear and trembling the meaning of this new and dire portent. They had not long to wait the answer."

According to an early chronicler of Deerfield, "this was the age of superstition. Women were hung for witches in Old England and New, and witchcraft was believed in everywhere." Indeed, just twelve years earlier, from February 1692 to May 1693, a witchcraft hysteria had gripped Salem, Massachusetts. The contagion spread beyond Salem. More than two hundred people in Salem and beyond were accused of "entertaining Satan," and in Salem nineteen were hanged—fourteen women and five men—and one man, Giles Cory, was pressed under a board with heavy rocks piled on it to force him to enter a plea. Cory refused and was crushed to death. The chronicler continued: "Every untoward event was imputed to supernatural causes. Did the butter or soap delay its coming, the churn and kettle were bewitched. Did the chimney refuse to draw, witches were blowing down the smoke. Did the loaded cart get stuck in the mud, invisible hands were holding it fast. Did the cow's milk grow scant, the imps had been sucking her. Did the sick child give an unusual cry, search was made for the witches' pins by which it was tormented. Were its sufferings relieved by death, glances were cast around to discover the malignant eye that doomed it. Tales of events like these, so fascinating and so fearful, sent the adults as well as children to bed with blood chilled, every sense alert with fear, ready to see a ghost in every slip of moonshine, and trace to malign origin every sound breaking the stillness,—the rattle of a shutter, the creaking of a door, the moan of the winds or the cry of the birds and beasts at night."

On the night of February 28, the people of Deerfield tucked themselves into bed, oblivious that encamped two miles north of where they slept, just across the river on the frozen hayfields of Petty Plain, a raiding party that had departed Canada one month earlier and had marched three hundred miles to kill or capture them was about to strike. That was far enough away to avoid accidental discovery by any stray soul venturing out from the town, as unlikely as that might be. The French and Indians had built no campfires that day—the orange glow could be spotted for miles, columns of smoke might stain the sky, and the scent of burning wood could drift impossibly far in the cold, crisp winter air. They spoke in hushed voices, and were careful to avoid making any sharp, accidental clanking sounds of metal striking metal. After sundown, the townspeople had failed to post pickets or vedettes to patrol the surrounding snow-topped fields. Nor had any watchmen been posted outside the palisade to guard the entry gates. Nor did they double or triple the guard inside the walls. No, no one but a single sentinel inside the palisade was entrusted to stay awake and sound the alarm in the event of trouble. As Deerfield slumbered, the fate of three hundred souls depended on that one man. The ticking clock that had started a month ago in New France was winding down fast.

On Petty Plain, a few hours before dawn, perhaps around 3:00 a.m., the raiders fitted their snowshoes, so they could glide swiftly atop the deep snow. They loaded their flintlock muskets and pistols with black powder and bullets, and secured their scalping knives, tomahawks, and war clubs. They packed extra moccasins and snow-shoes, and lengths of rope. The spare footwear was not for them. It was for the townspeople they did not kill and whom they hoped to take alive and march back to Canada as captives. The stiff, heavy, buckled leather shoes that the colonists wore were not suited to hike three hundred miles across snow, ice, and freezing rivers and streams. The rope was to bind the prisoners so they could not slip away.

In town, almost three hundred people slept crammed into the houses and temporary shelters protected by the stockade—up to fifteen people per house. Many felt safer in such close quarters, surrounded by so many people. They ranged in age from the Widow Allison, who was eighty-four, to John French, just four weeks old. That night Deerfield numbered about two hundred and seventy residents, twenty garrison soldiers sent to guard the town and who had arrived just a couple days ago, plus a few out-of-town visitors—two from Hatfield and four from French Canada. A few families still slept in their houses outside the fort, near the north and south ends of The Street.

About an hour before dawn, the raiders moved toward their objective, timing the tramping of their muffled snowshoes to mimic the sound of the gusts of wind. They paused in the meadows under the starlit heavens. They sent a few scouts ahead to confirm that no early birds from town were out and about who might raise a premature warning. It was still pitch-dark.

The main body advanced to the outskirts of town and spotted the first houses at the north end. The French and Indians made no sounds. They did not break down doors, wake and roust the occupants, utter the war cry, or set the houses ablaze. No, this was not their mission. Their target—the fort, its closely built houses, and the bulk of the population—still hunkered down several hundred yards ahead of them, behind the palisade walls. If they attacked the scattered houses outside the fort, they would alert the whole town that Deerfield was under siege. Total surprise was necessary for success. Any premature alarm, even one minute before the attack, would spoil the surprise and give the English just enough time to spring from their beds, dress in a hurry, and grab their muskets for a fight. So the raiders ignored what they saw, and passed over the houses that they encountered on the way to the fort. As on the original Passover from the Old Testament, the French and Indians spared these houses on their way to unleash a massacre. They continued south to the fort. Surprise still favored the raiders: Not a soul had spotted them.

The deep snow had drifted high, almost to the top of the ten-foot-tall palisade that protected the town. In silence, an advance party of Indians scampered up the drift, straddled the palisade, and dropped down to the other side. The soft white carpet softened their landing and muffled the sound. Not even a dog barked. Then they unlocked the north gate. Competing legends describe what happened next. In one account, a sleepy watchman finally spotted the Indians teeming over the palisade, discharged his musket, and screamed "Arm!"—but few people heard the shot or his cry. In another account, the guard had been lulled asleep by a woman singing a lullaby to her restless baby. In another account the guard was simply missing in action. Who knows where he was? In Rev. Williams's ambiguous version, he said only that the watch had proved "unfaithful," a vague accusation subject to many interpretations. Williams never elaborated, assigned responsibility, or named a guilty party. He must have known more, but the rest of the story has remained a mystery for more than three centuries. Whatever happened, the people had no timely warning.

A horde of French and Indians pouring through the north gate split into three columns, each rushing toward a different cluster of homes. War whoops, musket fire, the din of tomahawks and axes chopping on locked doors, and the flames and smoke from burning torches in the predawn darkness startled the disoriented sleepers awake. John Williams recalled that "the enemy came in like a flood upon us . . . they came to my house at the beginning of the onset, and by their violent endaevors to breach open doors and windows, with axes and hatchets, awaked me out of sleep" as twenty Abenaki, Mohawk, and Pennacook

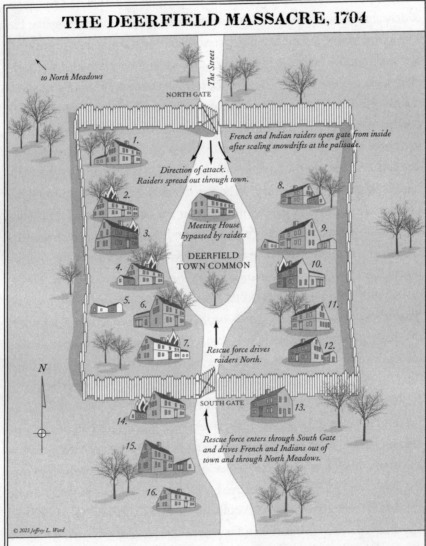

THE DEERFIELD MASSACRE, 1704

to North Meadows

The Street

NORTH GATE

French and Indian raiders open gate from inside after scaling snowdrifts at the palisade.

1.

Direction of attack. Raiders spread out through town.

8.

2.

3.

Meeting House bypassed by raiders

9.

DEERFIELD TOWN COMMON

4.

10.

5.   6.

11.

7.

12.

Rescue force drives raiders North.

N

SOUTH GATE   13.

14.

Rescue force enters through South Gate and drives French and Indians out of town and through North Meadows.

15.

16.

© 2023 Jeffrey L. Ward

1. SHELDON HOUSE. (2 killed, 4 captured, 3 escape)

2. STEBBINS HOUSE. (1 killed, 14 escape, house burned)

3. WILLIAMS HOUSE. (3 killed, 8 captured, 1 escapes, house burned)

4. HAWKS HOUSE. (1 killed, 2 captured, 1 escapes, house burned)

5. TEMPORARY SHELTERS. (In several families 12 killed, 11 captured, 4 escape)

6. HINSDALE HOUSE. (1 killed, 3 captured)

7. RICHARDS HOUSE. (1 captured, 5 escape, house burned)

8. CARTER HOUSE. (1 killed, 7 captured, 1 escapes)

9. FRENCH HOUSE. (1 killed, 7 captured)

10. CATLIN HOUSE. (2 killed, 2 captured, 1 escapes, house burned)

11. FRARY HOUSE. (3 killed, 1 captured, 2 escape)

12. NIMS HOUSE. (7 killed, 4 captured, 1 escapes)

13. SMEAD HOUSE. (unscathed)

14. N. BROOKS. (house burned)

15. J. BROOKS. (unscathed)

16. WELLS. (unscathed)

warriors broke down his front door. He leaped from his bed to barricade it, but he was too late—the Indians had already pushed inside. He shouted to wake a slumbering garrison soldier stationed in his house, but the Indians "with painted faces and hideous acclamations" grappled with the man before he could grab his musket. Williams reached for his flintlock pistol. "Taking down my pistol," he remembered, "I cocked it and put it to the breast of the first Indian that came up; but my pistol missing fire, I was seized by three Indians, who disarmed me, and bound me naked . . . in my night shirt." That misfire saved Williams's life. If he had shot the Indian to death, his comrades might have tomahawked and scalped the minister on the spot. "My pistol missing fire was an occasion of my life's being preserved," Williams conceded. One of the Indians was killed by musket fire coming from a neighbor's house, but there were too many raiders for Williams to escape.

Now the Indians turned on the rest of his family, including his wife Eunice, who had recently given birth. His son Stephen (age ten) was taken by a Pennacook Indian named Wattanummon, while Mohawks claimed his daughter Eunice (age seven) and son Warham (age four). And his daughter Esther (age thirteen), who shared a bed with her sister Eunice, was taken by Abenakis. They were the lucky ones. John (age six) and the new baby Jerusha (six weeks) were murdered on their doorstep by having their skulls smashed in front of their father's eyes, as was Parthena, one of Williams's two slaves, who might have been slain trying to protect the children, or perhaps because she was Black. "Some were so cruel and barbarous," Williams recalled, "as to take and carry to the door two of my children and murder them, as also a Negro woman." The Indians made her husband, Frank, their captive.

Only then was John Williams allowed to dress properly, under careful watch: "They gave me liberty to put on my clothes, keeping me bound with a cord on one arm, till I put on my clothes to the other; and then changing my cord, they let me dress myself, and then pinioned me again." All the while, Natives menaced him with hatchets. Eunice was allowed to dress their remaining children while the fresh blood of her two murdered little ones still flowed across the threshold.

It was time to go. "About sun an hour high, we were all carried out of the house," Williams recalled, "for a march, and saw many of the houses of our neighbors in flames, perceiving the whole fort, one house excepted, to be taken." All around them their town was burning—indeed, his own home was now aflame. "Upon my parting from the town, they fired my house and barn."

The French and Indians rampaged through Deerfield killing or capturing bewildered townspeople as they emerged from their homes, which the raiders then set afire with torches, sometimes even burning them down with the occupants still inside. The English tried to fight back, but this was not an organized, pitched battle. Taken by surprise, the unprepared settlers had no time to mount a proper defense or fight together as a group, or stand in neat lines arrayed in ranks to fire coordinated volleys of musketry. On European battlefields the English army was the best in world at holding the line and firing volleys in massed ranks while under enemy fire. But tonight, no redcoats were stationed in Deerfield. These were civilians and poorly trained militiamen, many of whom had never seen combat before. This was a chaotic melee, not a proper battle. Instead, many heroic individual combats between men fighting in the street occurred that night, as well as multiple assaults on individual homes. Muzzle flashes all over town illuminated the night sky like miniature lightning bolts. According to John Williams, the raiders "immediately set upon breaking open doors and windows" and taking more captives. They burned houses to flush out the occupants and kill or capture them the moment they stepped outside.

A few buildings survived the onslaught, and their occupants escaped. Ebenezer and Elizabeth Brooks and their two children, who lived near the north gate, hurried into their cellar and managed to hide during the raid. Benjamin and Thankful Munn scooped up their infant daughter and hid and survived because their home was not torched. But most members of the Carter and French families were captured almost immediately, and two small children murdered. Almost all the Hoyt, Kellogg, Beaman, and John Stebbins families were taken captive. Sarah Kellogg hid under a washtub in her cellar but had to run outside nearly naked when her house started to burn up around her. House after house fell to the raiders, and before they burned them, they looted them for valuables, money, food, alcohol, blankets, and guns. Then the raiders burned the barns and outbuildings and slaughtered sheep and cows and other farm animals. The French and Indians wanted to leave the survivors—if any—without food or shelter.

But two fortified houses fought back, resisting every effort to capture or burn them down. At Ensign John Sheldon's house, the double-thick front door, fashioned from dense New England oak panels and studded with iron nails, could not be battered down by brute force or splintered by tomahawks and axes. The stout exterior walls of the house were lined with brick and resisted all attempts to ignite them with flaming torches, and there were no big, unshuttered first-floor windows for the enemy to break through. This big house was built like a private fort. The Indians redoubled their efforts and launched another furious assault. The door was then all that stood between life and death for those who had taken refuge in the house. Indians and Frenchmen hacked at it maniacally with their hatchet and tomahawk blades. The defenders heard the chopping—the dull thud of tomahawks striking wood. And the metallic clank of the sharpened blades glancing against iron nails. Sparks flew in the black night when metal struck metal, while the defenders kept up a steady musket fire through portholes and second-floor windows.

The Indians finally chopped a small, irregular hole though the first, outer plank of the door. Then they cut a smaller hole through the inner plank. This breach measured only four by five inches, but it was big enough for them to peer into the house. A raider thrust the barrel of his musket through the hole and fired blindly. The random shot struck and killed Hannah Sheldon (wife of John Sr.) in her bed. But the stubborn occupants continued to hold out. It looked like they might survive this night of terrors—as long as that door held.

But one fainthearted soul inside the house could not stand the terrifying sounds of war whoops and howling voices, nor could he suppress his fear as the tomahawks chopped through the panels. He wanted to flee, but he could not run out the front door. The other occupants would have stopped him—the moment he did, Indians would have rushed in and killed or captured them all, as they did at John Williams's house. But the Sheldon House had a smaller, second door, hidden at the back wall. When no one noticed, the coward—his name and shame have been lost to history—fled through that door—and left it wide open behind him. The Indians discovered the breach and poured into the house. Mohawks took the three older Sheldon children prisoner, but poor Mercy, age two, received none. A Mohawk warrior beat her brains out on the threshold stepstone.

Once the Sheldon House fell, the French and Indians turned their fury to the last house still in the fight—the fortified home of Benoni Stebbins, about thirty yards away in the center of town and next door to the ransacked Williams house. Benoni had been taken captive before, in 1677, the era of King Philip's War, and he had vowed never to become one again. In his house were at least seventeen people: Stebbins, his wife and five children; David Hoyt and his wife and child; Joseph Catlin with his wife and child; Benjamin Church, three other men, and possibly a few additional women and children. The house contained a generous stockpile of gunpowder and musket balls, and the occupants kept up a steady fire, with some of the men shooting more than forty rounds each. This fusillade held the raiders at bay, and even killed a French officer who was second in command of the attack, plus several Indians, including a Mohawk chief. When Indians and French rushed the house in a mad charge to get close enough to set it afire with torches, the English opened fire again and killed three or four more of them. The attackers failed to understand why their musket balls weren't penetrating the exterior walls. The walls were lined with unfired brick for insulation and the balls bounced off.

But the luck of the colonists was running out. Eventually a musket ball found Benoni Stebbins and killed him. He had gotten his wish—the Indians never captured him alive again. Abigail Hoyt and one soldier (possibly Benjamin Church) were wounded and bleeding heavily. In a ruse, the raiders yelled out and offered "good quarter"—a promise to not kill them—if the inhabitants agreed to surrender. It was a lie. The colonists knew that the enraged French and Indians would torture and kill them to avenge the deaths of their comrades. At minimum they would take them all prisoner and march them off to Canada and sell for ransom those they did not kill on the journey. Natives tried again to burn the house. One of the defenders shot down in an instant the first man who ignited the fire—he fell into his own flames and burned to death. Another raider tried to light a fire at the other end of the house, but a colonist spotted him, slipped out the door, killed him with a single well-aimed shot, and dashed back inside to safety.

The Stebbins House could not hold out forever. The occupants had been fighting off the raiders for two and a half hours and were near exhaustion. Then, around 8:00 a.m., a surprise relief force of fifty mounted militiaman under the command of Colonel Partridge arrived from nearby Hatfield and charged through the south gate of the fort. Before sunrise they had spotted a bright orange glow in the sky hanging close to the ground. They knew what it meant. Deerfield was under attack, and its houses and barns were aflame. Even before the handful of people who had fled the raid on foot had run the twelve miles to Hatfield, the men there had already leaped from their beds, hurried to dress, grabbed their weapons, and made haste to save their besieged neighbors. "The light," Partridge wrote, "gave notice to the towns below a long time before we heard news from the distressed people."

It was a brave thing to do. The Hatfield men did not know the size or strength of the Indian force they might face in Deerfield. If the raiders had attacked in overwhelming numbers, as they had at Bloody Brook, the Indians might be waiting to ambush and kill them all. But they had to risk it. They honored the code of the frontier and spurred their horses toward the burning town.

The rescue force arrived at the very spot where the raiders were weakest and most widely dispersed. South of the fort, most of the houses and barns were not burning yet. Partridge's men looked north up The Street and saw Indian and French warriors ransacking and burning homes and rounding up captives closer to the center of town. They saw dead people sprawled across the ground. And they saw many Indians besieging the Stebbins house, which had not fallen. Captain Jonathan Wells, leader of Deerfield's garrison, rallied fifteen local men and five militia to join Partridge's horsemen, and together they charged north up the street. Taken by surprise and out in the open, the French and Indians ran away, dropping much of their plunder as they ran. "When we entered at one gate," Wells recalled, "the enemy fled out at the other." As the Indians quit the town, they slaughtered all the livestock and any other animals they found. Colonel Partridge realized that he had arrived just in time and noted that "if the enemy had liberty but one hour more, doubtless they would have utterly destroyed this place. Thus in the moment God was seen."

The colonists pursued the raiders out of town and across the North Meadows, toward the Deerfield River. Not more than an hour earlier, the enemy had already removed most of the captives from the town to prepare them for a long march ahead. But they were still nearby, probably no more than a mile away, still within reach. The English chased the French and Indian rear guard out of Deerfield and engaged them in a running skirmish through the meadows. The fighting was so fast and furious that the pursuers ripped off their "gloves, coats, hats, waistcoats, jackets, and neckclothes" so they could run faster as they charged ahead. At first, it looked like they might succeed, locate the main body, and free the captives. Indeed, one account reported that "we saw . . . many dead bodies [of raiders] and . . . manifest prints in the snow, where other dead bodies were drawn to a hole in the river."

Wells shouted at his men to restrain their zeal and slow their pace, but they "little minded" his call to retreat. They failed to notice that the French had set up an ambush about a mile from town that outnumbered them by three to one. Wells observed: "The enemy being reinforced by a great number of fresh men, we were overpowered." The colonists ran out of steam. "Our breath being spent," Wells confessed, and "theirs in full strength, the battle was sore against us." He ordered his men to halt the heedless pursuit: "We retreated with caution, facing [the enemy] and firing, so that those [of us] first felled might be defended." It was a disaster. In what went down in legend as "The Meadows Fight," nine English were killed and many were wounded before the survivors withdrew to the questionable safety of the breached fort and the burning town.

Later, the survivors of the Meadows Fight sought compensation for the property they had lost in the skirmish: numerous coats, jackets, hats, gloves, shoes, spurs, and guns.

Another document boasted of the pitiful catalog of so-called "plunder" that the English had captured from the enemy: five guns, six pieces from guns, eight blankets, seven hatchets, five caps, two pistols, two knives, four squalines, one pair of shoes, one pair of snowshoes, one musket case, one powder horn, and one glass bottle. A dutiful scribe listed each item and then wrote down next to each "trophy" the name of the man who had "captured" it. Later the goods were sold for a profit of a little more than sixteen pounds, with the guns fetching the highest prices. The haul was meager treasure given the high price that Deerfield had paid in lives: 9 killed in the Meadows Fight alone; 41 killed in the stockade in town—112 captive prisoners; property lost, destroyed, or burned during the raid. Today, more than three centuries later, no one knows the whereabouts of these relics—if they still exist, the link to their provenance was broken a long time ago. Today a collector or museum would pay an enormous sum for the only known musket or tomahawk carried during the Deerfield Massacre.

The morning light made clear the terrible cost of the raid. A force of over two hundred Indians and fifty French had killed almost fifty townspeople, plus five colonial soldiers and five militiamen. An unknown number had been wounded, some seriously. A few hours earlier Deerfield had contained about three hundred people. Now only 125 remained. The French and Indians did not leave the field unscathed. Twenty-two of the French had been wounded and three killed (about half the French force), and at least seven Indians had been killed and an unknown number wounded.

Deerfield had been devastated. Half the houses and outbuildings had been burned. Even the Stebbins house, which had held out so long, had finally been set ablaze by Indians during their retreat. An estimate of the property lost in the raid totaled some three thousand British pounds, the equivalent of thirty thousand days of work. For many people, the labor of a lifetime vanished in a few minutes of flames and destruction.

Godfrey Nims lost not only his burned house, barn, and all his possessions, but four of his children had been killed and his wife and three other children taken captive. John Williams saw his home burned, two of his children and his African slave woman, Parthena, slain, and his wife and five other children taken captive. All told, one hundred and twelve people, including Williams himself, the first Puritan minister captured during any New England conflict, had all been spirited away. He was to his French and Indian captors the greatest prize of the Deerfield Massacre.

The fires burned for hours. The only way to have extinguished them would have been to organize a fire brigade and draw buckets of water, hundreds of them, from the well all day long and splash the houses. The survivors were too dazed and exhausted to do that. And what was the point? The smoldering houses were too far gone to save. On the town common, two prominent houses stood unharmed. Although the Indians had taken the Sheldon House, they had not set it afire. The Stebbins house, defiant to the end, had survived.

As the raiders hurried John Williams and his family into captivity, Williams watched as the town he had served for eighteen years was ransacked and destroyed. He saw his house burning in the early morning sun. He had time for no more than a quick glance before the Indians took him across the river, "to the foot of the mountain, about a mile from my house, where we found a great number of our Christian neighbors, men, women and children, to the number of an hundred."

The raid had been a great success. The Natives had taken many captives, killed many of the English, and had driven them back at the Meadows Fight. Their own losses had been acceptable. Now they had to complete the second half of their mission, the turnaround; completing the three-hundred-mile trek back to Canada safely while evading pursuers, and with a large number of shocked and traumatized prisoners in tow. The greatest fear that worried the French was that the English might get up an expedition, chase them halfway to Canada, intercept them, and attack during their retreat.

The captives were forced to pause and remove their thin English shoes and put on so-called "Indian stockings" that covered the leg up to the knee, keeping the wearer dry and warm during long journeys. That tipped off the captives that they were going on a long march away from everything they knew, into the strange and terrifying world of uncharted Native territory. They knew that they might never return; they knew that they might not survive.

Half the captives were under the age of eighteen; forty were not yet twelve years old, and twelve of them were under the age of five. Although the Natives prized child captives, they had to be at least old enough to walk, travel, and eat on their own. Those who could not, such as babies, infants, and toddlers, were slain on the spot. Without the ability to walk on their own or eat solid foods such as dried corn or meat, they were especially vulnerable. In this harsh landscape, they could never survive the journey. Rather than abandoning them to a prolonged death in the woods by starvation, Natives chose to kill them quickly. To them it was an act of mercy: to the English, it was savagery. As the captives approached a hilltop, the devastation of Deerfield was laid out in plain view. As John Williams wrote, "We went up the mountain, and saw the smoke of the fires in the town, and beheld the awful desolation of Deerfield." For Williams the sight was God's anger made plain. And the suffering was not over. "And before we marched any further," he wrote, "they killed a suckling child belonging to the English."

Back in Deerfield, the survivors and relief forces from other towns debated what to do next. By the night of the 29th, the same day of the raid early that morning, eighty men had gathered in town, and more were on the way. Some wanted to pursue the raiders right away. But the snow was deep and most of them did not have snowshoes, which handicapped their mobility. The English had not mastered the Native craft of snowshoes or sleds that enabled them to glide above snow and ice and travel fast in winter conditions. The rescuers, by contrast, would have to lumber through the snow, literally walking in the footsteps of their enemies. It would be difficult to catch up to the war party, let alone get ahead of it and flank it to set up an ambush.

Another consideration was the safety of the captives. It was a common practice of Indian raiders to kill their captives en masse if counterattacked by a rescue party. On another occasion, a war party of the French and Pennacooks had taken thirty-seven captives from the village of Pascommuck, but killed nearly all of them when English troops approached. In the February 29 debate about what to do about the Deerfield captives, the majority decided against a rescue mission, even knowing that their families, friends, and neighbors camped out that night, and not very far away.

They decided instead to dampen the fires, salvage what remained, care for the wounded, and count and bury their dead. Firearms from this era inflicted traumatic wounds. The English Brown Bess musket fired a heavy .75-caliber ball at subsonic speed. Unlike a modern supersonic rifle bullet that can pass through flesh and bone, the soft lead bullet from a Brown Bess or its French equivalent could shatter any bone it struck into dozens of untreatable splinters. Amputation was often the best treatment for a shattered arm or leg bone. Otherwise, the wound could become infected, then gangrenous, killing the victim by blood poisoning.

In Deerfield, Samuel Church had been shot through the arm, a wound that would permanently disable him. John Smead was shot in the thigh and his bullet was never removed; he carried it in his body for the rest of his life. Benjamin Church was wounded in the foot, which disabled him for twenty-five weeks according to a petition he filed later, and he was awarded four pounds in compensation. John Bridgman, a garrison soldier, was captured after the English counterattack in the Meadows Fight. Natives severed one of his fingers. "They cut the forefinger of my right hand," Bridgman said. This ritual torture was designed to humiliate and incapacitate male captives. Such a mutilation meant that the subject could never pull the trigger of a musket or draw a bow again, handicapping him for life; Bridgman claimed later that the injury had cost him four months of work, and he was reimbursed seven pounds.

Many casualties in Deerfield had died not from musket, tomahawk, or war club wounds, but had perished by other means. On the morning after the raid, not all the corpses of the dead were found lying out in the open. Survivors and rescuers had to search for the rest. They began to excavate the cellars and underground storage rooms below the smoldering ruins of the houses that the French and Indians had burned. Descending into these dark, smoking caverns to recover human remains traumatized the searchers. Had anyone survived? Would anyone emerge from the wreckage? Some of the bodies were still warm. During the raid a number of people had sought refuge by hiding underground, beneath the fight that raged above them.

That worked for a few townspeople whose houses were not burned. But for others whose homes had been set afire, it proved disastrous. As their houses blazed above them, the occupants were trapped below with no escape. One cellar yielded ten bodies. Most horrifying was the fate of the children. The Nims family suffered terribly; twins Mary and Mercy, age five, and sister Mehitable, age seven, were recorded in a tally of the dead as "burnt in the cellar." As many as sixteen people might have burned to death, or died from smoke inhalation ("smothered" in the vocabulary of the time), including Philip Mattoon's wife and child; John Catlin and his son; Samuel Smead's mother, wife, and their two children; and the entire Hawks family—John, his wife, and their three children, along with Martin Smith, whose wife Sarah had been hanged in 1698 for the murder of her newborn baby.

The trauma of locating, identifying, and burying the bodies of family, friends, and neighbors victimized the survivors again. The Deerfield Massacre was a mass-casualty event that had occurred over the space of two days, a quick series of multiple traumas on the survivors: first, the raid; second, the killings; third, the Meadows Fight; fourth, the kidnapping of more than one hundred friends and neighbors; fifth, locating the dead; and sixth, burying them.

What to do with so many dead? Deerfield was accustomed to the occasional death and funeral of a venerable town elder, and the expected procession of mourners to an open grave in the Old Burying Ground. Or the sudden and sad passing of a newborn child. Childhood mortality rates in colonial New England were much higher than they are today. But almost fifty people dead at once, killed on the same day? How could the town handle so many burials?

The earth in the burying ground was frozen solid, too hard to excavate for multiple graves with pickaxes and shovels. Instead, it appears that the bodies were laid in a mass grave, marked today by a grassy mound of earth that rises at the southeast corner of the Old Burying Ground. Still, it would have been hard to dig such a deep hole in the middle of winter. It is possible that the bodies were stored in cold, ancient, natural caves nearby, until the spring, when the earth was more forgiving.

3

"FELL BY THE RAGE OF YE BARBAROUS ENEMY": ON THE MARCH

‖‖‖‖‖‖‖‖‖

The French and Indians faced their own challenges on the march. In the dreadful winter weather, the party of captors and captives, which included many women and children, could not travel fast. In what might have been acts of compassion or practicality, the Natives carried some of the small children on their backs. According to John Williams, "God made the heathen so to pity our children, that though they had several wounded persons of their own to carry upon their shoulders . . . yet they carried our children, incapable of traveling, in their arms and upon their shoulders." None of Williams's children were slain during the march, but not all Deerfield's children enjoyed that consideration. The motley party did not travel far on the first day. As night fell, the raiders began clearing snow to level the ground and setting up wigwams in which to sleep. From the trees they cut dense branches to make ersatz bedding and insulation from the frozen ground. They doled out a little food to their prisoners, but few had an appetite. Everyone was afraid; many were still in shock, and some were wounded or injured. After the captives had been bound and sent to bed, some of the Indians started drinking the alcohol that they had pillaged from Deerfield. It did not take them long to get drunk. In their inebriated state, they lost control of themselves and murdered Frank, dead Parthena's husband, one of the two enslaved

Black people owned by John Williams. Although exhausted, few of the traumatized captives slept well that night. What would tomorrow bring?

The morning of March 1 dawned cold and miserable. It had been a night of terror and uncertainty. Who among them might die this day? Would a rescue party arrive to save them? Nobody could predict what would happen next. For the French and their Native allies, the raid had been an unqualified success. They had achieved total surprise, won the fight to subdue the town, burned most of it, killed or wounded dozens of people, and captured 112 men, women, and children, about one captive for every three raiders. Their haul included a great prize, Deerfield's important minister and spiritual leader, the Reverend John Williams, and most of his family—after they murdered his two youngest children on his doorstep. The raiders awoke in an ebullient mood, thrilled with their success.

Deerfield welcomed news this morning. More reinforcements had arrived. Now about two hundred and fifty men were in town, equal in number to the French and Indians who had participated in the raid. The surprise appearance of one more man astonished and delighted everyone in town. Joseph Alexander, who had been taken captive during the raid, managed to escape from the French and Indian encampment and bolt home to Deerfield. He revealed that the raiding party was still close and within striking distance—only five or six miles away, on the northern bank of the Deerfield River.

At the raiders' camp, the previous night's alcohol-fueled revelry had turned to rage the moment they discovered that Joseph Alexander had escaped overnight. They were more than angry—now they were afraid. No doubt Alexander had run straight back to Deerfield. What intelligence could he give the troops who had assembled there about the attackers' strength, fitness to fight, supplies, number of dogsleds and teams to pull them, and more? What if the English pursued them with a large force of fresh troops and caught up to them? Alexander could report their last location and the pace of the march. If the colonists moved fast and got ahead of the raiders, they could lie in wait and set up an ambush just like several Indian tribes had thirty years earlier at Bloody Brook.

The captors spoke to John Williams in English and gave him a stern warning: If anyone else escaped, they would burn the rest of the captives alive at the stake. It was a bluff. If a rescue mission was already on the move, it would arrive before the Natives had time to make good on their hideous threat. But the warning worked. For the duration of the march to Canada, no one else attempted to escape.

The French and Natives hurried the captives to their feet and continued their long and cold journey north. To avoid future escapes the prisoners were yanked along by "halters." These would have been looped around a captive's neck, like a dog leash, with a captor holding the other end of the line. One surviving example is decorated with a repeating pattern of three figures, possibly of a captive flanked by two captors. The terrain of northern New England and the territory between Deerfield and New France was daunting—miles of woods, hills, and small mountains, through thick melting snow and cold rain. The raiders rushed the prisoners along, but those without snowshoes—the Indians did not bring enough extras to outfit everyone—found that they could not travel quickly. Anyone unable to keep up was threatened with death.

At last John Williams was allowed to speak to his wife, Eunice. He had not been allowed to see her or any of his children since the raid. Given her weakened condition (she had given birth only seven weeks ago), she was having trouble keeping up with the strenuous pace, so he helped her along. As they walked, they spoke about earthly and spiritual matters. John told her, "It is our reasonable duty to quietly submit to the will of God, and to say 'the will of the Lord be done.'" Eunice knew that two of her children had been murdered in Deerfield, and she had seen some of her friends and neighbors slain along the way. She understood the fate of anyone who faltered.

Eunice confided to her husband that she was too weak to continue much farther. She feared she would never make it. "My wife told me," John remembered, "that her strength of body began to fail, and that I must expect to part with her." She said that she hoped that God would at least preserve his life, and those of some of their children. The reverend recalled that "she never spake any discontented word as to what had befallen us, but with suitable expressions justified God in what had happened." Eunice's passivity might seem shocking to us today. Was she already resigned to her fate? Had she given up? On the other hand, she had listened to her husband's prayers and sermons for seventeen years. She had listened to him preach about the repercussions of God's anger, and the consequences of divine wrath. Did she believe that she was paying that price, and deserved God's punishment? It might appear alien to us that she accepted the possibility of her death with such equanimity. But then, Eunice would have believed that her reward awaited her in heaven, and that her earthly sufferings would be over soon. Is it possible that she desired or welcomed her end? Perhaps the quicker the better.

John did not set down in writing his response to Eunice's statements, whether he accepted them with Puritan stoicism, or if he disagreed and tried to persuade his wife to carry on and struggle to live. When John and Eunice stopped for a short rest, their Indian captors separated them. As they were torn apart, John remembered: "We asked each other for grace sufficient for what God should call us to." In his last sight of her, Eunice was reading a Bible that she had somehow managed to take with her on the night of the raid. It reminded John of happier days, of an image of her poring over the scriptures in their Deerfield home, praying daily and meditating on theology.

After their parting, John and Eunice did not know whether they would see each other alive again. He was now forced to march at the head of the column and help break the path for others. Soon the party crossed a small river, wading through the icy water that rushed above their knees, and then ascended a steep mountain. This was strenuous and backbreaking work, and John begged his captor to let him go back to his wife and help her, but he was denied. As others in the party reached the summit, Williams asked each captive: "What news of my wife?" Eventually someone revealed the truth. "Passing through the above-said river," a fellow captive told him, "she fell down, and was plunged over her head and ears in the water; after which she travelled not far, so at the foot of the mountain, the cruel and bloodthirsty savage who took her slew her with his hatchet at one stroke." It was more than John Williams could bear.

The "desire of my eyes," his beloved wife of seventeen years, almost half of his forty-year lifetime, was dead. He broke down and wept. His callous captors mocked him for his tears. John and Eunice had shared a hard life in Deerfield on their own errand into the wilderness, but they shared good times too. Despite harvest failures, years of Indian ambushes and attacks, and perhaps even the fear that God had abandoned them, there were plenty of times for love and celebration. They had known the joy of having children, raising a family, and cherishing the simple pleasures of a hearty meal, a warm bed, and their delight in togetherness. Outside their home life, they thrived in the town's close-knit sense of community.

That was all over now. That Deerfield no longer existed. John Williams was stranded in the wilderness. Within the last twenty-four hours, he had seen unimaginable horrors and experienced profound heartache. First, his two helpless little children had been murdered while he watched. Then he saw friends and neighbors dragged out of their homes and slain on the street. Then he watched his town burn. Then he, his wife, and his surviving children were taken captive with more than one hundred fellow townspeople and sent on a forced march to an enemy land far from home.

And now his Eunice was dead. What torments might God inflict upon him next? Whatever they might be, Williams vowed to survive. How else could he protect the lives of his motherless children? And how could he stay strong enough in captivity to sustain the faith of his flock in their despair and set an example to inspire the congregation with the will to live?

John fretted about Eunice's corpse. What would happen to her remains? Would her body be devoured by wild animals, as he wrote, "left for meat for the fowls of the air and beasts of the earth?" That outcome would symbolize the meaning of the massacre—the defeat of civilization by an unforgiving, savage wilderness. He lamented that his wife might not receive a proper Christian burial. Unbeknownst to John, a force from Deerfield had tracked the raiders as far as the spot where Eunice had been slain and found her. They carried her body back to town and interred her in the Old Burying Ground not far from the charred skeleton remains of her house. Later, they would erect a gray slate gravestone in her memory. Carved with skulls, bones, and winged hourglasses, it shouts an epitaph that sums up the colonists' view of their Indian foes: "Fell by the rage of ye Barbarous Enemy."

Eunice was not the only casualty that day. Before night fell, the Natives killed two more captives, a newborn baby and an eleven-year-old girl. Williams mourned all three of the day's dead: "My flock . . . a flock of slaughter, many being slain in the town, and so many murdered in so few miles from the town; and from fears what we must yet expect." The uncertainty unnerved the captives. Many wondered when it would be their turn to die from exhaustion, hunger, or the blow of a tomahawk or war club. That night the raiders stripped the captives of their clothes and valuables. Young Stephen Williams, John's young son, lost his "silver buttons and [shoe] buckles." In exchange for their English clothing, which was not practical for the difficult journey ahead, the Indians handed the captives worn and ragged Native clothing, warmer and more suited to the winter. Williams found the trade unsavory—his Indian clothes were swarming with lice. But his troubles that day were far from over. Later that night, before sleep, John Williams and his captor, the Indian who had seized him in his house and taken personal charge of him since the raid, were confronted by another Native possessed by bloodlust. That man demanded the right to kill the minister and scalp him as a war trophy. But Williams's captor had promised to keep him safe, and refused to allow the man bent on murdering Williams to lay a hand on him and dishonor the promise. That was not an absolute guarantee of safety for the rest of the trip—after all, anything could happen in this strange world—but at least John Williams could sleep that night without the fear of being scalped.

It was a cold, brutal journey to Canada. Many of the Natives had been wounded during the raid, and their comrades buried any who died along the way. The Indians killed at least nineteen captives during the march, and women and children were not spared. Indeed, the captors often singled them out for murder because they were the weakest. French officers

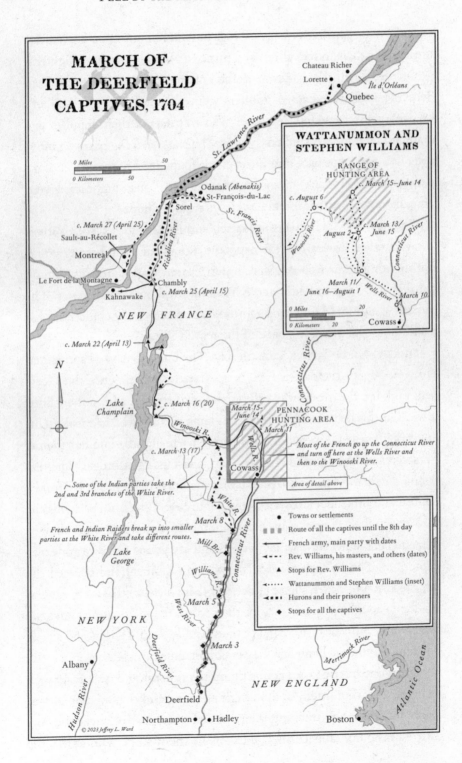

MARCH OF THE DEERFIELD CAPTIVES, 1704

Chateau Richer
Lorette
Île d'Orléans
Quebec

WATTANUMMON AND STEPHEN WILLIAMS

RANGE OF HUNTING AREA
c. March 15–June 14

c. August 6

Winooski River

August 2

c. March 13/ June 15

Connecticut River

March 11/ June 16–August 1

Wells River

March 10

0 Miles 20
0 Kilometers 20

Cowass

St. Lawrence River

0 Miles 50
0 Kilometers 50

Odanak (Abenakis)
St-François-du-Lac
Sorel

St. Francis River

c. March 27 (April 25)
Sault-au-Récollet
Montreal
Richelieu River

Le Fort de la Montagne
Chambly
c. March 25 (April 15)
Kahnawake

NEW FRANCE

c. March 22 (April 13)

N

c. March 16 (20)

Lake Champlain

Winooski R.

c. March 13 (17)

March 15– June 14

Connecticut River

PENNACOOK HUNTING AREA

March 11

Wells R.

Cowass

Most of the French go up the Connecticut River and turn off here at the Wells River and then to the Winooski River.

Area of detail above

Some of the Indian parties take the 2nd and 3rd branches of the White River.

White R.

March 8

French and Indian Raiders break up into smaller parties at the White River and take different routes.

Mill Br.

Lake George

Williams R.

March 5

West River

NEW YORK

• Towns or settlements
▪▪▪ Route of all the captives until the 8th day
— French army, main party with dates
-▲- Rev. Williams, his masters, and others (dates)
▲ Stops for Rev. Williams
····· Wattanummon and Stephen Williams (inset)
▪■▪ Hurons and their prisoners
◆ Stops for all the captives

Connecticut River

March 3

Albany

Hudson River

Deerfield River

Merrimack River

Atlantic Ocean

NEW ENGLAND

Deerfield
Northampton • Hadley
Boston •

© 2023 Jeffrey L. Ward

might have disapproved of the killings but did not possess complete authority over their Indian allies, and turned a blind eye to the slaughter.

On the fourth day, March 3, the column came to a frozen river. Here the Indians executed another woman, a neighbor of Williams too weary to continue. Here they also transferred their supplies and wounded men to sleds pulled by dogs. This allowed the party to move faster at a strenuous pace that the captives found hard to match. Toting a heavy pack on his back, the reverend struggled. "Near night I was very lame, having . . . wrenched my ankles bone and sinews."

The next day, March 4, the French and Indians forced the captives to march even faster. The townspeople, not all of them having warm clothing or adequate shoes, were hungry, tired, and scared, and found it difficult to keep up. Fear and adrenaline could not last forever. The Indians slaughtered four women that day because they could not—or would not—maintain the pace of the march.

Sunday, March 5, was Sabbath day. The entire party—captors and captives—spent the day at rest. It was nearly a week since the Deerfield raid, but the group was still only about fifty miles from the ruined town. On this occasion Reverend Williams was allowed to speak to his fellow captives and preach a short sermon. He chose a familiar theme: Personal sins had aroused God's wrath, and thus their ordeal. The text from Lamentations 1:18, he recited from memory, or perhaps read from a contraband Bible that he carried on the journey: "The Lord is righteous, for I have rebelled against his commandment; hear, I pray you, all people, and behold my sorrow: my virgins and my young men are gone into captivity." The Indians mocked this solemn moment and ordered the congregation to sing a song but derided them because their singing was not loud enough. One can imagine their words to God floating above the bare winter branches and rising to the sky above amid taunts and sneers spoken in a strange language they could not comprehend.

Everyone hurried into action again the following day. The French and Indians were jittery and on high alert, fearful that a colonial war party might still be tracking them. When a few Natives near the outskirts of the march fired their muskets to shoot some wild game, the main body mistook the gunfire for the arrival of a rescue party, panicked, and prepared to slaughter all the captives before the English could free them. "No! Stop!" the hunters yelled; it was only a false alarm. The captives were never allowed to forget that their lives hung daily on the whims of their captors.

On March 7, a week into the ordeal, a young pregnant woman named Mary Brooks stepped into the wigwam where John Williams was confined. Brooks and her entire family—husband Nathaniel, daughter Mary, and son William—had all been taken captive during the raid and their home burned. Brooks had begged her captor to let her visit Reverend Williams with a special purpose in mind: to bid him farewell. Why farewell? he asked. She was young, just thirty-one years old, and appeared healthy enough to continue the journey. But she had lost her unborn baby. "By my falls on the ice yesterday," she explained, "I injured myself, causing a miscarriage this night." Williams recorded their conversation:

"I am not able to travel far; I know they will kill me today." But she assured him: "God has . . . strengthened me to my last encounter with death. . . . I am not afraid of death."

Williams could say nothing to change her mind.

"Pray for me," Mary said, "that God would take me to himself."

Later that day, just as she had predicted—or, in her distressed condition, had longed for?—Mary Brooks was slain by method unknown, either by knife, tomahawk, or war club. Reverend Williams did not specify. The Deerfield Massacre claimed two more lives: Mary's unborn child on March 6, and the next day, her own.

On March 8 the raiding party reached the junction of the White River. Here the main party split into several different groups. One group took John Williams and the majority of the captives toward the Winooski River and the Green Mountains. His son Stephen, held by the Pennacooks, was sent north to the Cowass Natives, and then broke off along the Wells River. Williams wondered if he would ever see the boy again. That night John had to worry about his own life. Another Indian threatened to kill him. It was the same man whom he had tried to shoot in the chest when Natives broke into his bedchamber the night of the raid. "At night [March 8] my master came to me," Williams recalled, "with my pistol in his hand, and put it to my breast, and said, 'Now I will kill you, for' he said, 'you would have killed me with it if you could.'" Williams squelched his fear, knowing that bravery was one of the qualities that Indians respected and valued the most. Impressed by his courage, his captor let him live. It was not a good sign for what was to come.

The next day, on March 9, Williams's "master" separated him and two of his neighbor's children from the rest of the captives. The Native had been carrying six-year-old Elizabeth Hawks, his musket, and a heavy pack (likely containing food, bedding, and other supplies) during the march. Concluding that he could no longer carry this burden for the rest of the march, he decided that something had to go. He chose to keep his pack. He set down the child and killed her. The murder might seem to modern readers barbarous and cruel. The Native who slew the little girl viewed it as a coup de grâce. Rather than abandon her to die by starvation, exposure to freezing temperatures, or wild animal attack, he committed what was to him an act of mercy in a merciless wilderness. One might argue back that he should never have taken a helpless child captive in the first place. Reverend Williams's sole non-Native companion now was Elizabeth's brother, John Hawks, Jr., a scared nine-year-old boy.

On March 12, the Indians holding John Williams and the boy abandoned them to go on a hunting trip, leaving one man to guard them. During the entire march Williams had never been so alone. It was a Sunday and he had plenty of time to reflect upon the past two weeks. If not for the February 29 destruction of Deerfield, the reverend would, as usual, have been in his church standing at his pulpit and delivering a Sabbath day sermon to his congregation. Eunice would have been feeding her new, suckling babe. After the service his children might have frolicked about indoors at home. Yes, spring was coming and its scent was in the air, but it was too early and too cold to enjoy the outdoors yet.

It was then, Williams recalled, that he judged himself a failure. Was the massacre his fault? Could he have done something—anything—to prevent it? To lift this cloud of dejection he thought of several Bible verses to raise his spirits, including Psalm 118:17: "I shall not die, but live, and declare the works of the Lord." He considered his surviving children and parishioners, and how much they needed him. Whatever his earthly sufferings, he served a higher purpose to live not for himself, but for others. He had much for which to be grateful. Each of his children on the march had been well treated by their Native captors. His eldest daughter, Esther, and son Samuel had been ferried across the snow and ice, riding Indian sleighs when they grew too tired to keep walking. His namesake Stephen seemed to be faring well too, and it appeared that the Natives in charge of him had taken a liking to the boy. His youngest son, Warham, was also transported aboard a sled, while his youngest daughter, Eunice, "was carried on all the journey, and looked after with a great deal of tenderness." This careful attention lightened John Williams's burden in the hope that the Indians would continue to treat his family well. The French officers recognized that Williams was an important prisoner and knew that once the captives arrived in New France, the Catholic priests and government leaders there would want to make good use of him. The officers intended to protect his family from any depredations that the Natives might perpetrate against them. Indeed, it is possible that on the night of the raid, Indians might have murdered Williams's two youngest children by mistake without realizing who they were. The same might be true of the killing of his wife, Eunice.

The hunting party returned with good news—they had killed five moose. For three days the group rested to roast, eat, and dry the meat. With bellies full and packs heavy with cured meat, the group continued until they reached a river. Here the Natives removed their packs and pulled them along like little sleds down the river's frozen surface. But the route was not easy. The snow was knee-deep, and breaking through the icy crust with each step shredded the skin of Williams's shins. "My feet were very sore," he recorded, "and each night I wrung blood out of my stockings when I pulled them off." Without access to bandages, he used oak leaves to plaster over the cuts. "My feet were so bruised," he wrote, "and my joints so distorted . . . that I thought it impossible to hold out." By the morning he was in so much pain that he could barely stand up straight.

His Indian master had no mercy for his injured captive and demanded that Williams walk even faster. He refused. "Then," his captor said, brandishing his hatchet, "I must dash your brains out and take off your scalp." The threat was not motivated by malice, but fear. They were on a frozen river and spring was coming. Each day, the temperature warmed. A thaw was coming, and then the river ice would break up and melt. What then? They risked falling through thin ice if they remained on the river's surface too long. If forced to return to a land route, they would have to detour through difficult and dangerous terrain.

His Native master ordered Williams to start out on his own and cover as much distance as possible. But his captor overtook and passed him without speaking a word. Williams walked from dawn to dark, never stopping to eat, instead chewing frozen moose meat, which he carried in his coat pocket. Soon they passed from the river to a large lake, and then into the interior of a forest. There they met a party of Native hunters, who viewed Williams as a novelty and shared their food (moose jerky and dried nuts and cranberries) with him. He lamented that they had no bread. In the three weeks since the raid, the captives had eaten no bread, a main staple of their English diet. As the temperature warmed, Williams faced another problem—lice. The tiny creatures infested his borrowed clothes, and he complained about being unbearably itchy and uncomfortable.

Part II

THE AFTERMATH: CAPTIVITY
AND A TEST OF FAITH

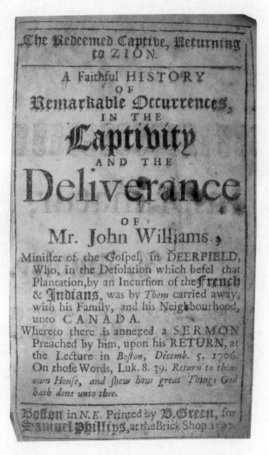

First edition of The Redeemed Captive, *John Williams's
epic account of the Deerfield Massacre and his captivity.*

4

TALES OF CAPTIVITY

||||||||||||||

Finally, almost one month after the attack on Deerfield, John Williams and his Indian master made a canoe from elm bark and rowed to Fort Chambly, on the Richelieu River, about a day's journey from Montreal. It was a French fort garrisoned by many soldiers, and it was there that John Williams would get his first taste of how he would be treated by other Europeans. The rest of the captives trickled into New France as their captors arrived piecemeal and concentrated there.

A new stage of his journey began: captivity in Canada.

Upon their arrival, the Deerfield colonists experienced many different varieties of captivity. They were not confined together in one place, as in a prison. Some lived in Native communities. Some lived with French families, including officers. Children were often separated from their parents to make them more vulnerable to conversion by the Natives to their culture, or by French Jesuit priests to the Catholic faith. A number of the children, especially the youngest among the captives, would soon forget how to speak English and gradually adopt the native tongue.

All shared one thing in common: Their captivity would not be short-lived. The fate and experiences of the captives depended on whether they were held by French or Native masters, and if the latter, on which specific tribe held them. Some Natives wanted ransom money. Others were "mourning tribes" who wanted to replace tribe members who had died with new captives who would, in many ways, assume the identities or the Indians' fallen loved ones. Such Natives were loath to free a captive for any sum of money. Other tribes wanted servants or slaves to do work or help hunt or fish. Natives tried to marry some of the English girls. The Natives were not monolithic. Some were cruel, some were kind. Some had murdered captives along the march, others had not. Some developed genuine affection for their captives.

On the other side, French priests tried to convert captives away from their Protestant faith to the Catholic religion. A French gentleman invited John Williams to his home, fed him a full meal, and gave him a room with a feather bed. He was told all the news, some of it good, and some of it bad. Most importantly, his children were still alive. Every one of them not slain during the raid had survived the march north. But now they were in Montreal, fifteen miles away—so close and yet so far. Two other prisoners from Deerfield informed him that the great bulk of other captives from the town had arrived in Chambly over three weeks ago and had long since passed on to other places. Williams was both relieved and anxious. He was glad to hear that his children had survived, but he was heartsick that they weren't there. He was even more worried because he had already seen several children who had been taken as captives from other New England towns the summer before. Now, in appearance and behavior, they were "very much like Indians." Two young Englishwomen visited him; one had been taken during the last war, and she remembered neither her Christian name nor how to speak one word of English. The other was known to Williams: Her name was Ruth, and she had lived in Wethersfield, Connecticut, some sixty miles south of Deerfield. She had "been often at my house," Williams remembered, yet she was dressed as a Native, and spoke as one too. Worse, both had converted to the Catholic faith, and urged Williams to do so as well. This must have been the reverend's first in-person experience with how quickly the "civilized" English could degenerate into Indian "savages." Even more worrisome, who knew if the process could ever be reversed?

The young were especially vulnerable to conversion to Native culture. In many cases, they were dressed as Natives, fed as Natives, grew their hair like Natives, and were spoken to in Native languages. The youngest of them who were old enough to speak English gradually forgot how to speak their native tongue. They forgot their English Puritan culture. They forgot their friends, forgot their community, and forgot their faith. Those who had learned how to read before their captivity found their skill diminished. There was a gradual, inexorable dwindling of all vestiges of their former lives until they became . . . Indians.

Why did some children do it? The Native life was enticing to some— there was camping out, adventure, fishing, hunting, and wilderness living. There was also less strict discipline than in a Puritan household, especially concerning religion. Finally, many of the young people were cast into a new world without any adult protection or guidance, except that of their captors. Without any European figures to rely on, without parents or guardians, they simply survived the best way they knew how—by adapting. Therefore, Reverend Williams worried about his future, and that of his children, and he was very relieved when word came that they were all moving on to Montreal.

The reverend arrived there, the capital of the French empire in Canada, on April 25, 1704. It had been nearly two months since the attack on Deerfield, and he had spent much of that time marching northward. In Montreal the captives were formally divided among the French and Natives. The French governor Vaudreuil—who had ordered the raid—now "redeemed" John Williams from the Natives, meaning that he bought or persuaded them to give Williams his freedom. This freed him of his Native master, but he continued to be "owned" by the French. Still, it meant that, for the moment, the reverend lodged with Vaudreuil and his family, was given his own room and a set of new European-style clothes.

The governor and his wife were sympathetic to Williams, and they both worked hard to "redeem" all his children as well as other Deerfield residents. His eldest daughter, Esther, was redeemed from her Native masters and "carefully tended in the [French] hospital" until she recovered from "her lameness," possibly injuries she had sustained on the march north. Williams's youngest son, Warham, was also redeemed, by a French gentlewoman living in Montreal. His eldest son taken captive, Samuel, was finally redeemed six weeks after a Montreal merchant purchased the boy, taking "a great deal of pains to persuade the savages to part with him." Williams's son Stephen had been purchased from his Native master with hard currency, but the captor reneged on the deal. It would take another year to retrieve him.

Still, that was nothing compared to the problems of even attempting to visit his youngest daughter, Eunice, then only seven years old, who was stuck with the Mohawks. Vaudreuil ordered a French priest to assist Williams. The priest's parish was near the Mohawk fort, and a letter was sent to the Jesuits at the fort asking to see Eunice. The priests said no: They replied that Williams was not allowed to see or speak with his daughter, or even attempt a visit. According to Williams, the Jesuits wrote that the Mohawks "would as soon part with their hearts as my child."

The reverend took the bad news back to Vaudreuil, exasperated and angered by the behavior of his Indian allies. After several days of negotiations, Vaudreuil went in person with Williams to the fort and demanded that the Jesuits produce the child. Eunice was brought forth, and John was able to speak with his daughter for about an hour. During those precious minutes, Eunice read to him from an unnamed text, which reassured John that she had not forgotten her education, or her catechism. She begged her father to save her from her Indian captors and "bemoaned her state among them."

"They force me to say some prayers in Latin," she complained to her father, "but I don't understand one word of them; I hope it won't do me any harm."

All the concerned father could tell her was not to forget her faith or the scriptures that she had learned by heart. Williams told her that "she must pray to God for his grace every day." But of what use were these Puritan consolations to a scared, seven-year-old girl? What comfort could his urgings provide for a daughter who might have witnessed her mother's murder and who longed for her father's protection in a strange world that she couldn't understand? Why had she been brought to this place where no one spoke her language, and why couldn't she go home?

John Williams left no account of exactly what else he said to Eunice. If she had not already seen it with her own eyes, did he tell her about the deaths of her two siblings in Deerfield? Did she know about her mother's death? Did they talk about it? Did he reveal to her that her older brothers and sisters were alive and not so far away from her? Did they even speak about the past, or were they both too traumatized by the present, and too worried about the future?

The reverend saw Eunice again, a few days later in Montreal. They spent only a few minutes together, and he gave her the "best advice" he could, probably more entreaties to pray well and often, in the Protestant faith, of course.

Governor Vaudreuil tried his best to procure her liberation. He sought a promise to release her if he traded a young Indian captive in return. That gesture was rebuffed. Then he offered hard cash—a hundred pieces of eight, a huge sum of money. This too was rejected. Vaudreuil's wife then went to beg for Eunice's release, in the hope that a woman's tender supplications might secure the desired end. The answer was still no. What else could be done but wait and see if time would ease such hardened hearts?

Two Faiths

In the midst of negotiations for the release of his daughter, the reverend was sent from Montreal to Quebec, where he stayed for seven weeks. In Quebec, the capital of New France, Williams was lodged with the Jesuit community. The Jesuits—members of the Catholic order of the Society of Jesus, founded by St. Ignatius Loyola in 1540—were radical missionaries. They had begun settling in the Americas in the late 1500s, with the purpose of converting Indians to the Catholic faith in an effort to "save souls." Although their initial efforts in Brazil and Florida were failures, they established themselves successfully in "Nouvelle-France." By the 1650s, the Jesuits had installed missions among the Iroquois. Many of these early missionaries were tortured and killed by the Natives, including eight in the 1640s alone. Their hideous sufferings transformed them into legendary martyrs of their faith.

Although small in number—about 320 Jesuits traveled to North America between 1611 and 1764—they were mighty. To advance their mission of saving souls, the Jesuits supported—if not actively influenced—French policy toward the English. The Jesuits rallied Indians to the French flag, and the French in turn supported Natives. One of the most famous Jesuit missions was Kahnawake, near Montreal. The mission's claim to fame was the presence of Kateri Tekakwitha, an Algonquin-Mohawk who had converted to Catholicism at age nineteen and was famous for her piety (so much so that she was formally canonized by Pope Benedict XVI in 2012).

John Williams, a famous and celebrated Protestant minister, abhorred the practices of the Catholic faith. He found them superstitious and unreasonable. For example, one afternoon the people of the town formed a great parade with a holy relic, supposedly the bones of St. Paul. The purpose of this procession was to bring rain, and indeed, it did rain. The Jesuits claimed that God had answered their prayers, whereas Williams replied that God would make it rain when he pleased, with or without any parades.

The Jesuits tried to persuade him to convert to the Catholic faith and stay in Canada. They offered him great sums of money and the promise that he would be reunited with all his children. But Williams held strong—he refused. He knew that converting him would be a great triumph for the Jesuits. If a famous Puritan minister were to renounce the faith, members of his flock might follow his example.

As Williams said to the superior of the Jesuits, "Sir, if I thought your religion to be true, I would embrace it freely without any such offer; but so long as I believe it to be what it is, the offer of the whole world is of no more value to me than a blackberry."

The French mocked him, his faith, and even his country. In Williams's words, "they boasted also of their King and his greatness, and spake of him as though there could be no settlement in the world but as he pleased; reviling us as . . . having no king, but being under the government of a queen . . ."

Soon Williams was sent to another town, Chateauviche, about a day's journey from Quebec. The reason for his continual movement was simple—the French did not want him to spur a rebellion among the English captives. They also did not want him to give them hope of rescue. Although the reverend had been released from Native captors, he was still a prisoner of the French, and they had great things planned.

They offered Williams more bribes and rewards to convert to the Catholic faith and remain in Canada. These offers were becoming ever more elaborate on the part of the French, but they were exhausting to Williams, who kept rejecting them. The French wanted to show off Williams as a trophy, an English Protestant minister who converted to French Catholic ways, so they could hold him up as an example of what other English captives should do. But the reverend refused: "What is a man profited," he asked, invoking Scripture, "if he gain the whole world, and lose his own soul?"

The Catholic priest of the town was courteous to the reverend—while he wished to convert him to what he considered the "true" faith, the priest also admitted that he disliked the French practice of sending Native forces into New England to attack the English settlements there. The priest considered it "more like committing murders than managing a war." In this—if nothing else—the Protestant and the Catholic must have been in full agreement.

Just as Williams started losing hope, he received letters from home, including one from Cotton Mather. It was now October 21, 1704—almost eight months since the Deerfield Massacre. Williams was relieved to learn that his wife's body had been found and properly buried, and that his oldest son, who was away at college at the time of the attack, had been provided for at school by Mather and others. The Puritan leader encouraged Williams to stay strong in his faith and withstand his trials. That was easy enough for Mather to write from the safety of faraway Boston.

Williams was allowed pen and paper, and he wrote not a religious sermon or letter with news, but a poem entitled "Some Contemplations of the Poor and Desolate State of the Church at Deerfield." The poem began with his thoughts about the state of his flock, the residents of Deerfield taken captive in the raid:

The sorrows of my heart enlarged are,
While I my present state with past compare.
I frequently unto God's house did go,
With Christian friends, his praises forth to show;
But now I solitary sit, both sigh and cry,
While my flock's misery think on do I.

Although Williams had once been able to preach in "God's house," to his neighbors and family, now he was isolated in a strange land without the ability to see or speak to those he knew. He was unable to provide comfort or offer advice, or to be the respected and revered leader he had once been.

Williams continued the poem with a review of the raid:

Many, both old and young were slain outright;
Some in a bitter season took their flight;
Some burned to death, and others stifled were;
The enemy no age or sex would spare.
The tender children, with their parents sad,
Are carried forth as captives. Some unclad,
Some murdered in the way, unburied left,
And some thro' famine were of life bereft.

This section of the poem reveals how much of the raid and its aftermath he had seen. He had read no written accounts of the event; in fact, he had not even seen or spoken at length with other Deerfield residents to compare their eyewitness accounts to his. In that "bitter season," Williams had seen much.

But worse than death was the threat of eternal damnation, or in Williams's view, conversion to the Catholic faith.

Crafty designs are used by Papists all,
In ignorance of truth, them to enthrall;
Some threatened are, unless they will comply

In heathen hands again be made to lie.
To some, large promises are made, if they
Will truth renounce, and choose their Popish way.

Through threat or promise, some English captives did convert to Catholicism. Perhaps they felt they had no other choice. Perhaps they found the Catholic faith more uplifting or appropriate in such troubled times. Because he was a longtime Puritan minister steeped in religious theology, conversion was unthinkable to John Williams. For others, the pressure might have proven impossible to resist.

Williams offered a prayer in his poem, beseeching God to intervene and save his flock from such temptations:

O Lord! mine eyes on thee shall waiting be,
Till thou again turn our captivity.
Their Romish plots thou canst confound, and save
This little flock. This mercy I do crave.

He concluded his poem with a wish for better times. "Save us from all our sins," he prayed, "And in thy house again, rest let us find."

What John Williams did not know was that there would be little rest for the weary.

Rescue and Redemption

Just one month after the Deerfield raid, Governor Joseph Dudley had sent a blazing letter to the French governor general in Canada: "You have boasted of massacring my poor women and children," it began, castigating the French for their conduct. But he received no reply. In August, he wrote again, proposing a prisoner exchange. Again, no reply. Unknown to the English officials, neither letter had ever reached Governor Vaudreuil. There was no postal service at this time, and letter carriers could be killed, their packages waylaid or simply lost. Meanwhile, the English had raised the bounty for Indian scalps to one hundred pounds in Massachusetts. To the French, this hardly seemed like evidence of a rapprochement.

Some officials in French Canada thought that the attack on Deerfield had been too brutal and might have violated the rules of civilized warfare. They feared that it might provoke the English to invade Canada in retaliation, which might expand the war throughout all the colonies. Perhaps it might even trigger the siege of Quebec or Montreal. And it might upset the intricate alliances or neutralities that France had cultivated with several Native tribes, which had different interests, motives, and allegiances.

The survivors of Deerfield, and the whole population of Massachusetts, remained preoccupied by one overriding question: How could they rescue the captives? An official military expedition to save the hostages was out of the question. It was beyond the ability and military resources of the colony. There were simply not enough men or weapons. A smaller mission was not practical, either. Even if an expedition did make it into French territory, not all the captives were located in one place. They were not simply locked in a central prison, but rather spread out among many French and Native captors, as John Williams had learned. A rescue mission could neither locate nor save all of them at once, and would endanger the lives of both would-be rescuers and those awaiting rescue.

In fact, any attempt to save the captives by invading French Canada might have triggered a second massacre, a mass slaughter of as many captives as possible. And the English would suffer heavy battle casualties. Invasion would have resulted in a disaster, even worse than the Deerfield raid. Complicating all this was the fact that the French did not have absolute authority over the Indians on the issue of the captives. The French had to treat the Indians as allies and partners, not as masters. They could not simply order them to hand over prisoners under Indian control. The Natives considered the captives valuable assets and often refused to bargain for them.

That left only one option: negotiation. There were only two ways to negotiate: by letter or in person. Neither was foolproof. Letters were often delayed or "lost," and travel was dangerous and time-consuming. Massachusetts and New France did not have ambassadors in each other's cities, so correspondence would have to be initiated by Governor

Dudley in Boston and Governor Vaudreuil in Quebec. But correspondence would take time to go back and forth, and since Governor Dudley's first two letters had not received replies, it did not seem an auspicious route. In addition, letters would not necessarily reveal the condition of the captives. How many more had been murdered like Eunice Williams and all the others who had been killed during the march to Canada? How many were still alive? What was their health? The only way to know was to send a small negotiating party into Canada, deep into dangerous enemy territory.

In December 1704, ahead of the raid's first anniversary, Deerfield residents John Sheldon, Sr., and John Wells made the perilous journey to French Canada. Sheldon had volunteered to lead it. He had a personal stake in the outcome. He had not been wounded or captured during the raid. His front door held, but Indians found the back way in and captured his house by stealth—one of the first homes taken in the raid. But instead of burning it, they used it as a depot to collect captives. One of the unanswered questions about the massacre is, where was John Sheldon? One might expect that he was at home with his family that night, but no evidence proves that he was there. He was listed neither as wounded nor captured, and no records confirm his participation in the Meadows Fight. Later, a descendant claimed that Ensign Sheldon was "not at home" that evening. So the mystery endures. Three of his children and his daughter-in-law were now captives. Mary (age sixteen), Ebenezer (age twelve), and Remembrance (age eleven) had all been marched to French Canada, as had his son's wife Hannah, who had injured her leg jumping from a second-story window on the night of the raid. Sheldon's wife Mary had been shot to death by an Indian who thrust his musket barrel into the hole chopped through the front door and fired blindly. His daughter Mercy had been murdered on their doorstep, and her husband, Joseph Catlin, was killed in the Meadows Fight following the raid. Yes, John Sheldon had plenty of reasons to undertake this dangerous mission.

Sheldon and Wells went to Boston, where they received Dudley's blessing, and joined up with Captain John Livingstone, a noted scout and guide. He agreed to take them into French Canada for the sum of one hundred pounds plus expenses—far more than Reverend Williams earned in a whole year. Livingstone proposed to head west to Albany, and then due north, because he knew "the way thither from the upper towns . . . which he accounted to be more safe than to travail through the eastern country."

Accompanied by Livingstone and Wells, the latter of whom had seen his mother captured and his sister killed during the raid, Sheldon undertook the hazardous journey into enemy territory. They scaled the Hoosac mountains, then traveled past Lakes George and Champlain, and finally down the St. Lawrence River to Quebec. There was no such thing as a flag of truce. The Englishmen risked death if they encountered a Native war party that wanted their scalps. Natives might take them hostage and add them as prize trophies to their collection of captives. It had been brave of Sheldon to volunteer for the job. Several years before the attack on Deerfield he had once been taken captive by Natives. He was pushing his luck. This time, he might never return.

It was a hard journey, over snow and ice. The men used snowshoes, thus adopting Native technology. These were constructed by using basket-weaving techniques to make a "racket tied to each foot." They had no idea what to expect. Would Indians kill or capture them along their journey? Would the French even meet with them? Could they get a glimpse of the captives—see them and talk to them? Sheldon and Wells made it to Quebec by late winter and met with Governor Vaudreuil, handing over letters and proposals they carried from Governor Dudley. These documents informed Vaudreuil that Massachusetts possessed about one hundred and fifty French prisoners whom Dudley offered as bait in exchange for English captives.

The good news was that both men were also able to see John Williams. Sheldon learned that his children were also still alive. But the bad news was that Wells's mother had died on the journey north. Even worse, the French were not willing to negotiate for a full release of the prisoners. In fact, just three weeks later, Williams was sent from Quebec to Chateauviche during Sheldon's visit because the French Jesuits had complained that his presence hindered their ability to convert new Catholics. Sheldon lamented his absence: "Mr. Williams is sent down the river again about 18 or 20 miles. I did enjoy his company about three weeks [which] was a comfort to me. He gives his love to all the captives there."

Sheldon attempted to send written updates back to Deerfield, but the messengers returned due to "the badness of the ice." Finally a post got through to his son John Sheldon, Jr.: "This may let you know that I received a letter from your wife, the 29th of March, and she was well. I may let you know that I have seen none of my children, but I hear they are gone a-hunting." But Sheldon did achieve one success: He was able to free his daughter-in-law, Hannah Sheldon; his son Ebenezer; John Williams's eldest daughter, Esther; and two others.

Thus, in May 1705, the French sent Sheldon and Wells back to Massachusetts with a series of counteroffers for other redemptions, along with the handful of Deerfield captives that they had agreed to free as a sign of goodwill. The major sticking point was the fate of Pierre Maisonnat. He was a French privateer—more aptly, pirate—who sailed under the name "Captain Baptiste." Part of the problem in returning captives was that France and England captured very different kinds of people: France and her Native allies sought civilians, especially the very young, while England imprisoned political or military leaders (French or Native). This made for very unequal—and perhaps impossible—trades. The English held Baptiste for the unlawful capture of one of their vessels (in an act deemed to be piracy), which the French considered defense of their territorial waters. Vaudreuil indicated that if Baptiste and sixteen other French prisoners were returned, then the entire flock of English captives might be freed to return to New England.

But, at the moment, the majority of Deerfield captives, as well as many other English captives remaining in French Canada, were left there. Still, after the visit by Sheldon and Wells, the French town was abuzz with the news. Williams was grateful for their appearance because it "greatly strengthened many who were ready to faint, and gave some check to the designs of the Papists to gain proselytes." The fact that Sheldon and Wells made the hard journey to French Canada signaled to the captives that they had not been forgotten and might be able to return home soon. Even more so, Queen Anne's War seemed to be winding down: "And the English were many of them strengthened with hopes that the treaties betwixt the governments would issue in opening a door of escape for all."

But for some Deerfield captives, hope was not enough. It had been over one year since the massacre. Four young men decided to take matters into their own hands. Thomas Baker, age twenty-two, John Nims, age twenty-six, Martin Kellogg, age eighteen, and Joseph Petty, age thirty-two, made a daring escape from their captivity, outfoxed the manhunt for them, and undertook a harrowing, month-long winter trek on foot and by canoe back to Deerfield. During their journey they killed a white owl, which they ripped into four equal parts. Later, John Nims "insisted that a wing which fell to him was the sweetest morsel he ever tasted." Twenty-six days later they staggered into town—starving, bedraggled, and exhausted "in an imbecile condition," having been "guided more by instinct than reason"—to the astonishment and excitement of their neighbors.

John Williams was excited too, but he also worried about his children. He asked Vaudreuil again to help free his daughter Eunice, and to ransom his son Stephen. One of these prayers was answered—Stephen was finally released and sent to live with his father. The boy's appearance shocked him: "He was almost quite naked, and very poor." He appeared in Native clothes and with an Indian haircut, one side long and the other short. Stephen had suffered through his ordeal, and had been whipped by his captors. But he did not "go Native" and adopt their culture any more than necessary to stay alive.

In August 1705, Governor Dudley sent revised proposals to Vaudreuil. Delivered in person by none other than William Dudley, the governor's son, they signaled that negotiations were serious, and that a possible treaty between the English and the French might be in the works to allow all the prisoners to return home in the spring. John Williams and his son were brought up to Quebec for the diplomatic reception, but the reverend was sent back to Chateauviche again, after he had hindered Catholic conversion efforts once more. Vaudreuil seemed amenable, saying that wars between England and France "could never contribute to the glory of their sovereigns, or the aggrandizement of their states, but merely to the ruin and desolation of some poor families." The Deerfield captives must have agreed. Dudley's venture might have been a diplomatic failure, but it did succeed in gaining the release of eleven more New England captives, including three from Deerfield. Two were from the Williams family: sons Stephen and Samuel.

For the next several months, Williams shuttled back and forth between Quebec and Chateauviche. The French worried that he might inspire English captives to remain strong in their faith, or perhaps even foment an insurrection, so they never allowed him to stay in one place for very long. The quest to convert the English captives to the Catholic faith intensified. The English were kept isolated from one another. Letters were withheld, censored, or burned. Cut off as they were, captives must have succumbed to depression and despair. Perhaps resistance seemed futile.

When enticements to convert failed, the French tried threats. Jesuits said that they would send John's son Stephen, not quite sixteen, to live with Indians, who would torture him. At one point he was whipped with a stick made from a tree branch, fitted with leather knots.

When the French Jesuits learned that some captives had been redeemed, they tried one last time to persuade some of them to stay in Canada. It was too late in the season to undertake the dangerous sea voyage to New England, the French argued. Why risk a shipwreck and death at sea? Impressionable children were warned that if they returned to Massachusetts they would be damned and burn in hell.

Other captives were offered bribes or pensions to stay. John Williams recalled: "They told my child, if he would stay, he should have an honorable pension from the king [of France] every year, and that his master, who was an old man, and the richest in Canada, would give him a great deal; telling him, if he returned he would be poor, for, said they, 'your father is poor, has lost all his estate, it was all burnt.'" The French even tried to persuade young Stephen Williams to sail to France. And they continued to pressure John Williams to convert to Catholicism.

His resistance provoked his captors to treat him poorly. "Your obstinacy against our religion," a priest warned him, "discourages us from providing you with better clothes." "It was better," Williams retorted, "going in a ragged coat, than with a ragged conscience." His quip made it as far as Boston, where Judge Sewall, one of his friends, was so appalled that he ordered "a suit of clothes might be made here for Mr. Williams." Whether the garments ever reached him remains unknown.

Under immense pressure, Stephen Williams pretended to give in and profess the Catholic faith. The reverend's wife and two of his children were dead, and so were many of his friends. He also heard rumors that his sons Samuel and Stephen had converted to the Catholic faith. Could this be true? John Williams had been away from Deerfield for nearly two years. What would happen next? Would he ever be reunited with his family? Would he ever return home?

The Reverend's Recovery

In Massachusetts, Governor Dudley refused to give up on rescuing the English captives, especially John Williams. One motive for his continuing efforts to free Williams was that they knew each other, having been neighbors in Roxbury before John moved on to Deerfield. But Dudley's efforts also included others caught up in the conflict. He sent forty-seven French prisoners—including privateer William Rouse, but not the notorious Baptiste—back to Canada, and then arranged another diplomatic visit. At this point tempers wore thin. Dudley refused to "set up an Algiers trade," which would encourage more raids for captives to ransom. But Antoine-Denis Raudot, the intendant of New France, an influential government official who rivaled Vaudreuil for power, declared that he would send Reverend Williams "into prison and lay [him] into irons" unless Baptiste was released. It was a serious threat, and it was met with a serious response.

In January 1706, nearly two years since the raid, John Sheldon set out on another mission to Quebec, accompanied once more by John Wells and others. Sheldon arrived in Canada with new letters in March 1706, again seeking the release of the English captives. He stayed for almost three months, making two visits to Kahnawake, and racking up 809 livres in expenses, for which he sought reimbursement from Governor Dudley, given "the extraordinary difficulties, hazards, and hardships they have undergone." These costs indicate the hard effort yet delicate nature of travel and diplomacy. Sheldon spent 17 livres for a "tailor's work in making clothes," possibly for travel, and then ten times that at Mr. Dubenot's for "cloth for clothing, for stockings, shoes, a shirt and a hat and a pair of gloves and a neckcloth." Similar expenses were outlaid for John Wells, for silk, a shirt, a pair of stockings, and a hat. Likely they incurred these expenses in Quebec to outfit them suitably when they put their case before the governor general. It would have been hard to travel with such finery over hundreds of miles. Other expenses included Sheldon's lodgings in Quebec and Montreal, as well as the washing of his clothes and barbering. One couldn't visit the French officials without being styled first.

Sheldon incurred other expenses to visit the captives. He asked for money for "a canoe and men to go from Quebec to visit Mr. Williams." This must have been during one of the times when the reverend had been exiled from the city for his efforts to thwart Catholic conversions. Another expense was for "a carry-all to go to see the captives at the Mohawk fort." Once captives had been redeemed, they would require appropriate clothing—Sheldon spent more money, just under half of his own sartorial expenses, fitting out his daughter Mary with "necessary clothing" plus some spending money for her. John Wells and Joseph Bradley, who had accompanied Sheldon on the trip, also petitioned for reimbursement. They had purchased snowshoes, a dog (possibly to assist with pulling a sled), and "a gun hired for the voyage" that was "broken accidentally in the discharging."

After three months of bargaining, Sheldon secured more captives to bring home. The forty-four captives who set sail with Sheldon in May included his son Remembrance and daughter Mary. They also included Bradley's wife, Hannah, and the Burt family—Benjamin, a blacksmith; his wife, Sarah; their son, John; and toddler Christopher, who had been born on April 14, 1704, on the march to Canada. (The family would grow by one more on the return sailing with the birth of a baby appropriately named Seaborn.) Before the ship left port, Reverend Williams managed to smuggle a letter on board, to be read aloud to the passengers. "Pray for us that are left behind," he wrote, "that God would preserve and recover us, and give us grace to glorify His holy name, though He continue, yea increase, our trials."

This was all too much, and Governor Dudley gave in. He agreed to release Baptiste in exchange for his former neighbor, his man of God, John Williams, as well as all English captives. Messengers carried the news to Vaudreuil, and in response he tried to collect the remaining English captives from his Indian allies and send them home. But their Indian masters did not want to part with them. This problem vexed Vaudreuil, who worried that displeasing the Natives might provoke them to switch their allegiance to the English and then fight the French.

In the end, it took nearly seven more months, until October 25, for fifty-seven English captives, forty-six from Deerfield, to board a ship that sailed from Quebec to Boston. John Williams was on board, along with two of his children, Samuel and Warham. Almost three years after their capture, they were going home. As Williams said:

> We have reason to bless God . . . and yet pray to God for a door
> of escape, to be opened for the great number yet [left] behind,
> not much short of an hundred; many of which are children, and
> of these not a few among the savages, and having forgot the
> English tongue, will be lost, and turn savages also in a little
> time, unless something extraordinary prevent.

Williams rejoiced in his freedom but did not forget the other captives from New England who were still in French and Indian hands.

The cost to Deerfield had been terrible. Of the 112 captives, nineteen had died or been killed on the march north into New France, including two who were starved to death. There must have been many mixed emotions for those now sailing home to New England. On one hand was the relief and joy at going back to an English life, but on the other hand was the knowledge that at least thirty people captured in the Deerfield raid had decided to stay in Canada of their own free will.

Including John Williams's own daughter, Eunice.

The Captivity of Stephen Williams

What was captivity like for a young person? Stephen Williams (age ten at the time of his capture) had a very different experience in French Canada than that of his father, John. Eighty-nine captives from Deerfield had survived the brutal march to Canada. Fifty-nine eventually returned home, but others stayed behind. Most of those had been young children at the time of the massacre—most of the girls were younger than twelve, and the boys younger than fourteen. Young boys like Stephen often fared well among their captors, and many of the young Deerfield captives may have stayed in Canada and assumed new identities. Samuel Carter (age fifteen), Ebenezer Hoyt (age nine), and William Brooks (age six) may all have integrated into Native communities—no more is known of them or their whereabouts after the march north. They are now lost to history. Thomas Hurst (age thirteen), Ebenezer Stebbins (age ten), Josiah Rising (age ten), and Joseph Stebbins (age five) all acclimated to the French lifestyle and refused to return to New England.

But circumstances were different for Stephen Williams. Perhaps, raised as a minister's son, he felt he was destined for something better than a north-woods existence; perhaps he just disliked outdoor life. Whatever his reasons, Stephen had a unique experience as a captive, starting on March 8, when the raiders reached the White River. Here he was separated from his father and taken with his Pennacook master, Wattanummon, along the Connecticut River toward Cowass. Stephen recalled, "My master bid me go down the river with him very early in the morning, which startled me, for he did not use to be so early. There the river parted, and I went up one branch, [and] my father with my brothers and sisters the other." Stephen did not know it, but he would not see his father again for over a year.

Without a culture of adoption or ritual sacrifice, the Pennacooks usually sold their English captives to the French. The Pennacooks, including Wattanummon, had probably joined the raid for revenge against the English land grab of their ancestral homes. Wattanummon took Stephen to his new home in the mountains above the Wells River. It was a long, hard journey, and to make matters worse, Stephen was given hardly anything to eat. For his dinner, he had "one spoonful of Indian corn, in the morning five or six kernels."

At last they arrived at two wigwams, which were deserted. Stephen was left alone while his master and the others left their packs behind and headed off into the woods looking for food. Stephen ventured into the woods too, but soon became lost. Panicked, he shouted for help. His master located him but was furious with the boy and threatened to kill him for making such noise. Not only did the sound frighten away game animals, but the noise carried far in the bare winter mountains and might alert rivals or enemies to their location. As Stephen recalled, "The Indians will never allow a body to hello in the woods. Their manner is to make a noise like wolves or owls or other wild creatures when they would call to one another."

Stephen was no woodsman. Wattanummon installed him and a young Pennacook boy inside one of the wigwams and instructed them to stay put as he went out hunting again. Left alone, the boys made a fire to keep warm, but found there was very little food. Eventually they located "a moose's paunch and bones which the Indians had left." Stephen recalled, "We took that paunch and boiled [it], without cleansing of it, for what was in it served for thickening the broth." This broth served as their only food until the next day, when a Native girl brought the boys some dried moose meat. Stephen recalled that it "was the best victuals I ever ate."

The girl then took the two boys some ten miles away, to where Wattanummon was waiting. After a day or two, the group moved on to a place where several moose had been killed. The Indians built wigwams there: "Their manner was when they killed any moose to move to them and lie by them till they had eaten them up," explained Stephen. Here he encountered two other Deerfield captives—David Hoyt and Jacob Hickson—brought by their Pennacook masters. David, age fifty-three, had religious and military connections in Deerfield, having served as a deacon in the church and a lieutenant in the militia. Jacob, age twenty-one, was not a resident of the town, having been stationed there as one of the twenty garrison soldiers sent to protect against attack. They were not treated well, and they starved to death. Hoyt died, and Hickson was taken down to Cowass to do agricultural work. Farming for English settlers was a man's work, but in Native culture planting corn was a woman's job. Thus, Hickson suffered public humiliation. Older men were less valuable than young boys, who could be acculturated into Indian tribes.

At first, young Stephen was treated well. "When I first arrived here, they were extraordinary kind, took care of my toe, that was frozen, would suffer me to [do] any work, [and] gave me a deer skin to lie on and a bear's skin to cover me withal." In this way, he was brought into the community as a respected member. But soon Stephen was sent away to join his master's family at another location. Here he joined the Pennacooks in hunting "moose, bears, and beavers" for several months. Beaver skins were especially prized and valuable and served as a major part of the fur trade in French Canada.

Winter was a very hard time for the Pennacooks, who relied more on farming than hunting. Stephen and the Pennacooks remained in the mountains for over a month, but it was a hungry and desperate time: "[We] suffered much for want of provision for there was not much to be got a-hunting then, and if there was anything it was as nothing amongst so many. The chief of our provisions was roots of several sorts and bark of trees." In these hard times Stephen was put to work. He chopped wood for the fires and complained that he had to "carry it sometimes a considerable way on my back."

A rendezvous with other Natives allowed him to meet Jacob Hickson again. But Stephen was appalled at the man's condition: He "looked like a ghost. [He] was nothing but skin and bone." Hickson was not allowed to eat anything except what he could forage for himself; thus "he suffered

much for want of provision." Here Stephen also met other English captives, taken from the towns of Haverhill and Easthampton. There were
five women and one man. One of the women was Hannah Heath Bradley, who had been captured once before in 1697, before returning home,
only to be recaptured, in February 1704. She had fought back hard, killing one of her Native attackers by pouring boiling soap over him.

At this point, the Pennacooks decided to head toward Canada.
Wattanummon had accumulated so much "lumber" that it could not
all be carried in one go, thus forcing multiple trips. As Stephen complained, "this was an exceedingly tedious march to me, we being so
laden." Eventually they reached the river, but the water was so shallow
that the wood overflowed the canoe, forcing Stephen to walk along the
riverbank instead. Without any shoes his feet were "much galled and
one or two of my toes almost cut off with the stones." Their progress
was so slow that the other Pennacooks left them behind.

Stephen also complained about the lack of food: "I had little or any
thing to eat. My master killed a duck one day in the river and for my
part I had the guts, which I laid on the coals without cleansing them,
which seemed a sweet morsel to me." But once on the river, fish were
plentiful. They could be caught with lines and hooks, or by shooting
them, as Stephen relayed: "Two young Indians shot a fish with a bullet
and took it into the canoe; it was as large as I am."

The group arrived in Chambly in August, some six months after
the raid. Stephen was happy to be among Europeans again, and—like
his father—he enjoyed eating bread again, which the French provided.
He was also glad to hear news of his father and family, having feared
that they had all died. But his Native master was afraid that the French
wanted to take Stephen away—which they did—so he left town with
him and forbade Stephen to return to the fort. They ended up at the
Abenaki village of Odanak, with the Jesuit mission of Saint Francis.
Wattanummon did not like the Catholic influence and customs of the
town, so he decided to go to Albany. Before he left, however, he "gave"
Stephen to his kinsman "Sagamore George" and his wife.

During this time, several Frenchmen came to bargain with Stephen's masters for his release. But they refused to let him go for any price, and threatened to kill him for wanting to leave. At Reverend Williams's urging, Vaudreuil even stepped in and offered to buy Stephen. He sent so many messages offering to "redeem" the boy that the messengers were worn out. But nothing was agreed. While the negotiations continued, Stephen's new master, George, left for the hunting season. Stephen was left under the command of his wife, who ordered him to work. However, he proved to be a very unwilling servant. One day she ordered him to get more wood, but because he thought they already had enough, Stephen refused. When she returned home that night and discovered Stephen's disobedience, she ordered him to be punished by a Jesuit missionary in the town, who whipped him "with a whip with six cords [of] several knots in each cord."

Undeterred, Stephen continued his resistance. It was Native practice to make sugar from the sap of maple trees. This was a labor-intensive process of continually stirring large vats of boiling sap over a fire. Stephen kept the fire hot, but did not stir the mixture, thus allowing the whole kettle full to burn and spoil. When his mistress found out, she was furious and refused to feed him. Finally, in the spring of 1705, after much persistence, Governor Vaudreuil purchased Stephen for the price of forty crowns. After a year in captivity, Stephen was finally released. He was taken to Quebec, where he met other redeemed English captives. He was given English clothes (breeches and stockings, shirt and jacket) and had his hair styled in the European fashion (having had it kept in the Native fashion of one side being long and the other side being short). At this point, he was sent to live with his father at Chateauviche, and in October he boarded a ship to take him home to New England. After his return, Stephen stayed with relatives in Roxbury, where his father had been born. He did not go back to Deerfield. Eventually he followed his elder brother into Harvard in 1709, graduating in 1713. Three years later, in 1716, he was ordained a minister like his father, serving the community in Longmeadow, Massachusetts.

At age ten, Stephen had been considered by the Indians a prime candidate for adoption into a Native community. But he resisted all efforts at integration, and only pretended to convert to the Catholic religion when absolutely necessary. Stephen endured some abusive treatment and discipline in Native hands, but in general he was treated well. But he did not enjoy Native life and resisted adjusting to it at every turn, from getting lost in the woods to spoiling maple sugar. Still, Stephen's life was shaped by his experiences in captivity. Despite his ordeals, he was "solicitous for the welfare of the poor heathen, ever since I was a prisoner with them." For the rest of his life, he avoided the town of Deerfield. It was, he wrote, "a melancholy place to me."

The Captivity of Eunice Williams

And what of Eunice Williams? Just seven years old at the time of the Deerfield raid, she had been brought to the village of Kahnawake, the largest Native settlement in New France. By 1704, at least a thousand people lived at this Iroquois Mohawk settlement; it rivaled the size of French Montreal.

Three years earlier, in 1701, disease had ravaged the St. Lawrence Valley in New France. Smallpox devastated many Native communities, including the one at Kahnawake. Thus, it is likely that many of the Mohawks who had joined the Deerfield expedition went to seize captives and integrate them into their community following their usual mourning war customs. In places like Kahnawake Iroquois women grew corn, beans, and squash, while the men hunted and fished for protein. Women worked to tend the crops and complete other domestic tasks such as making maple syrup, while men trapped and sold animal skins.

Eunice was put to work. In addition to planting, growing, and harvesting the corn, women had to grind it for meals—something that required an hour each day from every woman in the community. In Kahnawake, every person had two names: first, a traditional Mohawk name, and second, a Christian name. Eunice was named Kanenstenhawi: "she brings in corn." Such a name spoke to her daily occupation as well as to her obedience. Here she would have lived in a typical Iroquois longhouse, where as many as sixty people could be housed under the single roof. These were built like large tents, with posts and bent saplings that created an arbor covered with bark. A row of hearths down the middle allowed for cooking, while platforms along the sides provided sleeping spaces.

Through 1704 and 1705, Vaudreuil and his wife worked to free Eunice, offering huge sums of hard cash and even an Indian girl in trade, but to no avail. Her father tried to visit her but was turned away until the governor general demanded that Williams be allowed to see his daughter. All efforts had failed, and so John Williams returned home to Massachusetts without his little girl. This would not be his last attempt to save her from the people he called "savages." But for now, she remained an unredeemed captive.

Memory

The Deerfield Massacre was a success for the French and their Native allies. Never again would they be able to achieve such unity in attack, or achieve such complete surprise or victory. Some Indian alliances broke down later. At Deerfield, the French and Indians may have won the battle, but they lost the long war.

The raid had provoked the opposite effect to what Governor Vaudreuil wanted. It made the English angry; it did not, as expected, cow them. The English did not want to show weakness or back down; they wanted revenge. That caused a huge buildup of defenses on the English frontier. Just months after the raid, in the summer of 1704, Massachusetts counted almost two thousand men in arms, about one of every five men in the colony. Garrisons from Deerfield to Wells, in Maine, were staffed with these new recruits.

Defense was no longer enough. The governor of Massachusetts, together with those of Connecticut and New York, called for a military invasion of French Canada that would climax with the expulsion of the French from North America. As Governor Dudley wrote, "The destruction of Quebec [would] forever make an end of an Indian war."

But there was a larger war to consider, and the rulers across the sea in London and Paris had other ideas. By the end of the conflict the wheel of fortune had turned. France, so powerful and dangerous at the beginning of the War of the Spanish Succession, known in the colonies as Queen Anne's War, was now weak and divided, whereas an emergent English (British, after the 1707 union of England and Scotland) empire ruled the colonies—and the seas.

Rather than turning away from the English empire, the residents of Deerfield embraced those links more enthusiastically than ever and supported future efforts of war and expansion more fully than they might have otherwise done.

5

REDEMPTION AND
RETURN TO ZION

Fifty-seven captives, including John Williams and many from Deerfield, arrived in Boston on November 21, 1706. It had been nearly a thousand days since the nightmare morning of February 29, 1704. Cotton Mather hailed their return as a bountiful "harvest," and the greatest star of all was the returning minister, John Williams—the "redeemed captive."

As Boston's outspoken Puritan leader, Mather had played an important role in Williams's return. Mather had been a cousin of Reverend Williams's now-dead wife, Eunice, and had corresponded with Williams during his captivity in Canada. From the beginning, Mather—perhaps for his own strategic purposes—saw the hand of God in all the events that unfolded. Two years into Williams's captivity, Mather had written to him: "You are being carried into the land of the Canadians for your [own] good." Mather believed that Deerfield's minister would have "a more than ordinary usefulness."

Even before Williams returned, Mather had made big plans for him. He ordered the printing of the reverend's "pastoral letter," the one that he had smuggled aboard a ship carrying other captives home when he was himself still forbidden to leave French territory. Mather published it as a tract titled "Good Fetched Out of Evil." The pamphlet included two other captive narratives, but Williams, whom Mather called "that suffering and shining servant of God," was the star attraction. Mather began by retelling Williams's experiences, and by noting that many English captives still suffered in French Canada, languishing in "horrid and howling wigwams," and "miserably circumstanced among those dragons of the wilderness." Yet, as Williams's letter had declared, "the best freedom is freedom by Jesus Christ from spiritual evils"—these words fit both Mather's and Williams's plans and goals. Mather reported that the tract sold one thousand copies in a week—an outstanding number.

When Williams finally arrived in person, Mather was probably the first to greet him. He immediately "sat with him and united counsels with him, how the Lord might have revenues of glory from his experiences." Even if Mather did not see Williams as a Puritan cash cow, he certainly saw him as a symbol for the Puritan religion. Mather recorded in his diary that he "particularly employed him, to preach my lecture, unto a great auditory (the [Massachusetts] General Assembly then also sitting) and, directed him, to show how great things God had done unto him."

Whether Williams knew he was a pawn in Mather's game is unknown. The reverend stayed in Boston and, on December 5, preached a sermon. He cited Luke 8:39: "Return to thine own house, and show how great things God hath done unto thee." He said that God had indeed answered the captives' prayers, to keep them safe while prisoners in French Canada, and then to return them to their homes.

On December 6, 1706, Williams preached a sermon entitled "Reports of Divine Kindness." Here, in front of a rapt audience, he thanked God for his rescue, but also hoped for the release of others:

> Do not be discouraged, and say, your friends and relations have
> (being captured when young) for a long time lived in popery,
> and therefore [have] no hopes of recovery; for God can make dry
> bones, very dry, to live, and can in ways unthought of by you,
> both recover them after they have fallen, and return them again.

But there was a difference between Mather's goals and Williams's views. For Mather, "irreligion and profaneness" were the real sins in Massachusetts, not the threat of a combined French and Native attack. "The sad condition of our frontiers" was due, in Mather's opinion, to the breaking of the Puritan faith by "drunkenness," "unchastity," "profane swearing," and "Sabbath-breaking." Mather struggled with the problem of how to sustain religious enthusiasm. Josiah Chapin agreed. His cousin Hannah Sheldon, John Sheldon, Jr.'s, wife, had been taken in the 1704 raid. He wrote:

> We are ready to complain of our French and Indian enemies, but they are not the cause. . . . So many New Englanders say that our sins have brought the sword of the wilderness upon us, I do therefore believe there must be a general Reformation before the rod of God will be taken off from us.

Although general sinfulness may also have been on Williams's mind, he was more worried about the very real threat of Catholicism. Having spent two years in French territory subjected to repeated and intense conversion attempts, his view was not surprising. For Williams, internal Puritan disputes were less important than defeating an existential threat: French Catholic power and influence, which he had suffered firsthand during his captivity.

John Williams did not return to Deerfield at once. Why should he? Boston welcomed him as a conquering hero who had stayed the course. French Catholic priests had offered him all manner of inducements to tempt him to renounce his religion—even freedom for him and his surviving children—if only he would betray the faith and convert to Catholicism. But he had refused. Even under the threat of death he would not abandon his beliefs. He had been tested, but stayed faithful. But was he faithful enough to return to Deerfield?

Unlike after earlier attacks, such as Bloody Brook in 1675, Deerfield had not been abandoned after 1704. But that was only because the region's military commander saw it as a valuable strategic outpost. That wasn't a strong selling point for future settlers: from a thriving town of almost three hundred souls Deerfield had been reduced to a sparse village of just twenty-five. On May 11, 1704—little more than three months after the raid—John Allen and his wife were captured and killed by attackers just south of town at the "Bars." Allen's body was found, but his wife's was not—only a later manuscript note revealed that her death occurred "about a mile or two from the place." It may have been that she was killed on the raiders' retreat, when she became an encumbrance to their hasty departure. If so, her body was never found, and likely was eaten by animals somewhere in the deep woods.

The survivors had wanted to abandon the town. But they didn't quite get that far—Colonel Samuel Partridge immediately drafted all the town's men to serve as garrison soldiers. Now any man who wanted to leave could not, unless he chose to break the law. As Jonathan Wells wrote to Governor Dudley:

> After the bloody desolation made by the French and Indian
> enemy in [Deerfield] . . . we were unanimously determined to
> desert the town and seek shelter and safety where we could find
> it; but the Hon. [Lieutenant] Colonel Samuel Partridge issued
> forth a warrant whereby we were impressed into Her Majesty's
> service and posted as garrison soldiers in the said town and
> our hopes of saving our lives by quitting our habitations [were]
> superseded by fear of incurring the penalty of deserting Her
> Majesty's Service.

Wells complained that soldiering took up to three-fifths of their time, when it should have been obvious that rebuilding and restocking should take place first. After all, the town's livestock had been killed, supplies plundered, and houses burned. How were those remaining supposed to survive? Was slow starvation better than a bullet or a quick blow from a war club?

Thirty-three captives returned to live in Deerfield, while as many as thirty decided to leave and settle elsewhere. Many moved to neighboring Connecticut, including John Sheldon, Sr.; John Hawks, Sr.; John Field; Samuel Carter; and John Richards, the school headmaster.

Sheldon might have quit Deerfield, but two of his sons stayed. Samuel Carter had been part of one of the founding families of Deerfield, but he lost his wife and three children in the raid, and three more children had been taken captive. Others moved farther south into Massachusetts, away from the dangerous frontier, including Joshua Pomroy and almost all of John Williams's children.

But, by 1712, more than two hundred people lived in Deerfield again. A significant majority of them—four out of five—had lived there before the war. Only twelve new families decided to risk settling in Deerfield. Of the sixty-two survivors of the 1704 raid, about half returned to the site of the massacre, rebuilt their houses, and farmed their fields. Of the fifty-nine Deerfield residents rescued and returned to the Massachusetts colony, thirty-three settled again in Deerfield. The average age of those who returned to Deerfield was twenty-seven; that of those who decided to stay in French Canada was just nineteen. A difference of almost a decade must have tipped the balance in feelings for home and family.

Why did half the townspeople who had survived the attack and not been captured refuse to abandon Deerfield? They were still in danger from possible attack. But, in defiance, they rebuilt their town. Was it because they wanted to keep faith with the captives, and give them a home to return to? Was it for religious reasons—part of a Puritan covenant with God? And when freed, why did many of the captives return to Deerfield to begin their lives again? They could have moved to the safety of Boston, or another community near the Atlantic coast and remote from danger. Why did they choose to remain on the frontier, where there was a good chance it could happen all over again?

We have no answers, except that they wanted to. They saw a future there.

John Williams had achieved celebrity status. He spoke again on December 20, at a meeting organized by a Mr. Bromfield. Many churches in Boston bid him to stay, but those in Deerfield wanted him to return—the town was able to obtain a large sum of forty pounds from the legislature to pay him to come back. On November 30, some nine days after he had landed in Boston, the Deerfield residents resolved to send representatives there to bid the reverend to return to Deerfield: "to go down to the

Bay for them, and in their behalf act and treat with their pastor, the Reverend Mr. John Williams, in regard to his resettling with them again in the work of the ministry." Those sent included Captain Jonathan Wells and Ensign John Sheldon—both with ties to the 1704 raid.

If Williams agreed to return, the Deerfield representatives offered further generous inducements: to build him a fine new house to his specifications, as big as John Sheldon's; to give him land and supply him with ample firewood for the cold winters. Still, these offers paled in comparison to what a cosmopolitan city like Boston could offer—prominence, prosperity, safety. As fellow minister Isaac Chauncey recalled:

> When he returned from captivity he was importunely invited
> to settle where his worldly interests might be more promoted,
> than if he returned to Deerfield; and there were plausible pleas
> he might have made for his accepting the invitations; since
> Deerfield was in a shattered condition, and reduced to a small
> number, and his own family had suffered so much there and
> might suffer a great deal more, if he returned.

Reverend Williams might have dreaded a return. Was he haunted by memories of what he had witnessed in 1704, and the horrors that he and his family had suffered that night? Of his two infant children murdered on his own doorstep? He'd had to pass their tiny, broken bodies when the Indians dragged him out the front door and smashed their skulls. And what of his wife, Eunice, torn from his arms and slain by a tomahawk, buried now under those words of eternal accusation: "Fell by the rage of ye Barbarous Enemy"?

If John Williams did elect to return to Deerfield, could he ever find relief from their ghosts? Not all the ghosts who haunted the survivors were dead. How could Williams ever forget his daughter Eunice, who still lived among the heathen? Other children of Deerfield too, remained captive in a strange land far from home. If he returned, Williams would have to live with the knowledge that as the days, weeks, and eventually years passed, these children, though still living, were growing up in a world not their own, but which they would come to be a part of, that they must be considered lost, having been transformed into Indians. Did Williams imagine himself, or Deerfield, as some kind of homing beacon that might draw them home?

And was it even safe to return? As the Natives would soon prove, they were not finished with Deerfield. Attacks on the town would continue. Returning to Deerfield presented more than a risk. Future violence by the Indians was almost guaranteed. Would it ever be safe to live there again?

Still, John Williams decided to return to Deerfield and took up the pulpit again. Less than three weeks after arriving in Boston, he returned to Deerfield, on December 28, 1706, just after Christmas. The meetinghouse, first built in 1695, was ready for him—it had not burned. What did he think when he laid eyes on the Sheldon House for the first time since the raid? Would the sight of the house and its scarred door condemn him to traumatic flashbacks every time he passed by?

It was Reverend Williams who brought Deerfield back to life. His very presence instilled confidence and hope, and brought back some of those who had fled. As the town committee noted, "many who deserted the place quickly after the desolation, by our Rev. Pastor's return and giving hopes of settling again amongst us has encouraged their return." His faith allowed the town residents to go back to their farming lives—literally to reap what they could sow. Rather than focusing on military defense, people were able to rebuild their agricultural foundations. Later, on September 23, 1707, in a sign that Deerfield had recovered enough to worry about an overpopulation of animals, the town issued a strict injunction against loose pigs on the common: "Voted that all swine that shall be found on the commons after the third day of October shall be ringed, and any that shall neglect to ring their own swine, *they* shall be forthwith rung by the hog ringer." Deerfield might still need Indian fighters but it had needed a "hog ringer" too.

True to their promise, his Deerfield neighbors built John Williams a new house, mercifully not on the site of the one that had been burned during the attack. Less than a year later, in September 1707, Williams remarried. His new wife, Abigail Allyn Bissell, was a cousin of his first wife, Eunice. Together, he and Abigail had five children. Three of his sons followed him into the ministry, preaching the Protestant gospel. His son Elijah lived in Deerfield as a merchant.

The Redeemed Captive Returning to Zion

Yet the memory of the raid must never have been far from the reverend's mind.

Only three captives ever wrote about their experiences at length: John Williams, his son Stephen, and Joseph Kellogg. In an era before widespread literacy, this may not be surprising. Few had the time or skills to read a book let alone take up their pens when crops needed planting, animals tending, and homes defending. Many former captives wanted to forget the trauma of the past and move forward. They saw little reason or profit in recording their experiences.

Getting a manuscript into print was also difficult, and usually required extended assistance of friends and family. In Reverend Williams's case, Cotton Mather, Boston's outspoken Puritan leader, played an important role in encouraging a permanent record of the minister's experiences. In the spring of 1707 Williams published *The Redeemed Captive Returning to Zion*. Given that he did not have a house yet in Deerfield, Williams likely returned to Boston over the winter of 1706–1707, which would have enabled him to complete his manuscript in comfort and safety. He preached a sermon there on March 6, entitled "God in the Camp." Judge Sewall recorded on March 8, 1707: "Mr. Williams visits us and tells me he goes to Deerfield 14 nights hence next Tuesday. His narrative is now in the press." The reverend may have elected to stay with friends to complete his manuscript and shepherd it into print.

The book was a bestseller for its time and, over the next century and a half, was reprinted sixteen times. The book must have been eagerly consumed by eighteenth-century readers. Few copies still exist, and those that do are in well-worn or damaged condition. Today it is a rare and valuable book. The reverend described his capture and captivity, but above all, he detailed his unwavering Protestant faith and fervent anti-Catholicism. The book must have inspired survivors of the raid, but neither diaries nor estate inventories reveal how many copies made their way to Deerfield.

Williams opened with an effusive dedication to Governor Dudley, thanking him for his "uncommon sagacity and prudence in contriving to loose the bonds of your captivated children" and for his leadership "in this dark and tempestuous season." Williams wrote a thrilling captivity narrative following the expected conventions of the genre. He described the violence of the raid, his dramatic capture, the ordeal of the march, the murder of his wife Eunice, the suffering of other captives, his failure to redeem his daughter Eunice, and his challenging experiences in Canada. But *The Redeemed Captive* is two books in one. The first part offers firsthand drama and action; the second part, not so much. Instead, it presents abstract theological arguments and polemics about what caused the raid—God's disfavor with his believers and their communal sins, or the designs of the French and Indians—and an attack on the evils of the Jesuits and the Catholic faith. Williams highlighted the spiritual trials of his townspeople and praised their heroism for resisting ceaseless attempts at conversion. For John Williams, the true enemy was not the Indians but the Catholic faith and its priests. A modern reader not versed in early eighteenth-century Puritanism might find this part of the book dry and hard to follow.

Part of Williams's reason for writing the book must have been to shine a spotlight on the plight of his daughter Eunice, still "unredeemed" in French Canada. He continued to seek news of her, but it was difficult to get reliable—or any—communication from the French. In the months ahead, occasional rumors and reports concerning Eunice reached the English colony.

Finally in February 1707—three years after the raid—news came in the form of a letter sent to Colonel Partridge: "As to Mr. Williams' daughter, our spies which we sent to Canada are returned, who as they were hunting, saw Mr. Williams' daughter with the Indian who owns her, she is in good health but seems unwilling to return, and the Indian not very willing to part with her." Partridge penned a swift reply: "Please to do what you can at all times to obtain Mr. Williams his daughter."

It was now a race against time to rescue Eunice. The longer she stayed in a Native community in French Canada, the less likely it was that she would ever want to leave. As captive Titus King wrote, "[captivity is] an awful school for children when we see how quick they will fall in with Indian ways. Nothing seems to be more taking. In six months' time they forsake father and mother, forget their own land, refuse to speak their own tongue and seemingly be wholly swallowed up with the Indians."

Female captives transitioned better into Native communities than their male counterparts, especially the young. Many of the girls and young women captured in Deerfield adapted to new lives in captivity. Mary Field, the daughter of John Field, was about the same age as Eunice. She was adopted by a Native woman and took the named Walahowey, probably meaning "she brings fruit." She married a Mohawk man in French Canada, and other than a visit to New England, lived for the rest of her life in Canada. Joanna Kellogg, age eleven, had been taken captive along with her two brothers and sister in the Deerfield raid. She married a Kahnawake Native, and remained in Canada, as did Mary Harris and Mercy Carter. Thankful Stebbins, age twelve, was ransomed from the Natives into French custody in Canada and converted to the Catholic religion quickly. On April 23, 1707, she was baptized into her new faith as Louise Therese Stebens. Just four years later, she married Charles-Adrien Legrain, called Lavalle, and proceeded to bear ten children, dying in childbirth with the eleventh. Attempts to redeem Eunice Williams continued throughout 1707, but by then—as feared—she claimed to have forgotten how to speak English and seemed unwilling to return.

In 1708, the English sent peace offers to the Kahnawake Mohawks, who accepted them after tiring of fighting a French war. Many at Kahnawake were angry with the French for forcing them to release so many captives, because without captives, such fighting had little meaning for them. The sachem Stiataque told the French governor general that the Mohawks would fight no more. Later, in 1710, the Kahnawake Mohawks pledged not to attack New England.

But the 1708 rapprochement with the Mohawks did not end the danger of Indian attacks in Massachusetts or Deerfield. That year, the Connecticut Valley experienced several small raids. In July, two sons of Captain John Parsons were scalped and killed in Northampton, some fifteen miles south. Later that month, three adults were killed near today's Chicopee; two children were tomahawked, but two-year-old Hannah Wright survived her injury. By August, the violence had revisited Deerfield when Martin Kellogg was taken captive for the second time.

The following year, Mehuman Hinsdale was captured by raiders once again. As he drove a team back from Northampton with a load of apple trees, Indians seized him just south of Deerfield. They took him to Chambly, where he was forced to run the gauntlet. After imprisonment in the dungeon and an aborted escape attempt, Hinsdale and another captive were ordered onto a French man-of-war that sailed for La Rochelle. Somehow, they managed to get from St. Malo to London, where they boarded ships to Rhode Island. After three and a half years, Mehuman returned to his wife Mary in 1712. In 1720, he became the first Deerfield resident to purchase an "innholder's license" to operate a tavern that served alcohol, which he operated until 1729. When he died in 1736, Mehuman Hinsdale's gravestone recorded that he was "the first male child born in this place and was twice captured by the Indian Savages."

His "son" Ebenezer did not fare well. On the surface, he appeared to live a charmed life. He attended Harvard, held office in Deerfield, and served in the militia as a colonel. He came from a wealthy family, and he married Abigail Williams—a daughter of John Williams. But his life was a troubled one, due to excessive drinking and lingering doubts about his legitimacy. When he died in 1760, he was buried next to his mother. Her single gravestone apparently answered the question once and for all: "Her husbands were Lieut. Mehuman Hinsdale and Mr. George Beal. By the first she had two sons, Samuel and John." Ebenezer, the son buried beside her, was not mentioned.

Although Eunice was at Kahnawake at this time, there is no record of her thoughts on the peace. But that year her name appeared on a document listing "English prisoners in the hands of the French and Indians at Canada." The possibility of a prisoner exchange was raised several times, in the hopes that Eunice could be brought home via diplomacy. But none of these efforts worked out: Eunice remained irretrievable.

6

END OF DAYS

||||||||||||||||

John Williams devoted himself to his fold. In Deerfield, he was renowned for preaching sermons not only on the Sabbath day, but frequently on weekdays as well. Isaac Chauncey, a fellow minister, recalled: "His custom was to preach a lecture once a month, and a sermon the Friday before the Sacrament, and frequently a sermon either to the Elderly, or to the young people." He reached out to people of all ages in the community to bring them together as one flock under God.

Williams was noted for keeping himself educated on current affairs, often indulging in "reading good books." His library contained 349 pamphlets and 190 books, almost all religious, and no fiction or poetry. He owned works by Plutarch, Thomas Aquinas, and John Calvin; several texts in French, "Mather on Earthquakes," and, tellingly, a volume on "Indian Converts." In an age noted for the Salem witch trials, he also owned a copy of Rev. John Hale's *Modest Enquiry into the Nature of Witchcraft*.

Chauncey noted "how careful he was to inform himself of the transactions and affairs of Europe, and to understand the state and circumstances of the province, that he might calculate his prayers accordingly." It was realpolitik for Puritan times. And in an era of limited literacy, especially on the frontier, Williams provided oral education and communication. He was Deerfield's one-man news service.

He often invited others to dine with him: "He cared not to eat his morsel alone." As one of the wealthiest men in town—and the most prestigious—he brought "persons from other towns . . . to rest and repose themselves under his roof." Such hospitality kept him well stocked on the latest news.

Williams also made a daily habit of visiting the sick, often of his own volition rather than just when requested. Isaac Chauncey recalled that Williams would "walk the circuit almost every day, and visit them all except they were remote from him." Given the possibility of ambush, raids, or attacks, his everyday visits were undergirded by a stubborn, even reckless, bravery—or perhaps his ultimate faith in God.

Williams was well paid for his service both to the Massachusetts government and the local Deerfield community. In 1709, he served as a chaplain for an expedition to French Canada, and was granted more than twenty-four pounds. He probably used part of the money to pay for a family pew in the town's meetinghouse: "The town granted Mr. John Williams a liberty to build a pew for his wife and family."

By 1711, Williams was being paid sixty pounds as a salary, and unlike earlier times he was now paid in hard cash rather than in kind. By 1718, he earned eighty pounds per year; by 1727 it had risen to ninety. He possessed "blue linsey woolsey curtains" and "calico curtains." He furnished sleeping quarters with "feather beds and bolsters." His dining room featured a set of "blue china"; silver tankards, cups, and spoons; pewter ware of platters, plates, basins, and porringers; and wooden ware, probably for everyday use. Outside the house, he was well furnished with farm animals and equipment. He owed multiple cows and a team of oxen, more than two dozen sheep, and, by 1729, eleven horses.

His personal appearance must have been striking. He owned at least two pairs of shoes, plus a pair of boots, numerous neck bands (appropriate for a man of the cloth), silver buttons, and silk muslin handkerchiefs. As he grew older, he invested in a cane for walking, and spectacles for his fading eyesight. He must have owned at least one pipe, for he possessed a steady stock of tobacco for smoking. He owned at least two muskets: "a long fowling piece" and "a gun of the old Queen's Arms."

This might have been when John Williams took the opportunity to sit for his portrait, though it is more likely that it was painted in Boston soon after he was redeemed from captivity and at the height of his celebrity. It would not have been unusual—or considered vain—for a man of his accomplishment and importance to memorialize his image. Perhaps painted by Nehemiah Partridge (1683–c.1737), the portrait depicts a respectable middle-aged man of the cloth, wearing the traditional black gown accented with Geneva bands, the two strips of white cloth draped from the front of the collar. The face of the man who looks back at us seems untouched by trauma—even three hundred years later, the eyes twinkle at the viewer. His round face suggests serene satisfaction—no gaunt lines of hunger, no creased stress wrinkles across the smooth forehead, and almost—perhaps—the crinkle lines of a smile around the cherry mouth. The curly hairstyle may be either a wig or the sitter's own hair, prominently parted in the middle. If a wig, it might have been made by Deerfield's own David Hoyt (son of prominent Deerfield settler Jonathan Hoyt), who was a noted "maker of wiggs and foretops."

The portrait had vanished for two and a half centuries after Williams's death. In all that time, no known likeness of him surfaced until 1980, when this picture appeared at a low-profile public sale by Weiss Auctioneers & Appraisers at a Holiday Inn in South Deerfield. A tiny label in type had been affixed to the back of the canvas, stating that the figure was none other than the Reverend John Williams of Deerfield. The painting had been salvaged from the attic of a local family with roots in the Deerfield area.

Resurrection and Rebuilding

A cessation of hostilities between the English and French in North America was agreed to in Boston in October 1712, and the Treaty of Utrecht, signed by dignitaries across the Atlantic Ocean on March 30, 1713, signified the formal end of Queen Anne's War. By this agreement, the undefined lands of French Acadia became British. Rather than ending a conflict, the treaty merely set the stage for another yet to come.

Slowly, Deerfield rebuilt itself. The town had suffered greatly in Queen Anne's War—61 had been killed and 112 taken captive. Those

who returned settled back into their previous lives, some into prominence, others into obscurity. Mehuman Hinsdale returned from captivity, along with his wife Mary. But it is unclear whether they returned
together, as Mary gave birth to a son, Ebenezer, on the way back. Whis-
pered rumors questioned whether Mehuman was the father; town records included a strange note: "Query: whether to record the birth of
Ebenezer?" No record was made, and shortly after they returned to
Deerfield, the Hinsdale family moved to Connecticut. Did they leave
out of scandal and shame? If so, the new location did not suit them any
better because a year later they returned to Deerfield.

Reverend Williams continued to pursue reunion and reconciliation
with his daughter in French Canada. He solicited all information available on her condition and continued to lobby for her release. In 1712,
Peter Schuyler, a New Yorker with ties to many Native groups, informed
Governor Dudley that he had tried to see Eunice but to no avail. According to Schuyler, the Native "squaw" who "owned" Eunice had not
appeared in town. Regardless, Schuyler assured the governor: "If they
do come together or be it the squaw alone I shall use all possible means
to get the child exchanged." Schuyler promised to search out all intelligence on the pair, in hopes of locating and then meeting them. He also
confirmed that he would use all possible methods to get Eunice: "either
as your Excellency proposes or what other way the squaw will be most
willing to comply with." In short, everything but outright murder and
kidnapping was on the table. By this time, Eunice had lived in the Native
community for eight years. Captured as a seven-year-old, she was now
fifteen, nearly an adult in Native and Puritan cultures.

But John Williams refused to remain a passive bystander to his daughter's
fate. Instead, he traveled on four missions to French Canada. In three con-
secutive years—1709, 1710, and 1711—he had served on three expeditions,
and in 1714 he served as a political emissary to the French. Williams must
have believed wholeheartedly in his mission to return captives to New England, including his own daughter. What else could explain these repeated,
arduous sojourns into enemy land? Every time he traveled to Canada, he
reenacted his own captivity and relived painful memories. These were

psychological journeys into the past where he confronted the demons that haunted him, although he also used them as a quest to save Protestant souls. The longer captives stayed in French Canada, the likelier their conversion to the Catholic fate. In Williams's absence, an adjunct minister was called in to serve Deerfield's religious needs. Williams must have felt he owed a greater duty to his former flock—those still held captive—than to his present one. Now, by 1712, Queen Anne's War was over. But the issue of captives still remained. Their fate was unresolved. What would happen to these missing people? And what about Eunice?

In 1713, Williams and Captain John Stoddard went north again under the new peace. The reverend's son Stephen would soon graduate from Harvard; the proud father had once advised him: "To get grace and learning should be your highest ambition." Stephen would go on to serve as a schoolmaster for the nearby town of Hadley before being ordained as the minister of Longmeadow, about forty miles due south of Deerfield, on the present-day border with Connecticut. John Williams's son Warham, who was just four at the time of the raid, was also on his way to Harvard. Esther, his eldest daughter, would soon marry. Eleazer, John's eldest son, was the most settled of the family. He had graduated from Harvard in 1708, having been safe in Boston during the massacre. He had settled as a minister in Mansfield, Connecticut, by 1710 and married Mary Hobart in 1711. In 1712, they named their first child, a girl, Eunice. It must have seemed like the moment for the elder Williams to focus once again on his own daughter Eunice.

In 1713, almost a decade after the raid, news came from Canada by way of John Schuyler, Peter's brother. John had been in Montreal since April and had petitioned Governor General Vaudreuil to assist in Eunice's release. He "gave me all the encouragement [I] could imagine for her to go home." One can imagine that Vaudreuil was only too willing to clear up a vexing mess that seemed never-ending. Although he could not compel the Mohawks to part with Eunice, he could help arrange a meeting, which was set for May 26. Schuyler was accompanied by Vaudreuil's representatives, as well as two interpreters—one to translate English to French, and one to translate French into Mohawk. They traveled by boat, on a river swollen with spring thaw. Thus, with the governor general's approval, Schuyler went to Kahnawake to convince Eunice, now age sixteen, to return home. An added sweetener was the one hundred crowns of Vaudreuil's own money he had set aside to purchase her from the Natives.

Schuyler had already learned some disturbing news. Eunice had taken a new name—Marguerite—having been rebaptized as a Catholic. This news added insult to injury—from the English point of view, Eunice had not only chosen a savage lifestyle, she had now endangered her Protestant soul, putting her eternal salvation in jeopardy. But this news—while shocking—was probably not unexpected. It had been nine years since the 1704 raid, and Eunice had reached the age of marriage for both Native and English societies. Still, her family wanted to know more—it was the "earnest desire" of her father who still dreamt and hoped to bring home his little girl—even if she was no longer so little.

Schuyler's entourage must have made quite an impression when it arrived. Jesuit priests were quick to inform the delegation that it would be impossible to convince John Williams's daughter to return—as she had just been married—and to a Native man, Arosen!

Schuyler refused to believe it. How could a Christian woman marry an Indian? A Jesuit priest assured Schuyler it was true. He had performed the wedding ceremony himself; in fact, he had only done so after much convincing from the young couple. The Jesuit claimed he had even taken leave of the fort so as not to be pestered by their begging. Finally, they played their trump card:

> Until at last, some days past they both came to me, and said that they were joined together, and if he would not marry them they mattered not, for they were resolved never to leave one the other but live together heathen-like.

If the priest was to be believed, the young couple took matters into their own hands, consummated their relationship sexually, and would live as a married couple whether or not the French priest provided a ceremony.

Schuyler demanded that the Jesuit produce the young couple in person so he could see for himself. They appeared, with reluctance. It is possible that no English representative had seen Eunice in more than five years, perhaps even longer. Her physical appearance shocked Schuyler, who might have expected an older version of the Puritan child who had been kidnapped a decade ago. This woman, no longer a child, stood before him dressed as a Kahnawake—in a tunic, leggings decorated with porcupine quills, and moccasins. Her hair would have been greased back (usually with bear fat, an early version of hairspray) and then combed and braided, and decorated with beads and feathers. She would have worn bracelets and necklaces and, if she followed custom, would have had paint applied to her face.

When Eunice and her husband entered the room, Schuyler noted, "she [was] looking very poor in the body, bashful in face but proved harder than steel in her breast." Eunice, now Marguerite, was no longer a frightened English child being held captive against her will. Now she was an adult woman who had chosen her path in life. If she was reluctant to meet him, it may have been because she feared that these English negotiators wanted to tear her away from the only life she had known and built over the last decade.

What happened next showed how much time had passed—and how much Eunice had changed. Schuyler invited her to sit down, which she did. Her husband stood behind her, surrounded by Catholic priests. Schuyler spoke to her in English, but she no longer understood the language, so he asked the interpreters for assistance. His first questions were all family related: Did she know how much her family missed her? Did she know how much they hoped for her safety and (Protestant) salvation? Schuyler asked if she would agree to return home to her father in Deerfield.

Eunice was silent. She would not—or could not—speak. Schuyler asked the interpreters, the priests, anyone in the room, to help. They tried, but she remained stonily silent. Schuyler implored her: Please, wouldn't she at least visit her father in Deerfield? Wouldn't she at least travel to see her English family? Then she could return to Kahnawake if she wanted. No one would stop her, and she could return safely. The priest spoke to her for almost thirty minutes without a reply.

At last, she said two words: *Jaghte oghte*.

The words were quickly translated into French and then into English. No.

She would not go. Not to return, and not even to visit.

Schuyler was at a loss for words. After two hours' time, he had been able to get two words from Marguerite. He recorded, "Upon this my eyes almost filled with tears, I said to her myself, had I made such proposals and prayings to the worst of Indians, I did not doubt but [I would] have had a reasonable answer and consent to what I had said."

But the conversation was not yet done. Now Marguerite's husband spoke, and offered Schuyler truth for her refusal. Arosen said, "Had her father not married again, she would have gone and see him, long ere this time." Eunice was her father's daughter, but she was also her mother's. Given that John Williams had such a prominent and public role, she may not have spent much time with him prior to the raid. In fact, as a young Puritan girl, she would have been brought up by her mother to study her letters, learn needlework, and help run the household through any number of domestic tasks. Eunice might have also felt closer to the enslaved Black woman, Parthena, whom the Indians had killed during the raid, than she did to her own father. Did Eunice's long-held resentment speak to something not recorded by Reverend Williams about his wife's death, something Eunice might have witnessed? On the night of the massacre, Indians had murdered two of her young siblings on her doorstep. Young Eunice might have seen that. On the march, she might have watched as an Indian tomahawked her mother to death. Did she blame her father for the loss of her mother and her captivity—for failing to protect his family from the French and Indians? For failing to rescue her when she was seven years old? For abandoning her?

We will never know.

Schuyler's reaction—and our own—must be tempered with Eunice's feelings. She had lived with the Natives in Kahnawake for almost ten years. She had made it her home. She had married into the community. Deerfield and her Williams family were her past; this was her future. Schuyler's arrival might have frightened her—for the second time in her life she might lose everything she knew and be taken away once again to a strange land—her old New England home. Eunice was now a converted Catholic and firmly integrated into the Kahnawake community. Even if she remembered her previous life in Deerfield, she had no wish to return to it. What could Deerfield offer her that she didn't already possess? In this light, her actions are understandable.

Schuyler could do no more: "The time growing late and I being very sorrowful, that I could not prevail upon nor get one word more from her, I took her by the hand [to say goodbye] and left her in the priest's house." He wrote to Governor Dudley that he had tried everything but had not been able to secure Eunice's release: "My indefatigable pains therein came to no purpose."

The next year, John Williams made a final journey to rescue his daughter. He and John Stoddard got as far as Albany by November, but unseasonably warm weather meant that they could not cross the unfrozen river, delaying their travel until late January. On February 16, 1714, ten years since the Deerfield raid, they arrived in Quebec, where Governor General Vaudreuil received them. The French assisted and set up a meeting with Eunice, but it did not go well. It was not a warm, loving reunion; her father recorded that she would "not so much give [him] one pleasant look." Eunice hardly spoke a word, having probably forgotten all her English. Through an interpreter, she insisted that "she is yet obstinately resolved to live and die here."

Eunice remained firm in her refusal to return to New England. Her steadfast Protestant father could not understand. He thought that being a captive was "rather worse than [being one of] the Indians." Whereas Natives might exist in a state of religious ignorance, some English captives who had been raised as Puritans now renounced their faith as firmly as any heretic of the European religious wars. After years, Williams conceded defeat: "We are like to be very unsuccessful." In fact, he admitted it would be easier to get anyone *but* Eunice to return with them: "It would be far easier to gain twice the number of French and Indians to go with us than English."

John Williams departed that day, and he never saw his daughter again. For the rest of his life, he offered prayers for his absent and "beloved and unfortunate daughter Eunice, who was in captivity among the Indians."

Deerfield and Father Rasle's War

The war years had been incredibly destructive to Deerfield and its residents. Over nine years of conflict, Deerfield had been the target of ten of twenty-nine recorded attacks or raids. The town's population was about 10 percent of the entire Connecticut River Valley—about three hundred out of some three thousand. Yet it had made up more than half of those killed, and almost all of those captured.

In 1714—ten years after the raid—a party of natives visited Deerfield. Among them was Aaron de Noyen, the son of Abigail Stebbins and her French husband, Jacques de Noyen. The ten-year-old boy had come to visit his grandfather, John Stebbins, but was so taken with Deerfield that he refused to return to Canada. Instead, he anglicized his name and became Aaron Denio. In 1734 he was baptized as a full member of the church.

But while many of the Deerfield captives had been redeemed, that did not end the threat. A decade after the massacre, the town was still in danger. People were still snatched from the fields and never seen again. Others ventured into the woods, only to vanish. Some were killed by war parties, others were taken captive again—including some of the original hostages of 1704.

In 1718, John Williams received an unexpected visitor. One of his former Abenaki masters traveled to see him for a reunion because he had been "so deeply impressed" that the reverend "was more than a common man." But new frontier policies increased tensions between the English settlers and the Eastern Abenakis, led by Father Sebastian Rasle. He was a French Jesuit who encouraged the Abenaki to fight the English, their enemies since King Philip's War. Rasle had been fanning the flames of conflict for years: In 1720, the General Court had offered the princely sum of one hundred pounds for the capture of "the incendiary that has instigated and stirred up those Indians." The English, in return, allied with the Iroquois and some Mohawks.

In these trying circumstances, a second edition of *The Redeemed Captive* was published in 1720. Williams's anti-Catholic narrative—comprising much of the book—was once again relevant, sixteen years after the massacre. Thomas Fleet reprinted the text alongside another famous captivity narrative, that of Mary Rowlandson, who had written about her experiences during King Philip's War. But Fleet's intentions may have differed from Williams's—in fact, there is no evidence that the reverend was consulted at all about a second printing. Did Fleet hope to reanimate anti-French feeling among the English and instigate war with the Eastern Abenakis? If so, Williams might not have been pleased to be part of such a project. He wrote to his son Stephen, questioning the fairness of such methods and whether they were "just."

In 1722 the long-expected war broke out between English settlers and Abenakis on the Maine frontier—the Fourth Anglo-Abenaki War, or Father Rasle's War.

This time Northfield, some twelve miles farther north than Deerfield, was the target, and the garrison there was staffed with fifty men. Not so far away, Deerfield was protected only by two dozen men at most. In 1723, a party of five Natives raided Northfield, killing two. Colonel Samuel Partridge, still in charge of defense of the Connecticut Valley, demanded gunpowder, lead, and flints to supply frontier towns in western Massachusetts. Still, nothing more happened, while a foreboding increased among the colonists. "The people of Deerfield grow uneasy . . . at their having seen but 10 men," Lieutenant Joseph Stoddard recorded.

The town residents were understandably worried, and they petitioned the governor for additional support:

By reason of the war [we] are much afraid to go about our occupations, expecting daily a descent of the enemy on our Western frontiers . . . indeed the difficulties of war lie so hard upon us, that several families, and also several young men have drawn off from us, and several more are going in a little time, to the great discouragement of those who are left behind.

Some people decided that enough was enough. William and Margaret Belding, who had survived the 1704 raid, left Deerfield for the safer location of Norwalk, Connecticut. He and his father had been taken captive in 1696. His mother had been killed in a raid on Deerfield in 1696, and his stepmother in the 1704 attack.

He and Margaret may have left just in time. In 1724, Deerfield was ambushed again. In late June, three scouts and their horses were killed just a few miles north of town. Ebenezer Sheldon's shiny silver shoe buckles proved particularly attractive, and the Indians tried to pull them off his lifeless feet. But they would not come off his shoes and got bent in the attempt. The bodies were brought back to Deerfield and laid to rest in the Old Burying Ground. Reverend Williams gave an "affecting service."

The violence continued in July. Houses not far from Deerfield were robbed of "rum, meal, cheese, meat, &c.," and many townspeople crowded into the confines of Deerfield's inner sanctum of the palisade for safety. The raids must have brought back vivid memories: for many, it must have seemed like 1704 all over again. In July, Colonel Partridge immediately wrote to the governor:

> We are much distressed by lurking enemies . . . we are confident
> they are still about us waiting to shed blood, so that we being in
> the midst of our harvest we are forced to go 30 or 40 men a day
> with their arms and a guard to accompany and work together.

The situation was precarious: If men went to gather the harvest, they might be killed by Natives in the fields; if they did not gather the harvest, they all might die of starvation over the long winter.

Days later Samuel Childs and Samuel Allen were attacked at dusk just one mile from the town. The two were wounded and fell from their horses but were able to escape; Childs did so "by dashing through an adjacent pond." Allen had been "wounded by a shoot [sic] going into his buttock." Childs was shot through both shoulders, one ball penetrating so deeply that it had to be removed through his back. He was also shot through a finger, which had to be amputated later.

Colonial forces were duly equipped to make a show of force. The experience of 1704 had taught settlers that winter was treacherous, when rivers froze over and snow muffled sounds. Snowshoes and moccasins were pro-vided for all British garrison soldiers, and scouts went out to patrol against surprise attacks. In February 1725, eight men from the town headed north in a preemptive scouting expedition. They were "men of estate and [who] have been prisoners with the Indians, and know their manners."

Not everything went according to plan. Lieutenant Timothy Childs submitted a bill for reimbursement to cover expenses for a sick soldier who lodged with Reverend Williams. Part of the charges were for "six weeks' attendance by Rev. John Williams' maid." The maid was likely in addition to the two servants Williams owned at the time: a boy of mixed race named Meseek and a Black boy named Kedar. He must have purchased these enslaved people to succeed Frank and Parthena, who had been killed by Indians in the 1704 raid. Williams billed Childs for four pounds of sugar, wine, and "spice of sundry sorts" that the ill soldier consumed. Sugar must have really made the medicine go down.

The next month, at least sixty-five men under the leadership of Captain Thomas Wells, Jr., of Deerfield traveled to the borders of New France. On their return from the scouting mission, one of the canoes was upset by a se-ries of rapids and three men drowned. In the end, the expedition returned home without anything to show—but the town was not attacked.

Many of those who had been captured by the Indians turned their experience and skills to good use later. At least two dozen Deerfield men became scouts or rangers, including Joseph Clesson, John Cat-lin, Jr., and Joseph Kellogg. Another ten or so served in the same capacity, having been young boys during the 1704 raid. James Corse, a "noted hunter and scout," was the son and brother of captives, and his sister Elizabeth had been taken captive. By virtue of their expe-riences, these men rose above being common farmers or settlers and achieved prominence as military men. Jonathan Hoyt won respect as "a skillful woodsman, scout and officer" and became an officer in the militia. Thomas Baker, Joseph Kellogg, his brother Martin Kellogg, and Samuel Williams became provincial officers. Three of them—the two Kelloggs and Williams—also became paid interpreters for the government, due to the linguistic talents they had gained.

During this time, Deerfield was spared—there were no killings. Three men had drowned, three were injured, and one was captured. No women or children were harmed or taken. In 1728, Dudley Woodbridge traveled to Deerfield and stayed with the Hinsdale family. He drew a sketch of the town, depicting the meetinghouse, "dwelling houses," and surrounding features including a few trees, a leaf, a dog prancing in the street, mathematical calculations, and some doodles. The largest drawing on the page was not the church, the town's religious center, but rather the Sheldon House, its beating heart of survival. Twenty-four years after the raid, this was the first known image of the house. Despite many challenges, Deerfield continued to endure.

An Anniversary and a Funeral

February 1729 marked the twenty-fifth anniversary of the Deerfield Massacre. Twenty-five winters had passed since the deadly, predawn raid. Nothing in the history books records whether, or how, the inhabitants of Deerfield remembered the day. Did John Williams preach a sermon in remembrance of the dead? Did the survivors gather for a public event at the meetinghouse, or at the Old Indian House? Or did they hold somber, candlelit vigils in the privacy of their homes? Even if there was no public ceremony, it is inconceivable that the significance of the day went unmentioned. Did unsullied snow cover the ground, a reminder that a quarter century earlier the raiders had stained the white snow red with their victims' blood?

On April 29, the town built a fine new meetinghouse to accommodate Deerfield's growing population. On June 10, John Williams suffered an attack of "apoplexy"—a stroke. He was sixty-five years old—a venerable age for a man in early eighteenth-century New England—and had served as the town's spiritual leader for the last forty-three years, since 1686. He had straddled two centuries of American history. And he had suffered an ordeal and test of faith unparalleled in the annals of early America. Paralyzed, bedridden for two days and unable to speak, but in full possession of his mental faculties, did Williams tally for a last time everything he had lost? A murdered wife and two slain children; dozens of friends and neighbors slaughtered; and a little girl lost, his beloved Eunice who never returned home to him? Or did he gain comfort from all the good he had done, the people whose faith he had sustained during their captivity, comforted during a time of blood and madness, redeemed and carried home, and worked alongside to rebuild their town?

John Williams died on June 12, 1729. Rev. Isaac Chauncy from nearby Hadley eulogized him as "one of the pillars of the land," and said that his death not only was "a grievous breach upon Deerfield," but also left a void in the religious faith and fervor throughout New England. "We are not born for ourselves," Chauncy stated, "but are members of communities." Williams was someone "who shone as the *Lights* in the world, and taught by *example* as well as preaching." John Williams had remained unbending and unwavering during his personal suffering, and his obituary proclaimed: "He was redeemed from the flames, passed through the wilderness and sea of danger, and . . . reached a temple eternal in the heavens." His coffin was borne to the Old Burying Ground, not far from the site of the house from which he and his family had been wrenched on that awful February morning in 1704. At last he was reunited with his beloved wife Eunice, under a headstone beside hers: "Here lies the body of Rev. John Williams, the beloved and faithful pastor of this place."

It was impossible to replace a man like John Williams. Deerfield struggled for three years to find a new minister until, in 1732, the town hired Jonathan Ashley.

Deerfield and King George's War

John Williams was dead, but his son Stephen, who served as minister in Longmeadow, wanted to remember. Nostalgic for the historic days of his youth, he began collecting stories about the role of his birthplace in what he called "the wars with the Indians." Given his experiences, almost unique among captives, he was also more compassionate in his dealings with Natives, and he even brought young Native boys into his home to educate them—a reverse of his own captivity story. Soon he would experience during his search for the past an unimagined epiphany.

In the meantime, at the end of Father Rasle's War, the Massachusetts government designated Deerfield as a place of negotiation. Native tribes came to the town to press their case. In August 1735, a peace conference was held there to commemorate the end of the Fourth Anglo-Abenaki War. Indians from various tribes arrived in the small town—the largest gathering of Natives since the 1704 raid. Perhaps some of the very Indians who traveled to Deerfield now had participated in the attack on the town some thirty years earlier. Reactions of Deerfield residents must have been equally conflicted, as the Massachusetts governor met separately with the Schaghticokes, Kahnawake Mohawks, Odanak Abenakis, and Mahicans. It was agreed that a missionary would be sent to the Mahicans to bring them to the "true" Protestant faith. What resulted was not only a religious conversion, but a political and geographical one as well, in which Native lands were claimed by the British, and the Mahicans removed to New York. One of the most active in the Mahican mission was Rebecca Kellogg. Her brother Joseph had nearly forced her return from Canada and ensured she would not go back. She did not, but her affinity for Native work was marked, and she was recognized as "an extraordinary interpreter in the Iroquois language."

This time of peace allowed people to move about and to travel in safety. Eleven years after the Reverend John Williams's death, an unexpected visitor arrived in Massachusetts. It was Eunice Williams, now Marguerite, wife of Arosen. She had asked her brother Stephen to guarantee her safety and promise that no attempt would be made to hold her in New England against her will if she agreed to visit him. Satisfied, she and her husband arrived in 1740. Almost no evidence of this visit remains, but Eunice returned next year, in July 1741. She and Arosen and two children stayed for several months at Mansfield, Connecticut. Here, John Williams's eldest son, Eleazer, had settled as a minister. During her journeys to New England, Marguerite never returned to Deerfield to revisit the site of the massacre or her capture almost four decades earlier.

Her cousin, the Reverend Solomon Williams, had become a minister in Lebanon, Connecticut, and he preached a special sermon about Eunice on August 4, 1741, as an object lesson. The sermon, which he published later as a pamphlet titled "The Power and Efficacy of the Prayers of the People of God, When Rightly Offered to Him," appeared "at a time set apart for prayer for the *revival of religion*; and on the behalf of Mrs. EUNICE, the daughter of the Reverend, MR. JOHN WILLIAMS, (formerly pastor of *Deerfield*), who was then on visit *there*, from *Canada*; where she had been in a long *captivity*."

In this time of the Great Awakening, people traveled far to witness this "strange, unusual, occasion and event of divine providence." After all these years, Eunice had finally come home—what could it mean? Her Native family accompanied her. Did they plan to settle in New England? In Deerfield? After all the expeditions, all the failed efforts to ransom her, all the begging and pleading, had Deerfield's prayers—and her late father's—finally been answered? One sticking point was Eunice's conversion to the Catholic religion. Obviously, given the vise grip that Massachusetts Protestants had on religion, she couldn't stay without returning to her first faith. As her cousin preached:

> That *person* here present with us who has been for a *long time* in
> a *miserable captivity* with a *barbarous*, and *heathen* people; now
> for more than *thirty-eight years*, yet among that people bred up in
> *popish superstition*, blindness and bigotry, who by the providence
> of God came *last year*, and *now again* with her husband, and two
> of her children on a visit to her friends in *New England*.

Solomon Williams related how her father had always prayed for her return to Deerfield—but even more for her return to the true faith. Solomon hoped that her visit signaled her readiness to revert to her original religion "of her *own accord*, to make a visit to her friends." "The poor Captive" by fault of her Catholicism existed in a "pitiable and sorrowful condition." Her old family wanted her to convert back to the true Protestant faith.

How much—if any—Eunice understood of any of his remarks remains unknown. By that time, it is probable that she no longer spoke or understood English. If Eunice had understood her cousin's harsh and insulting comments, she might have returned to Canada that day. In any event, she disappointed the larger Williams family by leaving them and returning to her home in Canada. Interestingly, Solomon Williams did not try to reprint his uncle's famous book on his captivity. After its second publication in 1720, *The Redeemed Captive* remained out of print until almost twenty years after Eunice's visit. The possibility of her conversion might serve a religious revival in which she had no interest.

Still, Eunice was not put off by her experience. She returned two years later, in 1743, this time to visit her younger brother, Stephen. She had become a celebrity, or at least an eccentric. She was taken to Boston to meet with government officials. And she was taken to Deerfield—the only time she ever returned to the scenes of her childhood and what had once been her home. The Massachusetts General Court offered a generous grant of land to settle in New England, but Eunice refused, saying in Native language that she feared it would "endanger her soul." Her conversion to Catholicism was long complete by this time, and she was not comfortable in the Protestant colony. The only other reason she gave for her refusal to stay was the one she had cited years ago, when she had complained that her father, now dead, had married a second wife. Although it was a common colonial practice to remarry, perhaps Eunice considered this a betrayal of her mother, who had died on the march.

No evidence survives to know if the sight of Deerfield unlocked memories of what Eunice might have seen on that night long ago: fire, blood, death, terror. As a seven-year-old girl, she had been dragged off into the night and into another world. Eunice never wrote about her experiences, and if she talked about them, she did so in the Mohawk language of her adopted family, having forgotten how to speak English. After this visit, she went home to Canada. She never returned to Deerfield again.

Peace was still fragile on the New England frontier. In the 1740s, yet another "French and Indian War"—the third, this one called King George's War—broke out in North America. Once again, this was part of a global conflict, this time over the fate of Austrian succession. In 1740, Charles VI, the Holy Roman Emperor and patriarch of the Austrian Hapsburg family, had died, leaving a power vacuum. France allied with Spain and several German polities to prevent an Austrian power grab. Britain, fearing French dominance, supported Austria and her ruler, the Empress Maria Theresa, daughter of Charles VI.

Preparations were made throughout the Connecticut Valley. Colonel John Stoddard, the soldier who had been stationed in Reverend Williams's house on the night of the 1704 raid, was now put in charge of defense of the western frontier. Captain Elijah Williams, the son of Reverend Williams and his second wife, Abigail, commanded scouting parties from Deerfield. He was thirty-two years old. Having been born eight years after the 1704 attack, he had no memories of it, though he had grown up surrounded by the past and by his family's memories and lore.

In August 1746, an expedition of nearly a thousand French and Native allies traveled in secrecy to attack Fort Massachusetts, a garrison about thirty miles west of Deerfield. The force was led by Pierre François Rigaud de Vaudreuil, the brother of the governor general. Only twenty-some men guarded the fort, more than half of whom were ill with dysentery. The fort's inhabitants fought bravely, but agreed to an honorable surrender when they realized that only three rounds of ammunition per man remained. No further defense was possible. As usual, captives were taken. Mary, the wife of John Smead, gave birth on the way to Canada, and gave her baby an apt name: Captivity.

But not all the raiders were happy with the outcome. Many Natives felt that they had not taken enough captives. They wished to gather more to sell in French Canada. Thus, about a week later, war came back to Deerfield.

On August 25, an attack at the "Bars," some two miles south of the town, left four dead. The news of the assault on Fort Massachusetts had not yet reached Samuel Allen and his family as they went to work gathering cut hay from the fields. Allen had provided lodging and care for sick and dying Natives in his own home. In addition to the six people working in the field, there were two armed guards. An ambush was thwarted when Allen's brother-in-law, Eleazer Hawks, stumbled across the hidden attackers when hunting partridges.

Hawks was shot, but it was too late. One of the guards ran away, but Allen and the other soldiers tried to deflect the attack to give the children time to escape. His children—Eunice, age twelve; Caleb, age nine;

and Samuel, age eight—fled. Caleb hid from the attackers in a field of corn and escaped notice. Eunice fell down and an Indian clubbed her in the head and "chopped a hatchet into [her] brains." She was left for dead, but not scalped, and survived. Her younger brother Samuel was captured and taken to Canada, where he remained for over a year. He was the only captive taken that day.

Lucy Terry Prince, a Black poet in Deerfield, was twenty-two years old at the time of the attack. She was enslaved by Ebenezer Wells until 1756, when she married Abijah Prince, a free Black man. She commemorated the "Bars fight" of 1746 in the first poem written by an African American woman, preceding Phillis Wheatley.

Seventeen hundred forty-six;
The Indians did in ambush lay,
Some very valiant men to slay,
The names of whom I'll not leave out.
Samuel Allen like a hero fout,
And though he was so brave and bold,
His face no more shalt we behold
Eleazer Hawks was killed outright,
Before he had time to fight,—
Before he did the Indians see,
Was shot and killed immediately.
Oliver Amsden he was slain,
Which caused his friends much grief and pain.
Simeon Amsden they found dead,
Not many rods distant from his head.
Adonijah Gillett we do hear
Did lose his life which was so dear.
John Sadler fled across the water,
And thus escaped the dreadful slaughter.
Eunice Allen see the Indians coming,
And hopes to save herself by running,
And had not her petticoats stopped her,

The awful creatures had not catched her,
Nor tommy hawked her on the head,
And left her on the ground for dead.
Young Samuel Allen, Oh lack-a-day!
Was taken and carried to Canada.

Samuel Allen, the father, was laid to rest in the Old Burying Ground; his gravestone read: "In memory of / Mr. Samuel Allen who / fell by the Indian Savages / August the 25th 1746 / valiantly defending his / own life and children's in / the 45th year of his age." The epitaph on his stone warned: "Listen to me ye mortal men beware / that you engage no more in direful / war, by means of war my soul from / earth is fled, my body lodged in / mansions of the dead."

This was the last Indian attack on Deerfield. After decades of ambushes, raids, scalpings, kidnappings, killings, and more, warring Indians would never return to Deerfield again. The surrounding areas were not so lucky.

Deerfield and the French and Indian War

In 1748, the Treaty of Aix-la-Chapelle formally ended the War of the Austrian Succession. The treaty provided an uneasy truce in North America before the next conflict broke out. France continued to push southward down the Mississippi, building a string of forts as they went and sealing the British into a strip of the Atlantic coastline. No one knew what the French were really up to in the Ohio Territory, so the governor of Virginia sent someone to find out. His name was George Washington. He wrote in his diary: "We were agreeably surprised at the sight of thirty odd Indians coming from War." What he learned was that the French and their Native allies would fight to keep all territory west of the Alleghenies.

Deerfield, on the northern frontier, went into alert mode once again. Elijah Williams—now a major—was in charge of guarding Deerfield's military depot containing powder and lead. In September 1754, Colonel Israel Williams wrote, "It is open war with us and a dark and distressing scene opening. A merciless miscreant enemy invading us in every quarter."

Once again, vivid memories from the past must have incited déjà vu in everyone living in Deerfield. In July, Major Williams wrote, "We have so few men for guards at Deerfield and Greenfield and other places that the inhabitants are discouraged and think that they shall lose almost all the crops they have on the ground." A month later, he begged for more support: "We in Deerfield are being reduced by so many of our peoples being gone into service of the province that we have but about 70 men left in the town and how we shall be able to get hay to keep our stock and seed our ground I know not—hope the province will afford us some relief."

By the 1750s, however, Deerfield no longer sat on the edge of the frontier. It was no longer a strategic military outpost. No longer was it at the crossroads of trading routes, or the intersection of cultures. The memories of earlier times faded and were lost in the day-to-day drudgery of farming and the everlasting cycles of births, marriages, and deaths. By mid-century, the Deerfield raid was almost fifty years in the past. The majority of the participants had died; the rest were elderly outliers, living memorials to an earlier and deadlier time.

In August 1757, news of a climactic and dreadful event spread through the colonies. French general Louis-Joseph de Montcalm, his six thousand French troops, and his nearly two thousand Native allies had laid siege to Fort William Henry, located on Lake George. The fort was commanded by Colonel George Munro and contained a poorly supplied British force and a few provincial militiamen—perhaps just over two thousand men total, about a quarter of the combined French and Native forces. There was intense fighting and artillery shelling; some British cannons burst from overuse. After a few days, and without receiving requested aid, Munro honorably surrendered to Montcalm, who promised safe passage to Fort Edward, on the Hudson River. As they left the fort, the defeated train of soldiers, along with women and children, were attacked by Montcalm's Native allies, breaking the promise of safe conduct. There were some Deerfield residents under command of Colonel Munro; in the thick of the fighting, one of them, Salah Barnard, managed to fight off his attackers and escape to Fort Edward. About two hundred were killed, and several hundred taken captive, many of whom were marched into Canada and whose release had to be engineered later through Governor General Vaudreuil.

James Fenimore Cooper immortalized these events in the second volume of his *Leatherstocking Tales*. But, as George Sheldon, Deerfield's preeminent historian, later confirmed: "The readers of 'The Last of the Mohicans,' [Mahicans had been spelled with an 'a' earlier] may take the assurance that the writer did not overdraw the bloody scenes of this faithless and cowardly massacre."

In 1758, a third edition of *The Redeemed Captive* was published by Thomas Prince of Boston. Stephen Williams, the reverend's son, had encouraged this printing in the aftermath of the debacle at Fort William Henry. His father's text, with its anti-Catholic and anti-French emphasis, was a perfect tool to intensify support for the war. Stephen added two appendices to this edition: a list of those captured or killed in the 1704 raid and "an account of the mischief done by the enemy in Deerfield, from the beginning of its settlement to the death of Rev. Mr. Williams, in June, 1729." The sales of the book were recorded by Elijah Williams, the reverend's youngest son, with his second wife. At the time, he owned a tavern in Deerfield and sold the book there. In one month (January 27 to February 27, 1758) he sold seventeen copies. His father may have died thirty years earlier, but his experiences were still relevant—and in demand.

By 1758, Deerfield residents apparently felt safe enough to sell the timber they had set aside to build a new garrison in the town, and they dismantled and disposed of wood from the old garrisons. In September 1759 at the Battle of Quebec, British General James Wolfe defeated the French army under the command of General Louis-Joseph, Marquis de Montcalm, on the Plains of Abraham, just outside the walls of Quebec City. In 1763, after the French lost the Montreal campaign, France ceded its territory to Great Britain in the Treaty of Paris that formally ended the French and Indian War. France would never again be so powerful in North America, and the threat of Native attack in the eastern colonies—whether encouraged by the French, Catholic priests, or colonial governors—had dissipated.

In 1761, Eunice Williams visited her brother Stephen again at his home at Longmeadow. By now, he had become an important figure in his own right. Like his father, he had his portrait painted to mark his status. When viewed side by side, the resemblance of John and Stephen Williams in their portraits is noticeable. Eunice was now sixty-five years old. Her daughter Katherine and her grandson Thomas accompanied her. They visited for ten days before returning to their home in Canada. Stephen was unsuccessful in converting Eunice or her family to the Protestant faith; they remained, to his dismay, staunch Catholics.

What did he think of the repeated visits of his "savage" sister? Did New England, Deerfield, and faint, glimmering memories of her earliest days exert a gravitational pull on her and awaken a longing to touch her origins? It is hard to know. This would be Eunice's last visit to the British colonies. After she left, Stephen might have examined the gifts she and her husband had given him, and thought about how different their lives had turned out. One of those gifts was a fine leather bullet pouch decorated with fringe and porcupine quills. Another was a red slate gorget, a piece of armor worn to protect the throat. Eunice and Arosen gave Stephen an intricate finger-woven sash and a brightly decorated tobacco pouch. Such bags were daily accessories for Native men, who cultivated and smoked tobacco. For decades, earlier historians had described these objects as "Arosen's gifts"; now scholars interpret them as Eunice's gifts, or joint gifts from the couple.

Years later, Stephen received an update about Eunice. "Your sister lives comfortably and well and considering her advanced age enjoyed a good state of health. . . . She retains still an affectionate remembrance of her friends in New England: but tells me she never expects to see them again; the fatigues of so long a journey would be too much for her to undergo." In 1781, Stephen received a letter from her in which she admitted that this was "the last time you may hear from me." Four years later, she died at age eighty-nine. In all likelihood, she was the last survivor of the Deerfield raid of 1704.

She remained, until her end of days, the "unredeemed captive."

Deerfield and the American Revolution

In the 1770s, war came to Deerfield once more. But this time it was not a battle against France, but against England, the mother country. In 1704, such a conflict would have been unimaginable. But many colonists no longer saw themselves as British—they had become Americans. More than a century later, George Sheldon, Deerfield's nineteenth-century historian extraordinaire, observed "but amid all the harassing distress of this dark period the men and women were not the subjects of abject, helpless fear. They were brave and determined and held their own by sheer force of character—and we must not forget that they were the fathers and mothers of those who fought at Bunker Hill, Saratoga, and Yorktown."

Proto-Americans of the 1600s and early 1700s had gone far and survived much. Separated from England by a vast ocean, the colonists learned how to thrive in an unknown wilderness, build towns and farms, raise families, fight battles against Indians and the French empire, and survive. They learned how to take care of themselves, and they formed the core of the American character—an independent spirit that led to the American Revolution. And how times had changed since the Deerfield raid of 1704 and the subsequent Indian Wars of the 1700s. Colonists looked back at the previous Indian Wars and reshaped them into a propaganda tool against the British. As the Reverend Nathan Fiske observed:

> When [the first settlers] purchased lands of the natives, they
> thought them their own; and when they cultivated them for their
> children whom they hoped to leave free and happy, they little
> thought that their posterity would be disturbed in their possessions
> by *Britons*, more than themselves were by savage Indians.

Memory was now reworked in the bright flare of revolutionary politics.

For Deerfield residents, the 1704 raid was once again relevant, even if they were no longer fighting beside the English, but against them. Their past was now important to their future. As Fiske continued:

We are not anxious lest the frightful Savage should spring from his thicket with his murderous tomahawk, or drive the leaden death through our bodies before we are aware; nor lest, when we return home, we should find our dwellings in ashes, our little ones dashed against the stones, and our wives carried captive through a perilous, dreadful wilderness, by those whose tender mercies are cruelty.

Death or captivity at the hands of the Indians had now been replaced by the fear of tyranny under the British Empire. Now the colonists were captives once again, but of their king. And what could make those connections more clear than reprinting a popular captivity narrative? Captivity was a theme that began with sin, and worked through with suffering, and finally ended with redemption. For Deerfield residents as well as others, the conflict with the British—like those of the Indian Wars—had an end point.

The story of the Reverend John Williams resonated once again in this atmosphere of war. *The Redeemed Captive* was reprinted again in 1773, 1774, and 1776. Furthermore, its anti-Catholic sentiments were once again relevant in the aftermath of the Quebec Act, passed by Parliament in an attempt to transform the formerly French colony into a part of the British Empire. The act not only extended the territory of French Canada beyond the treaty of 1763, but also granted freedom of worship to its French Catholics.

Not quite seven decades after the raid of 1704, New Englanders understood their present conflict in light of the past. And the tension was about to become more intense: "A big dish of tea made in Boston Harbor, December 16th, 1773, stimulated the blood of two continents," wrote George Sheldon. Deerfield resident David Field happened to be in Boston on the day of the momentous brewing, and brought home all the news. After a long night at David Saxton's tavern, the Whigs of Deerfield danced throughout The Street, singing:

Who went aboard the British ships their vengeance to administer,
And didn't care a tarnal bit for any king or minister;
Who made a duced mess of tea, in one on the biggest dishes,
Steeped the Bohea in the sea, and treated all the fishes.

Deerfield contained both ardent Whigs who supported revolution and loy-alist Tories. Many families in the town had strong ties to Britain, having received military commissions, as had George Washington, during the earlier wars. These local loyalists included the minister Jonathan Ashley, the judge, the sheriff, three doctors, the town clerk, a storekeeper, and two of the three tavern owners. But the rest of the town seemed energetically Whiggish, so much so that Ashley's devout loyalty to King George pro-voked his congregation to cut off his salary and supply of firewood in re-taliation.

In July 1774, several Whigs brought a liberty pole, symbolizing in-dependence from Great Britain, into town. Generally, these were tall, straight pine trunks, from which flags could be flown. The pole could also serve as a bulletin board for posts and public taunts. One night, when it was left unguarded, several Tories sawed the Deerfield liberty pole in half. The wielder of the saw wrote in a letter:

> Where are things going, that so sensible people as you know
> the town of Deerfield are, should suffer these rascals to carry
> matters on so. I cannot help feeling, and very sensibly, when I
> think what the consequences of these things will be and have no
> reason to think but that they will issue in blood.

Patriots erected a second liberty pole in front of David Field's store. Field had served during the Indian Wars and was a prominent townsman.

At a Deerfield town meeting on April 20, the people voted that the town would provide a "Minute company" of soldiers. The vote was none too soon: The day before, on April 19, the "shot heard round the world" had been fired at Lexington and Concord, Massachusetts. Those events were some eighty miles from Deerfield; news must have traveled fast because men left Deerfield so quickly to join the fight that they lacked even basic supplies. One wrote, "After I had got from home I found myself destitute of so necessary an article as a blanket."

On May 6, 1775, Deerfield was graced with a visit by none other than dashing Benedict Arnold, on his way to capturing Fort Ticonderoga. Arnold appeared in a resplendent uniform—"bright epaulettes, gold lace and waving plumes"—and stopped at Salah Barnard's tavern (now the Frary House). He then sent for Thomas Dickinson and before rushing north to Vermont, presented him with a commission from the Committee of Safety, to provide supplies. Dickinson's first task was to provide fifteen cows (fifteen thousand pounds of beef) for the patriot armies. Deerfield men also served at the Battle of Bunker Hill in June 1775.

The people of Deerfield declared independence nine days before history was made in Philadelphia on July 4, 1776. On June 25, Deerfield declared:

> Voted that *this town will (if the Honorable Congress shall for the safety of the United States declare them* INDEPENDENT *of the Kingdom of Great Britain) solemnly engage with their* LIVES *and* FORTUNES *to support them in the measure.*

Deerfield resident Colonel David Field was selected to attend the Constitutional Convention. In 1787, his son followed in his footsteps: Samuel Field attended the State Convention in Boston and voted to ratify the United States Constitution.

But this was not only a white man's war. About nine thousand Black soldiers fought with bravery and valor on both sides. During the Revolution, several Native tribes also fought for the British, while others supported the Americans. Kahnawake Mohawks allied with Britain, and in 1777, the British—who now controlled Canada—recruited Abenaki warriors from Montreal, some of whom may have been descendants of Deerfield captives who did not return. Yet after the American Revolution, Indians were treated with the same disdain—if not more—than before. The Indian Wars of the 1700s had set the template for another century of Indian wars in the American West. The conflicts on the New England frontier—including at Deerfield—had inaugurated more than two hundred years of bloody conflict between whites and Indians.

Part III

MEMORY, MYTH, AND LEGEND

George Sheldon passes the torch to a new generation.

7

ANTIQUARIAN SANCTIFICATION

February 1804 marked the one hundredth anniversary of the Deerfield Massacre. Rev. John Taylor, Deerfield's minister since 1787, preached a sermon about it. Taylor admired his predecessor and had even edited two editions of *The Redeemed Captive*, in 1793 and 1800. In the atmosphere of the French Revolutionary and Napoleonic Wars, John Williams's anti-French rhetoric took on a new tone and dimension. In the 1790s the United States fought a quasi naval war with France, prompting President John Adams in 1798 to recall George Washington, now in retirement at Mount Vernon, into military service. Taylor's sermon compared the raid on Deerfield to the destruction of Jerusalem, concluding, "Perhaps no town in the Commonwealth, suffered, in early times, from the depredations of the natives, equally with Deerfield." Taylor noted, however:

> I am sensible that it is not in my power to describe; nor, indeed, is it in the power of language to convey to your minds an adequate idea of their sufferings. To obtain such an idea it is necessary that you should be placed in a similar situation; should endure similar trials, and should drink of a cup equally bitter.

In fact, in a time when all living memory of the 1704 raid had long been buried, the psychological repercussions continued. Taylor was the first author to describe the events of 1704 as a "massacre." Those who lived through it had never called it that.

In reviewing the events of 1704, Taylor blamed "the French, who united with, and instigated the savages to some part of their cruel conduct," noting that "the French encouraged a war of extermination." Taylor was an ardent Federalist and likely doubted the actions of the French government in his own time, especially as it had moved from revolution to terror. But he did not excuse the conduct of the English, in pursuing similar methods, and he urged reconsideration of Native conduct: "We are too much inclined to treat the natives with severity." In fact, Taylor praised the Indians for their "benevolence, the laborious and generous attention" that they paid to captives in treating their wounds, assisting their travel, and sharing food.

> This shows that the real character of the natives is but little
> known; and, that those traits in their character which appear
> to mark the extremes of cruelty, must be considered rather as
> the effects of habit, and of their national ideas of the honors,
> and duties of war, than the effects of an inherently cruel
> temper.

Yet even as Taylor bade his audience learn from the lessons of history to inform the present, he found himself looking straight into that very human past. Sitting in the congregation that day was Eunice Allen, who had survived an attack at the Bars in 1746. Taylor singled her out: "We still have among us the living witness of Indian barbarities, one of whom bears the mark of the tomahawk on her head." One can imagine every person in church that day turning to stare at her and search for evidence of the scar. Long after the threat of Native raids had passed, Eunice Allen remained a living reminder—and a haunting one—of Deerfield's not-so-ancient and violent past. She had been forever marked by that one event, and for the rest of her life had had to live with the visible scars. How many invisible scars she and her community carried, we can never know.

One Blood

In August 1837, a surprise expedition of twenty-five Abenaki Natives from the St. Francis mission came down from Canada and arrived at Deerfield. As a local paper, the *Greenfield Gazette and Mercury*, recorded:

> Our people were thrown into a state of considerable emotion last
> Monday evening and Tuesday, by the encampment of a body
> of Indians from Canada, about twenty-five in number who . . .
> went to Deerfield where they encamped, and still remain.

It had been 133 years since the destruction of the town in 1704. But this was not a war party, and no one raised an alarm. Those times were long past in this year of Queen Victoria's accession across the ocean.

Instead, the visitors had come with a purpose. The party included an eighty-six-year-old Abenaki woman who, before she died, wanted to see Deerfield. Her name was Eunice, and newspaper reports identified her as a granddaughter of Eunice Williams, the daughter of Rev. John Williams who had stayed in French Canada and married a Native man named Arosen. This Eunice, her granddaughter, called the town "Williamsecook," which meant "the Williams' place." She had come, after all these years, to see with her own eyes the place where her story had begun, and she had brought her extended family with her: daughter and son-in-law (Marie Eunice Agent and Louis Watso) along with their children (twin sons Simon and Joseph Louis and daughter Suzanne). Also along were Eunice's great-grandson and his pregnant wife (Jean Baptiste Watso and Marguerite Obomsawin). Her son-in-law's daughters from his first marriage came as well (at least one with her child), along with his unmarried sister. That meant at least eleven of the twenty-five were from the same immediate family group, six of whom were descendants of Reverend Williams's daughter.

Not everyone was convinced of this Eunice's supposed genealogy, however. The *Hampshire Gazette* stated: "We do not think there is any evidence that she is descended from Eunice Williams except her word."

Still, whether related by blood or wishful thinking, the Abenaki visit was nonetheless a meaningful event. Over the years a number of Williams descendants continued to return to the Connecticut Valley and Deerfield, as if irresistibly drawn by a genetic memory of their common past. Native versions of past events and family descent had been kept alive via oral traditions. On the Native side, the story went that the first Eunice had started a tradition of naming girl children after her. Thus, this Eunice was the granddaughter of the first Eunice. She passed the name on to her granddaughter, Marie Eunice Agent, who accompanied her on the trip. Her grandson and his wife celebrated the birth of a child on the return journey to Canada. But because the child was a boy, they named him William. When a baby girl was born later, she was duly named Eunice, according to her great-grandmother's wish: "This child will be called Eunice, as I was called by my grandmother, Eunice Williams the white papoose." Grandmother Eunice may have been very old and blind by this time, but she was insistent that traditions were continued—and she got her way.

Thus, this was a visit of remembrance and reconciliation. It was not a winter raid, but a cordial summer visit. There were no snowshoes, or muskets, or war clubs, but rather gifts and tokens of friendship. As the *Greenfield Gazette and Mercury* noted with relief and approval: "They appear to be comfortably well off for Indians, having several horses and wagons, and a goodly supply of blankets and buffalo robes," implying, in other words, that these Indians were respectable and not thieves or beggars, a common nineteenth-century racist trope about Native Americans. What this Abenaki visit started in 1837, if it had not begun earlier, was the formation of a new Native attachment to this place. This visit was likely also related to tensions in their Canadian homelands; the Patriots' Rebellion (*Guerre des Patriotes*) in Lower Canada flared precipitously in the summer of 1837. For the Abenakis, who wished to remain neutral, an extended visit to New England may have been the perfect excuse for a timely absence.

But such visits were not unusual. As in America today, it was a custom among the Abenaki to take family vacations over the summer months. Extended families often banded together on these travel holidays with their elders and young children. As Deerfield's Rev. John Fessenden recalled, "at various times" several groups had visited the town: "several of her [the original Eunice's] descendants have visited Deerfield and other towns in New England, claiming relationship with the descendants of Rev. Mr. Williams, and have been hospitably received." In a complete reversal from a hundred and thirty years previous, the Abenaki Natives were now invited into Deerfield homes. They walked invited through doors rather than chopping them open. Eunice was offered a comfortable room in a house but preferred to remain in the temporary Abenaki encampment. Like her grandmother, she had, according to a stereotyped, racist account, "a relish for the savage mode and habits of living." As the *Gazette* reported, "She scorns the effeminate comforts of civilized life as much as her grandmother did when she visited her afflicted Father and resists every importunity to lodge indoors." The paper erred in claiming that the original Eunice had come to Deerfield to visit her father, Reverend Williams, years after his return from captivity. She never did so.

The visit turned into an impromptu celebration and spectacle. White Williams family descendants called the visitors "our cousins," and Deerfield residents congregated with them in various activities. Several Natives unpacked the canoes that they had brought in their wagons and paddled on the Connecticut River with Deerfield residents. Decades later, Jonas Wilder recalled the visit: "The Williams Indians came down from Canada, and camped on the riverbank. A real pretty young squaw took me out on the river in a birch bark canoe, and we had a good time." This Eunice was toured around the town, and "she was shown many things among which was the house the door of which had resisted the attacking Indians on that memorable night of the sack of Deerfield in 1704." What must this Eunice have thought when she saw the ax marks in the door, cut by Natives who were as much her ancestors as the white captives that had been taken from inside these houses? In a more serious vein, the Abenaki group visited the graves of John and Eunice Williams, and attended Sunday church services in an "orderly and reverent manner." In all ways they behaved "decently and inoffensively." (In other words, they did not behave like stereotypical savages.)

Several of the Abenakis and villagers even exchanged gifts. Catherine Williams from Deerfield, twenty-one-year-old descendant of Reverend Williams, received a gift of a fine ash-splint basket from her twenty-six-year-old distant Indian cousin Sophie (Marie Saraphine Watso Denis-Paul), also descended from the Williams family. The beautiful item still bears a handwritten inscription: "Basket given me September 1837 / By Sophie one of the St. Francis Indians / Connected with the Williams family."

During this visit, Stephen West Williams, a sixth-generation Williams descendant, was also gifted with the knowledge of Louis Watso, elderly Eunice's grandson-in-law, who taught Williams about indigenous plants and herbal medicine. As Williams wrote, "When the tribe of Indians from Canada were here in 1837, Louis Watso, their doctor gave me an account of the principal medical plants which they used in their practice." One can imagine the two men spending multiple afternoons examining specimens such as narrow-leaved laurel and wild ginger ("snake head plant" to the Abenaki). Watso and the others, however, were "much offended" with Williams when he refused to try the remedy for his own malady: heart palpitations. Still, Williams noted many Native recommendations of plants to treat various ailments: blue cohosh ("colic, sore throat, rheumatism, dropsy," and "female complaints"); witch hazel ("sedative and resolvent in painful tumors"); mountain ash ("tonic in diseases of the heart"); and common lousewort ("to cure the bite of the rattlesnake"). While we can't know how much of this information he gleaned specifically from the Abenakis in 1837, he did give them much credit. In the entry for *Mitchella repens*, or partridge berry, he noted: "The Indian Dr. Louis uses it in combination with the *Spiraea alba*, a species of hardhack, for the cure of salt rheum [eczema]." In 1849, Williams published this research in the *American Medical Association Transactions*, titled "Report on the Indigenous Medical Botany of Massachusetts."

As minister of the First Congregational Society Church of Deerfield, Reverend Fessenden delivered a special sermon on the occasion of the visit. He reminded his congregation of the events of 1704 and their aftermath. Fessenden revealed that while Reverend Williams's daughter Eunice had eventually visited her relatives in Deerfield "dressed in the Indian costume," nothing could persuade her to remain, so she returned to Canada "and there ended her days, a true savage." Yet, for his sermon, Fessenden selected as his biblical text Acts 17:26: "And hath made of one blood all nations of men for to dwell on all the face of the earth; and hath determined the times before appointed, and the bounds of their habitation." Fessenden was determined to bury the hatchet, as it were. He did not dwell on all the blood spilled during the attack. Instead, he argued that the Bible spoke of "a common origin for all the differing tribes and races of men," and that "all mankind are of one blood." He cited a universal "common parentage," and added that in visiting the Williamses' graves, the Natives showed that "that ancestor [was] our own no less than theirs."

Despite his insult that Eunice was a "savage," Fessenden spoke of forgiveness as well as compassionate understanding. "I would say as ye have buried the hatchet whose traces still remain on the ancient portal," he offered, referencing the tomahawk and hatchet cuts that scarred the Old Indian Door, "to remind us of by-gone days of blood and violence, of suffering and captivity, so sleep the sword by which these wrongs—if wrongs they were—have been fully avenged." That phrase, "*if* wrongs they were," was an astonishing gesture of reconciliation in the context of that time and place. In closing, Fessenden invoked the night of February 29, 1704, by referencing the Sheldon residence, the landmark known as the Old Indian House:

> We look at the mouldering moss-covered house of strength,
> which has survived the perilous times of which we are
> speaking, and as we behold the deep indented marks of savage
> and mortal weapons, the record of "dreadful summoners," at
> dead of night, storming the bolted doors of maternal tenderness
> and sleeping infancy, we shudder at the thought of those
> barbarous cruelties, which were preparing for the defenseless
> and unsuspecting inmates.

And yet, Fessenden asked, who were they to question the designs of Providence? "Judge not, lest ye be judged."

A few weeks later, on August 29, 1837, the *Greenfield Gazette and Mercury* published another story about the visit: "Civilization Rebuked by Savages," read the headline.

> We are informed that a party of men from this town went over to Deerfield Sabbath before last, to make a visit to the Indians who were encamped there. On going into their lodges, one of the "savages" enquired what the party had come for. "To visit you" was the reply. "We don't receive visits on the Sabbath, please to withdraw"—was the answer. They did withdraw with "a flea in their ear," and these "natives of the forest" quietly and decorously attended divine service. Their revered progenitor, Rev. John Williams, would have rendered heartfelt thanks, to have known that his aboriginal descendants would thus respect divine institutions, and so pointedly and justly rebuke those of his own race, who had so far forgotten their duty to their MAKER as to profane his holy day.

As the article concluded, it was a rude response, but the right one: "This party of Indians have demeaned themselves with impudence, and yet with the utmost propriety." They were better and more proper descendants of Reverend Williams than the curious New Englanders searching for a racially stereotyped exhibit.

As welcomed as they were, the Natives were still viewed as curiosities. The temporary camp was swarmed with visitors, with brisk trading by the Natives, "on account of the rarity of any of the descendants of this race in our vicinity at the present day." Note the implied trope of the "vanished race." They were living relics from Deerfield's storied past, not partners in telling the story of 1704, or valuable sources possessing hitherto unknown information about the raid, the captives, or those who were never redeemed and remained in Canada. In fact, the same editions of the Greenfield newspaper from August 29 and September 5 that described the Native visit also included promotional advertisements for Stephen West Williams's new memoir of the Reverend Williams, his ancestor. No one was interested in an alternative, multicultural Indian perspective on the meaning of the events of 1704. No article about their visit refrained from, at some point, resorting to the word "savage" to describe them.

But many Indians regarded the Connecticut Valley as their ancestral homeland, which they had been forced to abandon. This was therefore a significant return, in which by their presence Natives not only reclaimed their spiritual connection to these lands, but participated in rewriting past history and attempting to restore balance to a largely white narrative. Gifts of baskets and swaps reinserted a Native presence into Deerfield's history and brought it literally into parlors across the town. In addition, this Abenaki visit reclaimed what had been assumed as Mohawk heritage. After all, Reverend Williams and his son Stephen had been taken by Abenaki masters, so how did Eunice end up with the Mohawks? This retelling of Eunice with Abenaki heritage was about staking a claim to a different Native past.

The following year, the *Courier* newspaper in nearby Northampton, Massachusetts, published on June 3, 1838, a much different, thoroughly racist view about visiting Natives and the myth of the vanishing race:

> The Miserable Remnants of a tribe of Indians from Canada,
> squatting in the woods a mile or two from town have been,
> and continue to be, the lions in this vicinity. Strange how
> demoralizing the contact of civilization with that of savage
> life, where it is but partial and of a loose and anti-Christian
> character . . . The lofty bearing and noble demeanor of
> the primitive Indians are gone, and nothing is left but the
> abject and debased exterior of the red man. . . . Altogether
> considered, they are merely a wretched remnant of a race of
> noble and proud Red men, who once tenanted this valley, and
> whose stealthy tread and uplifted tomahawk, carried death to
> hearts terrified by their appalling war-cry.

The alleged pitiful state of the visiting Indians prompted some New Englanders to ask: What had their colonial forefathers been so afraid of? Fessenden's radical egalitarian sentiments may have been too much for

Deerfield residents to bear. In an age that saw *The Last of the Mohicans* become a bestseller and the violence of King Philip's War performed on stage to sell-out audiences in the play *Metamora; or, The Last of the Wampanoags*, some people may have found it easier to accept fictional accounts rather than come to terms with real past history. Although Fessenden had served in Deerfield since 1830 (when Dr. Willard had stepped down due to blindness), he was "dismissed" in 1840, just three years after Eunice's visit and his sermon. For an outsider, it was all too easy to dismiss the past and move on. But to those in his audiences, whose ancestors had lived and died by Native hands, it was a different story.

Deerfield's Sanguineto

A year later, in 1838, Deerfield commemorated its heritage and the men slain in 1675 by erecting a new public monument at Bloody Brook. The original, installed just after the massacre, is likely the oldest monument to veterans in America. In 1728, Dudley Woodbridge had visited Deerfield to see the monument, then just a stone in the ground and already in need of repair. In 1793, the Reverend William Bentley of Salem, Massachusetts, observed: "We passed Bloody Brook and the monument erected to the memory of the men, who perished by the stratagems of the Indians." But over the course of time, that original memorial had fallen down and a repair or replacement was now needed.

This new memorial had been years in the planning. Before another monument could be erected, however, the sponsors wanted to be sure that they were honoring the right location. Perhaps X didn't mark the spot after all? The original marker had all but disappeared. Still, a visible capstone remained, so the surrounding ground was excavated. Several feet down, the diggers unearthed what they were looking for—the skulls and bones of seventy-six men who had once feasted on those "dear and deadly grapes" before they met their doom. "The bones were found much decayed," it was reported, "or rather changed into terrene substances, yet still retaining their primitive forms, with some degree of solidity, yet easily crumbled to dust by pressure of the fingers, and generally exhibiting a chocolate color, and often that of a bright scarlet, in masses of dark earth." The spot was directly in front of the home of Stephen Whitney—no one recorded what he thought having a monument or a mass grave in his front yard. The monument would be placed just north of the gravesite, which would be marked with a flat, flagstone slab.

At the same time, about two miles away, another site of buried bones was discovered; these were likely Indians who had been killed in the battle. They received no marker or recognition.

The cornerstone ceremony began at 11:00 a.m., on September 30, 1835. A procession gathered in front of Russell's Hotel. They joined with a military band, which escorted the participants and spectators to the monument site, and then fired a volley of introduction. A star-studded event awaited, supervised by the Honorable George Grennell, Member of the House of Representatives for Massachusetts, with military units supervised by Brigadier General James A. Whitney, who became the collector of customs for the Port of Boston. Grennell had attended Deerfield Academy, and Whitney had been born in Bloody Brook, which was later given the more neutral-sounding name of South Deerfield.

The cornerstone was then laid, followed by a prayer by Reverend Fessenden of Deerfield, then a short address by General Epaphras Hoyt, also of Deerfield and author of *Antiquarian Researches: Comprising a History of the Indian Wars*. As Hoyt opened, "Too long have the valuable men, who fell on this ground, slumbered in obscurity—lost to the world." He continued on a solemn note, "Long have the residents of this soil traversed over the hallowed spot unconscious that they were treading upon the ashes of the fallen heroes."

After Hoyt had finished, the band played a mournful dirge, and an original hymn, written by Dr. Samuel Willard, was sung. One verse chorused:

Ye Patriot Dead, whose ashes lie
Interred beneath this smiling sky,
To you this monument we rear,
And memory sheds a grateful tear.

The audience then walked to an open field in front of the Whitney house, where there were seats and a stage shaded by a large walnut tree. There was additional music, praying, and singing until Edward Everett rose to give the official address. Everett was one of the most sought-after and celebrated orators of his time. He had just stepped down from the U.S House of Representatives and would later serve as minister to the United Kingdom, governor of Massachusetts, president of Harvard University, and secretary of state for President Fillmore. He had met the Marquis de Lafayette and would, during the Civil War, deliver an oration before Abraham Lincoln took the stage in November 1863 to dedicate the national cemetery at Gettysburg. More than six thousand people listened raptly as Everett began. He was a celebrated, nineteenth-century luminary, a man of real achievement famous in his time but today lost to history, remembered only as a footnote to the Gettysburg Address, where his longwinded speech took two hours to convey what Lincoln could communicate in two minutes.

Speaking to the assembled crowd "on this hallowed spot," Everett evoked the "unimaginable hardships" in a "hostile wilderness." He recounted the story of early Deerfield, climaxing with tragedy at Bloody Brook. He honored the heroism of the dead and the obligation to remember:

> No, we ought never to forget, we ought this day especially
> to remember, that it was in their sacrifices and trials, their
> heart-rending sorrows, their ever-renewed tribulations, their
> wanderings, their conflicts, their wants and their woes,—that
> the corner-stone of our privileges and blessings was laid.

Everett was hard on the Natives: "We must look on the Indian," he proclaimed in typical racist language, "not with the eye of sentiment and romance, but of truth and reality. See as he really is, he stands low in the scale of humanity." He called the Natives "degraded, ignorant savage[s]" and decried Indian life as "an indolent, a squalid, and a cheerless existence." These sentiments were widely held and unquestioned by most whites. Everett then shifted to what he believed was a genuine, conciliatory tone:

> The ground, on which we stand is wet with the blood, which
> flowed beneath the tomahawk of [King Philip's] young men;
> and the darkness of night in these peaceful vales was often
> lighted up, in days of yore, by the flames of burning villages,
> kindled by his ruthless warriors. But that blood has sunk, not
> forgotten, but forgiven, into the ground. Havoc and dismay no
> longer stalk through these happy fields;—and as we meet today
> to perform the simple and affecting rites of commemoration
> over the grave of the gallant victims of the struggle, let us drop
> a compassionate tear also for these the benighted children of
> the forest,—the orphans of Providence, whose cruelties have
> long since been expiated by their fate. It could not be expected
> of them, to enter into the high counsels of heaven. It was not
> for them, dark and uninstructed even in the wisdom of man,—
> to comprehend the great design of Providence, of which their
> wilderness was the appointed theater.

Everett's comments were wildly racist and patronizing, yet he worried that he might be too *generous* in forgiving the Indians, and insulting to the brave men whose bones moldered in the grave before him.

He spoke in the context of the late 1830s, after nearly a decade of "Indian removal" efforts. These forced migrations had been signed into law by President Andrew Jackson in the Indian Removal Act in May 1830. Any Native Americans living east of the Mississippi River were now ordered to remove themselves west into current-day Oklahoma. This act mainly affected southern Native tribes, including the Chickasaw, Choctaw, Creek, Cherokee, and Seminole, which led to the infamous "Trail of Tears." But more easterly tribes were also affected. In 1832, the Black Hawk War in Illinois was a failed attempt by Native Americans to take back their ancestral land. Many Natives had already been displaced from New England, and these actions catalyzed negative national opinion about Indians in general. Everett pandered to these prejudices. Because the Natives led a nomadic existence, he claimed, their "removal from one tract of country to another is comparatively easy." That was easy to say in an empty field where Native Americans had "slaughtered" early settlers some one hundred and sixty years ago. As Everett concluded:

> Very different was an Indian War, a century and a half ago, from those which are waged at the present day, in which, from the bosom of the overswarming population of the states, regiments of infantry, artillery, and dragoons are sent out, to trample down the enervated remnants of once warlike races, with the certainty on both sides, if that force should fail, that another twice as powerful would instantly take its place.

No longer did New Englanders have to fear reprisals by Indians. Instead, whites had "won" the larger war, had written the victor's history, and could erect monuments wherever they pleased, praising the white settlers who perished on Native lands.

Bloody Brook continued to attract attention. In June 1838, Lucy Thurston Goodale visited the location with a small group. "The master of the house" (probably Stephen Whitney) came to greet them and toured them around the area. The marble monument had not yet been installed, so he showed them the stream and the old grave marker; he "lifted the old gravestone which had fallen down, that we might see the inscription." Last, he showed them a presumably authentic piece of living history, much like the sycamore tree in Deerfield's common. According to Goodale, he

> pointed out a venerable looking grapevine which was clambering over some trees near his gateway, and said that he thought it probable that it might have been growing at the very time that the unfortunate band was killed by the Indians.

At the end of the 1835 commemoration, the sponsors passed the plate for donations to complete the monument. Contributions failed to cover the full cost, so additional fundraising took place over the next three years. That explains why there was no monument for Goodale to visit in summer of 1838. Later that year, a white marble column rose to memorialize the second most significant event in Deerfield history besides the raid of 1704, the battle of Bloody Brook in 1675. An inscription carved near the base summarized the disaster:

> On this ground Capt. THOMAS LATHROP and eighty four men under his command, including eighteen teamsters, from Deerfield, conveying stores from that town to Hadley, were ambuscaded by about 700 Indians, and the Captain and seventy six men slain, September 18th, 1675. The soldiers who fell, were described by a contemporary Historian, as "a Choice company of young men, the very flower of the County of Essex, none of whom were afraid to speak with the enemy in the gate." 'And Sanguinetto tells you where the dead Made the earth wet and turned the unwilling waters red.' The grave of the slain is marked by a stone slab, 21 rods [about 400 feet] southerly of this monument.

For educated audiences of the 1830s, the last lines referenced *Childe Harold's Pilgrimage*, by Lord Byron, and the Battle of Lake Trasimene in the Second Punic War. In 217 BC, Carthaginian troops under the command of Hannibal slaughtered the Roman army. The legend arose that for three days, blood drained into the nearby waters, resulting in the renaming of the stream the "Sanguineto," or "Blood River."

This was hardly a river, but it was close enough. For Deerfield, it had indeed been a very Bloody Brook.

The Old Indian House

More than one hundred and fifty years after the Deerfield raid, the John Sheldon House—now known as the Old Indian House—still stood as a venerable witness to that night. In 1744, forty years after the attack, it was purchased by Jonathan Hoyt. Hoyt had been a six-year-old boy in 1704; he had survived the raid, been taken captive, endured the march to Canada, and been redeemed. What terrifying memories from his childhood did living in the house awaken? Every day he passed through the scarred front door. He beheld the musket-ball holes in the walls. Now that danger was almost over. After the fight at the Bars in 1746, the Indian wars in Deerfield were done. Of course, there were more Indian wars, including the French and Indian War, but violence came no more to Deerfield.

Hoyt died in 1799. The property remained in the Hoyt family until it passed to Elihu Hoyt (1771 to 1833) in 1814. He had been born and raised there, and he enjoyed receiving visitors and regaling them with lore about the attack. In 1833, the last year of his life, Hoyt published a book, *A Brief Sketch of the First Settlement of Deerfield, Mass.: Together with a Few Events which Took Place There in Early Times.* Unsurprisingly, among the "few events" that Hoyt wrote about, he devoted the most attention—fourteen pages—to the raid of 1704. In a clever marketing ploy, Hoyt sold the book to tourists who wanted to know more about the house.

In October 1728, the first representation of the Sheldon House had appeared as a charming sketch on a page in Dudley Woodbridge's personal journal. The house and its famous door became a tourist attraction. In 1793, the Reverend William Bentley, of Salem, Massachusetts, visited Deerfield for the second time, and he recorded: "At Hoyt's we saw the house which alone escaped the flames when Deerfield was taken, and the door of which is preserved as a specimen of the attack on it." Some twenty years later, in 1819, Benjamin Silliman wrote:

> One house still remains, as a painful memento to posterity. The
> front door was hacked and hewn with hatchets . . . this door,
> which still bears its ancient wounds, and the hole (closed only by
> a board, tacked on within) remains now, as the natives left it, and
> is now a most interesting monument.

Not everyone felt it was a "painful memento," however. Stephen West Williams, a descendant of Rev. John Williams, declared it "the pride of our village" in 1835 and was thrilled that it attracted the attention of so "many strangers of distinction."

However, the first published image of the building did not appear until 1824, when a copperplate engraving appeared in Epaphras Hoyt's book. Hoyt had been born in the house in 1765. Over the years many tourists had mentioned seeing the house, even if they didn't draw any pictures. The diary of Seth L. Andrews, a Dartmouth graduate, records a visit to Deerfield on September 22, 1831.

> Left Brattleboro this morning at three o'clock and arrived here about one. Visited the old house in Deerfield, which was left at the destruction of Deerfield by the Indians . . . the marks of their tomahawks still remain on the door, and three or four bullet holes are shown in one room, one of which is supposed to have been made by a ball which passed through a woman.

By 1838, the house had become a noteworthy tourist destination, probably because of the publicity for the new Bloody Brook monument. Lucy Thurston Goodale recorded a visit on June 26, 1838:

> We went on our way to old Deerfield to see the house once attacked by the Indians. . . . It is a quiet, old-looking village evidently the residence of rich farmers and well supplied with shady trees. We stopped first at the public house warm and weary but after a few minutes of rest, sallied forth in quest of the ancient building, not forgetting to take some travelling baskets which had been provided for the occasion. The house stands by the church, near the centre of the village. It is still in comfortable repair and is inhabited. On going to the door we stopped to look at the hole cut in it by the Indian hatchet, and the nails driven in by the whites to prevent it from being cut

to pieces. We gave several knocks before the people opened to us, but at last an old woman came and showed us the room in which the bullet holes are to be seen. Perhaps we had not come at the right hour, for she did not seem remarkable pleased at us, or perhaps it was an old story which she was tired of repeating.

Venerated by longtime Deerfield inhabitants as an ancient symbol of their early colonial heritage, the house gained wider prominence through an 1839 newspaper article in the *Greenfield Gazette and Mercury* that honored it as a "silent, eloquent monument of ancient days." The story lured more tourists to come to Deerfield and visit the house.

On September 28, 1841, the *Gazette and Courier* (the paper changed its name in July of that year) reprinted an observation by a Mr. Brockway, identified as the editor of the *Sentinel*, that had been published in the Westfield, New York, *Messenger*:

The village of Deerfield, though a little rusty and time-worn, is nevertheless a pleasant one. . . . I went to see the old house which was attacked by the Indians during the early settlement of the country, and saw the hole cut through the door by the tomahawks of the savages. The marks of the instruments are legible as if they had been made but yesterday.

These jottings from the 1830s and 1840s must represent many other visitor experiences that were never put down in writing or, if they were, have gone undiscovered.

By 1847, the Indian House showed its age. While still structurally sound, the house had seen better days. It looked unkempt; the exterior had never been painted. The roof sagged, and loose roof shingles had fallen off. Its antique appearance was out of style compared to the more modern and fashionable eighteenth- and nineteenth-century homes that lined The Street. The house was the sole survivor from the night of February 29, 1704. This longevity was a tribute to the quality of its construction when Ensign John Sheldon put it up in 1699. Built to withstand the fury of an all-out Indian attack, it had, for a century and a half, also withstood time and the elements. The threat from Indians had long passed. For the last one hundred years, Deerfield had been safe from that.

Despite its celebrity and direct link to one of the most famous episodes in early American history and the history of New England, Henry Hoyt, a direct descendant of one of the captives, revealed his plans to tear it down. He was about to get married and wanted to offer his bride a new home. He claimed that "the old house had become so much out of repair that it was untenantable." He wanted to build a stylish, modern home—"a more convenient dwelling"—something the Old Indian House was not. Word spread about Hoyt's plans, and caused an uproar. A man from Boston named Henry Williams wrote: "I should consider its destruction as the vilest vandalism that could be perpetuated." In Deerfield, concerned citizens met to appoint a committee to save the house. It was probably the first organized effort at historic preservation in America, preceding by six years the work of the Mount Vernon Ladies' Association in 1853 to preserve the home of George Washington. The members drafted a public letter in the form of a printed circular to mail far and wide and launch a fundraising drive to save the house. On December 15, 1847, they addressed a handbill "To All Who Feel an Interest in The Antiquities of New England":

> For the purpose of considering and applying the best means
> of obtaining the necessary aid in preserving and securing for
> future generations, that memorial of the dangers and sufferings
> of our fathers, in the infancy of our country, commonly styled,
> "THE INDIAN HOUSE."

The circular sounded the alarm that the historic landmark was now in imminent danger of being destroyed. But in lieu of tearing it down, the owner had agreed to sell it: "He is willing to sell it for a Hundred and Fifty Dollars, and our first plan was, to procure another place and remove it."

It should not have been difficult to raise that sum in Deerfield. If every adult resident had been willing to contribute just one dollar, that would have more than covered the cost of purchasing the building and moving it to a new location. But then the fickle committee complicated things. Now they decided that they needed to grab more than just the house—they wanted the land on which it sat too: "Two objections [to saving the house alone] . . . have led us to vary our plan. First, The House would lose much of its interest, if removed; and Secondly, it may not be in a state to be removed without material injury." That would mean buying the whole six-acre lot at a price of twenty-three hundred dollars. This was a wildly high sum at the time. Given that the current house occupied the only good building spot on the premises, the rest of the lot and superfluous land was not viable for erecting any other dwellings, so the price could not be offset by selling this extra land for homes. But the committee had a solution for that too—they could sell or rent out some of the land for farming: "Should we buy the whole, our proposal would be to sell or lease five acres more or less, for cultivation or other objects, which would probably save from Six to Eight Hundred Dollars on the whole cost of the place, viz: Twenty-Three Hundred Dollars, the price set upon by the owner." The effort was already starting to get overcomplicated with multiple contingencies.

To make matters worse, the committee insisted that the owner deserved *more* than market price for the building and land: "The [Hoyt] family have a strong attachment to the ground so long occupied by their ancestors, and it is reasonable that the sacrifice of such a feeling should [justify] pecuniary compensation." Not only was the inflated price meant to flatter family pride, but it was also to pay them years of back-remuneration for showing the house to curious tourists. As the committee argued, the public was indebted to the Hoyt family "for the cheerful and courteous reception, which for successive generations, the family have given to visitors at all hours of the day, although it has often been attended with personal and domestic inconvenience." The vast sum of over two thousand dollars was thus explained away as what the American people owed the Hoyt family for their years of care and chaperonage. That was ridiculous. If the house was so important to Hoyt, why did he want to tear it down in the first place?

An even bigger surprise awaited readers: The committee revealed that if their plan succeeded, and if supporters actually donated twenty-three hundred dollars, the preservation effort would actually need even *more* money—and right away. "Should our plan be carried into effect, it might require Two or Three Hundred Dollars to put the House into such repair as would be necessary to its preservation," stated the appeal. And a live-in caretaker would have to be installed to pay all "necessary attention to all the strangers [who were] curious to view the antiquities." The final goal was to turn the house into a living museum, into "a repository of such Indian Antiquities as we can collect."

These were ambitious goals. But the skyrocketing estimates and conflicting information made the case for saving the Indian House less and less persuasive. The committee members had done a good job of making a case *against* themselves. After all, why should contributors give money to pay an inflated price for the house and the land upon which it stood? And why should anyone from other places in New England (or America) bother to send money? Why couldn't Deerfield residents simply pony up and pay the price if they wanted to see the house preserved? After all, why help Deerfield, if the town was unwilling to help itself? The committee accused Deerfield residents of having none of the "antiquarian spirit" needed to preserve the landmark, and more so, they didn't want to sacrifice any money to do it.

Still, wasn't this a part of New England history that deserved to be saved? Not just for Deerfield, but as an important shrine for the history of *all* the "infant settlements" of early New England. As the circular persisted:

> It is, in a sense, common property; interesting to the antiquary,
> wherever he may dwell. If it be suffered to perish for the want
> of a little attention and exertion, it will be a subject of regret and
> self-reproach, more perhaps to the people of Deerfield than to
> those other places; but not peculiar to them.

The circular petered out on a timid note by failing to solicit money up front. Instead, it instructed potential donors to state in advance how much money they *might* contribute at a *later* date. This contradicted the alleged urgency of their mission: "What is done, must be done soon, as the Owner of the Old House wishes to be providing his materials for the new building, if he does not sell."

The gentlemen of that committee could not have written a more dispassionate, indecisive, unconvincing, contradictory- and self-defeating public letter. No records survive indicating how much, if any, money it raised. Likely it was not much, and their half-hearted effort ended in utter failure. Two weeks after the preservation committee mailed its circular, on December 28, 1847, the *Greenfield Gazette and Courier* published an article supporting the idea. The campaign needed all the support it could get, and the article spread the news and aroused the passions of "all who feel an interest in the antiquities of New England." But it was already too late. Mrs. Jennie Saxton Rose, who had been fourteen at the time, recalled: "I remember how everyone in Deerfield felt it was almost a sin to let that wonderful relic of those terrible times be torn down. *Protest* ran high, but there was no one who seemed to have enough money to save it."

So came the day. After waiting one year, Henry Hoyt finally gave the order to bring it down. By May 23, 1848, the *Gazette and Courier* reported that workmen had moved in to begin dismantling the house. It didn't take long. On May 30, Thomas Williams Ashley recorded in his diary: "H. Hoyt finishes pulling down the Old Indian House." Piece by piece, the building that had withstood the raid of 1704 was dismantled. The fabric of the past was torn apart and discarded. Hoyt did have the foresight to save a few bits and bobs. The frame, a window, some cornices, and some miscellaneous woodwork were saved. Hoyt collected bricks from the chimney, not as relics, but to incorporate into the walls of the new house he planned to build. Some of the house was still perfectly sound—the main timbers and doorsills—and could be reused. Perhaps Hoyt even allowed some of the witnesses to salvage a piece or two for their own collections and memories.

One more artifact from the house was saved: the massive oak front door.

Only after the building was gone did people comprehend the meaning of its loss. In 1852, just four years later, William Gould recounted in his guidebook to the area the "anxiety manifested by stage-passengers . . . to see the old house." It was gone but not forgotten. In 1704, the Sheldon House had survived an assault by three hundred fierce and battle-hardened French and Indian warriors. But a century and a half later, it could not survive the apathy of the citizens of Deerfield and the rest of New England. The house that had withstood assault of February 29, 1704, the home that the Natives had failed to burn as they fled after the assault, was intentionally destroyed by the descendant of a man who had survived the raid and subsequent captivity. The effort in Deerfield failed, and the house that had survived one of the bloodiest nights in the history of New England was felled not by violence and fire, but by indifference.

But the irony was that the destruction of the building transformed the Old Indian House into a greater icon in myth than it had been in life. Now that the house was gone, it would live on in memory and myth as a symbol of a lost age. Its loss also gave birth to a new movement: the cult of the Old Indian House. Relics were fashioned from salvaged timbers. Like fragments of the True Cross, pieces of the wood were doled out as favors to people who would have them carved into keepsakes. A number of walking sticks and also a chair were made by these early mythmakers. A special cane was presented to the Massachusetts governor, George Nixon Briggs (Briggs having produced the 1849 "Report of the Commissioners Relating to the Condition of the Indians in Massachusetts"). George Grennell, the former representative, now a resident of nearby Greenfield, wrote to John Wilson in Deerfield, acknowledging a prize gift:

> I thank you for a piece of oak from the "Old Indian House" in Deerfield, to be formed into a cane. I shall use it, and value it as a memorial of the sufferings and virtues of our forefathers. I shall value it too as a gift from an old friend.

Other material was used for less exalted purposes. As Jennie Sheldon reported, "the boards which composed the wainscoting of the room in which Mrs. Sheldon was killed, now make the floor of a workshop, and in one of them Mr. H. points out the hole made by the ball which killed her." Other wood was used to construct outhouses.

In time depictions of the Old Indian House would appear on virtually all types of souvenirs: paintings, rugs, textiles, picture postcards, baskets, spoons, ceramics, and more. Of course, the mania spawned a series of spurious items as well, including a woven basket featuring the Old Indian House that was claimed to have been made by the child captive Eunice Williams herself.

One of the witnesses who watched the dismantling of the house was a man named George Sheldon, a descendant of Ensign John Sheldon. For him, the destruction was a catalyst. The loss of this important history galvanized him. It changed Sheldon, and changed the future of Deerfield. It inspired his mania for local research and an obsession for historic preservation to ensure that the events of 1704 would never be forgotten, that not a scrap more of Deerfield's history would be lost to the vicissitudes of time or indifference. Soon he would emerge as Deerfield's historian laureate. In the years to come he would dominate the collecting of facts and the construction of myths in Deerfield.

The Old Indian Door

In 1851, three years after the destruction of the Old Indian House, *Gleason's Pictorial and Drawing Room Companion*, a large-format, illustrated weekly in the style of *Frank Leslie's* and *Harper's Weekly*, published a piece about Deerfield by J. R. Chapin. Founded by Frederick Gleason in 1851, the *Companion* had an ambitious mission of presenting a "weekly literary mélange of notable events" by "the best American authors." During its brief life (it ceased publication in 1859), *Gleason's* published a number of fine articles on American history and culture, including its piece about Deerfield in the Saturday, August 16, 1851, issue.

Though the article mentioned famous events such as Bloody Brook and the raid of 1704, it focused on the loss of the Sheldon House, which until recently "was standing and was an object of great interest to travelers until three years since, when it was pulled down to make room for a more modern structure." The page included a fine woodcut of the house based on Chapin's own sketches when he had visited Deerfield three years earlier, during the height of the campaign to save the Old Indian House. But the highlight of the article was the preservation of the Sheldon House's front door, what became famous as the "Old Indian Door." The article included an elaborate description:

> The door was made of two thicknesses of inch plank, studded and fastened with wrought nails, which must have required much force to wrench apart. After cutting through the outer plank, a hole was cut through the inner one, through which they thrust their muskets.

The article still described the Indians as bloodthirsty savages, but *Gleason's* revealed a new and obsessive—almost voyeuristic— fascination with the door:

> One can tell almost tell the exact number of the savages by the marks of the tomahawks. In the center, the blows were struck by a vigorous arm, and cut almost through the inch board—lower down are the marks of a tomahawk which must have been in the hands of an Indian on his knees, while above the aperture, on the right, are marks of blows given by one standing on the right of the door, one of which, as will be seen, struck the head of a nail, and the dent is as fresh as though given but yesterday.

Chapin failed to notice one of the most remarkable features of the door: the presence of unusual, repeated hex marks etched on the black iron inner latch of the locking mechanism. And he neglected to explain the true purpose of the iron horseshoe nailed above the front door. It was not for luck, a modern sentiment. In the time of Salem witchcraft hysteria, superstition said that no witch could pass under iron.

The door was living history. Like a *CSI* episode before its time, examination of the door led to a new, and hands-on, history. One could see by the marks on it how many attackers had hacked away at its surface, and from what locations, and at what trajectories. Even the strength of the arm—whether a strong blow or weak—was remarked upon.

The "Old Indian Door" was a time machine, a secular reliquary, a portal into the past. As the *Gleason's* article continued:

> It still bears the marks of the tomahawks, and in every respect
> presents the same appearance it did the day after the massacre.
> It is intensely interesting to stand before this relic of olden time,
> round which 150 years ago was grouped a savage band, thirsting
> for the blood of their victims.

But the past came at a price, or rather, with one. By 1863, in the midst of a civil war, Deerfield had sent many of her sons into battle, a sacrifice commemorated by the Civil War monument erected in 1866 in the center of the town common, beside the ancient well from which the fort drew its water in 1704. Deerfield now faced another existential, antiquarian crisis. After Henry Hoyt had the Old Indian House torn down in 1848, he retained possession of its door until his murder in Bloody Kansas during the antebellum conflict there between proslavery and antislavery forces. After Hoyt's death, the door remained in his family. Occasionally someone in Deerfield offered to buy it, but the Hoyts always refused to sell. Over time the door had attained the status of a holy relic. Now, fifteen years after the destruction of the Old Indian House, a threat to its door emerged.

It began with a letter sent from Deerfield on September 29, 1863, just after the Battle of Chickamauga in Georgia, in which the Confederate army under General Braxton Bragg defeated Union forces. The note was addressed to Dr. D. D. Slade, a noted antiquarian and collector:

> Friend Slade—I write to inform you that the old Indian door
> which you saw when you were in Deerfield, is for sale. It is
> the property of the orphan granddaughter of the late David S.
> Hoyt, who was murdered during the early Kansas troubles.
> This is nearly or quite all the patrimony the poor deaf girl has,

and I feel interested in having this ancient relic sold at a fair
price on her account.

Today, given the strong market for rare, one-of-a-kind Americana, if the door ever came up for auction, it might bring a million
dollars or more. Even in 1863, when the market for colonial antiques
was in its infancy, the door should have easily been worth several
hundred dollars. But the letter's author told Slade that he could snap it
up at a much lower bargain price:

I think it can now be bought for $100, securely boxed and
delivered at the express office, consigned as may be directed.
The door is in a good state of preservation and has the knocker
still attached to it. It has heretofore been held at a much higher
price, but an aunt of the girl is about to return to Illinois and
take her niece with her. The friends desire me to do what I
can to make sale of the property. I write to give you the first
chance. I think $100 a reasonable price for so rare a memorial
to Indian warfare. I shall be happy to render you any service
in my power in reference to it. An early reply is desired. Very
truly, your friend, R.N. Porter.

The signer, "R.N. Porter," was Dr. Ransom Noble Porter, whose
names "ransom" and "noble" couldn't have been, respectively, more apropos. Porter was a newcomer to Deerfield, having moved to town only
in 1856, when he opened a medical practice; he then became a justice of
the peace in 1862. What he was about to unleash on Deerfield was anything but peaceful. Because, unbeknownst to anyone in the town, the
fate and ownership of the Old Indian Door were now in play.

What possessed Porter to sell out his new home and community? As
the town doctor and owner of a milling business, Porter should have had
the funds to buy the door himself and keep the treasured object in Deerfield. It is possible that he experienced financial problems. Later, the Massachusetts Medical Society suspended him for five years' delinquency in

dues payments, and by 1872 he had declared himself bankrupt. It is possible that his financial problems had started much earlier, prompting him to reach out to Slade to sell Deerfield's valuable heritage. Did he instigate the sale with the majority of revenue going to a five-year-old deaf girl, but receiving a profitable cut for himself? But then, why never offer the door to any Deerfield resident, who might also have paid for this incredible object?

Slade, an experienced and canny collector, recognized this once-in-a-lifetime opportunity. He wrote back immediately, on October 2. "Sold!" he replied. He had not even tried to bargain. He knew he was getting the door—the single most famous surviving relic of the seventeenth-century colonial Indian Wars—for a steal. Slade received a letter from Porter on October 8 confirming the deal, and on October 10, 1863, the Old Indian Door arrived by express freight from Deerfield, Massachusetts. Slade immediately uncrated it and displayed it in a place of honor in the study at his home on Chestnut Hill, a leafy suburb just west of Boston.

By the time anybody in Deerfield discovered what had happened, the precious object was literally out the door and on its way to Dr. Slade. To add insult to injury, Slade had bought it for a pittance, less than one year's pay for a single, lowly Civil War private in the Union army (which was just $13 a month).

News of the transaction soon leaked out and spread through town. The Indian Door was gone! It had been sold in secret, and Hoyt's family had not even given Deerfield the courtesy of the opportunity to purchase it. Many residents considered it a profane act, as offensive as selling off the gravestones of John and Eunice Williams. Deerfield acted quickly and appointed a committee of three men—Rev. R. Crawford, E. W. Stebbins, and J. C. Pratt—to reach out to Dr. Slade and retrieve the door, their town's proudest and most valuable heritage. The question was, would this committee prove any more effective than the incompetent panel organized in 1847 to save the Old Indian House?

The Price of the Past

The campaign did not begin on an auspicious note. Reverend Crawford's first letter to Slade, dispatched from Deerfield on October 28,

1863, had an overwrought, presumptuous, and annoying tone. He started off by stating his intent to "repurchase" the door as part of Deerfield's rightful heritage. As he penned, "A good deal of feeling was expressed, regret, & also something approaching to indignation" by Deerfield residents upon the loss of this venerated object.

According to Crawford, Hoyt had purchased the door from his family relatives. After much negotiating and pestering, the Hoyt descendants had agreed to let him have the door, "on the *express condition* that it should not go out of the place, nor out of the Hoyt family." The family was rightly upset about this betrayal, which was so concerning that they dared not tell the family matriarch, "mother Hoyt, now an old lady over 80 years and bedridden." How and why had the door been sold to an outsider, Crawford queried, when numerous Deerfield residents had attempted to buy it over the years?

As Crawford continued:

The feeling is that the door belongs here. It belongs to our history as a town. Every citizen feels a personal right & claim to it. All our traditionary pride, not to say, self-respect, is touched & wounded at its removal. We feel that associated as it is with our memories of the past, it has a value here which it cannot have anywhere else. . . . [It is] a most significant link—connecting the present and future generations with the venerated & sorely tried ancestry of our town. For us they suffered & toiled, and we would keep their memory green & sacred.

He made an emotional claim on behalf of Deerfield that the door belonged to the citizens as part of their communal patrimony.

Then he got to the gist of the matter:

You will see—as we do—many good reasons why we should have the door restored to us. . . . Though private property to be sure, yet the public had a deep interest in it, if not claim to it. Then again, had we been careless about it, unwilling to give a

fair price for it—it being for sale—it might be said we ought to
lose it; but as already signified, we have cared, and do care for it;
& had we known that the price given for it was wanted, & would
have purchased it—so that it should henceforth be the property
of our people, that price would have been forthcoming. You can
see then our position; & in view of it may I not ask—on behalf
of the Committee & our whole people, whether we may not rely
upon your honor & your generous feelings to further measures
for restoring the door to us again?

Slade was not persuaded by this initial salvo, and several years of
sporadic and inconclusive correspondence ensued between Crawford
and Slade. As a sweetener, Crawford begged for an in-person meeting
and offered Slade a stick of coveted wood from the Old Indian House:
"I brought with me for you a specimen of the timber in the form of a
cane,—that is the material for a cane." It was an odd half gift. But rather
than present Slade with a beautiful, custom-finished cane, he gave him
the raw material and expected him to go to the trouble of having one
made himself from the valuable fragment of raw lumber.

The next five years passed in weary negotiations. With each passing year, worry deepened that the door might never return to Deerfield and that it would be lost forever. Slade might never agree to sell
to Deerfield, or he might choose to sell it to another collector or museum. Slade might die, and his heirs might refuse to return the door to
Deerfield. Or Slade's collection might be sent to auction and scattered
to the winds. Anything might happen to the Old Indian Door. Would
Deerfield repeat history and squander its chance to save its storied
relic, just as it had failed to save the Old Indian House?

Then, in October 1867, Slade wrote to Crawford with wonderful
news: he had decided to return the door to Deerfield. As he explained:

Since [the door] came into my possession, I have always felt
some compunction in regard to it, not that it was not fairly

mine by the right of purchase, but that it rightly belonged to the town of Deerfield, and should forever be retained by the town as a most sacred relic.

Unbelievably, Slade offered to sell it back for the same bargain price he had paid for it in 1863—one hundred dollars plus ten dollars for transportation. It was a generous offer. Slade could have easily marketed the door at a higher price for a nice profit. It had taken Reverend Crawford five years to coax Slade to this point, but now, so close to his goal, he claimed that the town was too poor to buy it!

Crawford's dithering, excuse-filled reply of October 29, 1867, must have surprised Slade:

> When the matter was in agitation, a few years ago, it would have been very easy to raise among the citizens the amount required according to your present generous offer to bring it back. And I have no doubt it can be raised ere long. But just at present we have the balance of some accounts connected with our soldier's monument to settle up, and this matter comes the heaviest on just those on whom we would depend for the price of the door.

Crawford cited the expense of the town's new Civil War monument, which would be dedicated in 1868, three years after the war's end. He claimed that Deerfield was, after all, just a village of farmers, and that many of them "have little care about such things—especially where it costs anything." That was the identical excuse that the committee appointed to save the Indian House had made when it claimed in 1847 that Deerfield alone could not be expected to save its own historic shrine.

What must Slade have thought when the desperate man who had once begged him to return the door now confessed that in all of Deerfield, the trivial sum of a hundred dollars could not be raised to bring home this priceless relic? Reverend Crawford's tone-deaf response to Dr. Slade's generous offer risked alienating him and losing the door forever.

Luckily for Deerfield, Slade was a patient man. He agreed to wait while Crawford begged and pleaded to raise the hundred dollars. It took him just four months to make the payment, and Slade shipped the door back to Deerfield, where it arrived safely by express service on Wednesday, February 19, 1868. But Slade attached some conditions to the sale:

The said door shall be kept in a convenient place, as near the place as may be where it was at the time of the destruction of the town, and near where the monument stands which was erected to the memory of our fallen heroes, who fell in the late rebellion.

Furthermore, the door had to be "kept in a situation where it will be accessible to all who take an interest in the many trials and sufferings of the founders of . . . Deerfield."

To welcome the door home, Deerfield held an ecstatic festival at the town hall on the evening of Friday, February 28, 1868, the eve of the 164th anniversary of the sacking of the town in 1704. The *Greenfield Gazette and Courier* of March 2, 1868, gave this account of the homecoming ceremony:

Over [the door] was draped the American flag, and here, too was the old horse shoe found over the door when the house was taken down, put there as a preventative against witchcraft. In a small room was a collection of relics, and a lady and gentlemen dressed in full Indian costumes, which had actually been worn by the savages. The fatal bullet which killed Mrs. Sheldon at the attack on the Indian House, was exhibited.

It was an intriguing promotional spiel, but it was highly unlikely that anyone—white or Native—appeared in actual Indian apparel that had been worn during the raid.

The unavoidable speeches followed. Josiah D. Canning, vice president of the newly established Pocumtuck Valley Memorial Association (PVMA), composed an ode to honor the door that proved popular enough to be memorialized in two separate broadside printings. Canning's verses on "The Old Indian Door" spoke directly to the door itself, as though it were alive, and not an inanimate object:

> *Door of Old Memories! thy battered face*
> *We welcome home again, its fittest place . . .*
> *Here, where you stood in those dark days of yore,*
> *And did brave duty as a Bolted Door:*
> *Where you withstood the Indians' fiendish rage,*
> *Who on your tablet scored a bloody page;*
> *Where you survived the havoc and the flame,*
> *And float Time's tide to-day, a Door of Fame . . .*

Canning thanked the door for luring tourists to Deerfield ("you've served attractor to this grand old Town") and rejoiced that it would serve forever as "Attractions Door." The poet marveled at the door's "silent face" scarred by "the Indian's hatchet and the scythe of time." Canning concluded that, while other towns might have their own traditions and legends, only Deerfield possessed the "Door of History."

The Old Indian Door was paraded through Deerfield like a Roman hero returning in triumph, or like a holy relic that possessed mystical powers. And did not the door possess such powers? It had passed through history and memory into myth.

All seemed well. No one on that celebratory night could have known it then, but the Old Indian Door had not seen the last of danger. After its return, it was placed in an unusual repository for a priceless relic: the front entrance hall of the Pocumtuck House, a hotel owned by Charles O. Phillips. Here, of course, it would have been viewed and admired by a steady stream of tourists and visitors. It was propped up in a glass case, mainly for protection from vandals. In 1875, author "Thirsty McQuill" (real name Wallace Bruce) called it "the most venerable thing of all our country's relics"—quite an honor when compared to the Liberty Bell or the Declaration of Independence. As he continued, "It is a living representation of that great contest between barbarism and civilization. . . . In the wide hall of the Pocumtuck House the door is kept secure in an upright glass case (to guard against the pen-knives of modern knight errants)." It definitely needed the protection, not only against the era's graffiti artists, who wished to scrawl initials into its scarred surface, but also apparently from inconsiderate visitors. In 1873, the glass case was damaged by traveler's trunks being smashed up against it.

And nine years after its arrival, tragedy struck. On May 18, 1877, the hotel caught fire. The wooden door was perfect kindling, and only the courage of Frank Nims, a descendant from a family that had suffered many killed or taken captive in 1704, saved it. Nims rushed into the flaming hotel and, with the help of a few other men, rescued the door. How appropriate that the door to the Old Indian House, which had not been consumed by fire in 1704, was now saved from flames by a man with a direct connection to the raid. And how ironic that the door that had survived all attempts by the French and Indians to burn down the Sheldon House 1704, as well as the vicissitudes of time since then, over the next 175 years, had almost perished in something so mundane as an accidental hotel fire.

This was the second time that Deerfield had almost lost its storied door. Now the Pocumtuck Valley Memorial Association chose to tempt fate for the third time. It moved the door to an old corner store, which it owned. When that building was sold, the door was toted to the corn house of one Nathaniel Hitchcock. There it languished until the PVMA could move it into its new, fireproof home. It was, after all, a very large object—not something one could place in a cabinet or on a mantel. It had proven it could weather Indian attacks and a century and a half of exposure to the elements, but perhaps not the fecklessness of its caretakers.

In the late 1870s, the PVMA took possession of the old Deerfield Academy building designed by the American architect Asher Benjamin and built in 1799. After structural renovations for exhibition space and fireproofing, its leaders planned to open to the public in 1880. By September 1879, the building was well enough along to retrieve the Old Indian Door from Nathaniel Hitchcock's corn house and install it in Memorial Hall, the name the PVMA had chosen for its museum. Finally, the door would be secured in a special room designed to serve as its sanctuary forever, where it would serve "as an unmistakable landmark in the tragic history of Deerfield."

By the autumn of 1882, the PVMA had accomplished its grand project—the creation of a memorial room within the museum to honor for all time the victims of 1704. As George Sheldon wrote, "It was for [such] a memorial that should perpetuate these names that the Association was formed." The PVMA placed the Old Indian Door at the center of the room, set between its massive, original posts, so the door could be viewed from all sides. A visitor could now visualize both sides of the events that night, literally from the side of the attackers and from the side of the inhabitants.

By the late nineteenth century, the Old Indian House and its door had come to symbolize many things. They had been built to last, like the English colonies in America. They were plain and unadorned, suggesting the honest simplicity of the people who built them. Rugged and raw, they were designed to withstand the cold, harsh New England winters and hot, humid, and sun-drenched summers. They proved strong and almost impervious to assault. The characteristics of the house and the door suggested the durability and resilience of the people.

To the people of New England, the house and the door symbolized something larger: a clash of cultures. Double-thick doors and sturdy, fortified houses had been built for one purpose: the Old Indian Door was a real, physical barrier to keep others—in this case, French and Indians—out. So the door served the practical purpose of safeguarding the physical security and the lives of the occupants behind it. But to the colonists it had meant something else too. It represented a barrier between savagery and civilization, Indians and English colonists, Puritan godliness and Catholic corruption, good and evil. On the night of February 29, 1704, that door had been breached. The dividing line was crossed. And for the people of Deerfield, the consequences were unimaginable.

In its apotheosis, the Old Indian Door had been transformed. It was more than a venerated, inanimate object. To the people who cherished it, it had become, like the Old Indian House, a living character in the story. Poems had been written about the house. Daguerreotypes froze it in time before its destruction. Artists had painted dozens of portraits of it before and long after it was gone. It was pictured on commemora-

tive china. Canes, knickknack boxes, picture frames, and chairs have
been fashioned from its sinews. Hooked rugs, tapestries, and baskets
have been woven in its honor. Silver-plated spoons had been cast with its
image at one end and an Indian brave at the tip of the handle. The material culture of this iconography conjured up memories of a house that
no longer existed, but it was a poor substitute for experiencing the real
thing. In contrast, the Old Indian Door *was* the real thing and required
no substitute. It was alive, eternal, and forever present, just like the values that New Englanders believed it represented.

Colonial Cenotaphs

But to fully explain the important role the Pocumtuck Valley Memorial
Association (PVMA) played in Deerfield means backtracking to 1870.
This was a seminal year in the history of Deerfield, and for the story of the
raid of 1704. Still smarting from the loss of the Old Indian House twenty-
two years earlier, and traumatized by the more recent near loss and then
recovery of the Old Indian Door, a group of civic-minded antiquarians
vowed "Never again!" According to George Sheldon, a few like-minded
men met on a street in neighboring Greenfield and started "talking about
the dark and bloody memories of February 29, 1704." They discussed the
raid, the taking of the captives to Canada, the destruction of the town, and
the killing of Rev. John Williams's wife. They resolved "that in some way
the spot where she fell should be permanently marked," George Sheldon
recorded. "That street corner discussion was the seed from which the Memorial Association sprang as a fitting tribute not only to Mrs. Williams,
but the other victims of the 1704 massacre."

From a small acorn sprung a mighty oak. These men and others
banded together to create a new organization dedicated to preserving the
past and a vanishing New England heritage. In September 1869, a local
newspaper announced a meeting "to test the feeling of the people concerning associated action in perpetuating the memory of our ancestors." The
answer was a resounding yes, the founders named the new organization
the Pocumtuck Valley Memorial Association, and the state legislature
granted it a charter in May 1870. This group would dominate the history,

memory, and myth of the Deerfield Massacre for the next one hundred and
fifty years. No organization has had a more far-reaching influence on the
narrative, interpretation, and meaning of the events surrounding February
1704. History is not just the story of what happened, but also *how* the story
of what happened is told. And one man, more than any other, was the
guardian angel of that story. His name was George Sheldon.

George Sheldon was elected president of the PVMA, and Josiah D.
Canning, poet laureate of the Old Indian Door, was elected vice president. The association's mission statement was simple:

> Collecting and preserving such memorials, books, records,
> papers and curiosities, as may tend to illustrate and perpetuate
> the history of the early settlers of this region, and of the race
> which vanished before them, and the erection of a Memorial Hall
> in which such collections can be securely deposited.

From its creation, the PVMA embraced and perpetuated the myth of
Indians as a "vanishing race" that had walked off history's stage and just
disappeared. At the beginning, the PVMA existed only on paper. It had
no building and no collection, but it had ambitious plans and a natural
leader who possessed a prodigious talent for collecting. In that regard,
George Sheldon turned out to be a treasure-hunting human ferret.

During its first decade, between 1870 and 1880, the PVMA flour-
ished. Sheldon proved himself an indefatigable researcher, writer,
catalyst, and, perhaps most important, collector. He dreamed of
cramming its headquarters with the rich material culture of Deerfield
and the Connecticut River Valley. He had already gathered, largely
through donations, an amazing collection of colonial furniture, Hadley chests, paintings, textiles, books, documents, diaries, photographs,
trade signs, tools, kitchenware, ironwork, military relics, maps, pewter, and silver. Sheldon's genius was that he decided to collect *anything*
that he believed possessed intrinsic historical value, even if it had little monetary worth. He wanted things with provenance from the old
families: things that had never left the valley, or that had been crafted

locally; pieces whose intertwined stories spoke to one another; anything with a local history. As he realized, "Hidden away in nooks and corners, buried in chests and closets, rotting in leaking garrets or selfishly hoarded in private hands, are hundreds of manuscript papers, rich with material for local, national, or family history." If it was connected to Deerfield or regional history, George Sheldon wanted it. A legend formed that it was not safe to allow Sheldon into your home or attic unsupervised, lest he ransack it for historical treasures to put in his museum: "A certain horse and wagon became a familiar site in the country round about, and the driver was allowed to forage at will by the long-suffering housewives." Decades later, residents would claim when they heard strange noises upstairs, that it was just George Sheldon rooting through their possessions for his collections.

The purpose of creating a "memorial hall" was to enshrine the town's history. Rev. John Williams had immortalized the dead and the captives in his book *The Redeemed Captive*. Sheldon and the PVMA now followed in his footsteps by doing the same in Memorial Hall through the enshrinement of the Old Indian Door and the white wall of cenotaphs that made the room resemble a tomb or burial chamber.

A central tablet explained the purpose of the room:

ERECTED A.D. MDCCCLXXXII, / BY THE / POCUMTUCK
VALLEY / MEMORIAL ASSOCIATION: / IN HONOR OF
THE PIONEERS / OF THIS VALLEY, BY WHOSE COURAGE
/ AND ENERGY, FAITH AND FORTITUDE / THE SAVAGE
WAS EXPELLED / AND THE WILDERNESS SUBDUED;
/ AND TO PERPETUATE THE REMEMBRANCE / OF
THE SUFFERINGS AT DEERFIELD, / FEB. 29, 1703–4, /
WHEN BEFORE THE BREAK OF DAY, 340 FRENCH AND
INDIANS, / UNDER THE SIEUR HERTEL DE ROUVILLE, /
SWARMING IN OVER THE PALISADES ON THE DRIFTED
SNOW, / SURPRISED AND SACKED THE SLEEPING TOWN,
/ AND KILLED OR CAPTURED / THE GREATER PART OF
ITS INHABITANTS.

Mounted to the walls of the room, on either side of the largest one bearing the main inscription, were eighteen smaller marble slabs. On the tablets were carved the names of the captured and the slain:

> On the tablets at either hand, recorded in love and reverence
> by their kindred, are the names and ages of those who lost their
> lives in the assault, or were slain in the meadows in the heroic
> attempt to rescue the captives, or who died on the hurried retreat
> to Canada, victim to starvation or the tomahawk.

One of the smaller tablets is representative of the style and sentiment of the rest:

> SARAH FIELD, 2. / MARY, HER MOTHER, 28, / WIFE OF
> JOHN, / with children, / MARY, 6, AND JOHN, 3, / were
> captured. / Mary, adopted by an Indian, / WAS NAMED
> WALAHOWEY. / She married a savage, / and became one.

Because they resembled tombstones, the array of tablets near the door heightened the drama of the setting. The room—even today— has the hushed and reverent aura of a mausoleum, giving the impression that the dead are entombed behind the tablets. But these are only cenotaphs, memorial tablets honoring the absent dead.

In 1883, George Sheldon reported on the dedication ceremony:

> The crowning event of the year at Memorial Hall, Deerfield,
> was the placing of the Mural Tablets, inscribed with the names
> of those slain or captured in the memorable sacking of the old
> town, in the room set apart for their reception.

As Sheldon continued, "We can now properly call this building a Memorial Hall." Ever the frugal Yankee, he boasted that the whole expense of "this crowning act of the Association" had been "just $299." Donations from living descendants funded the project, including the Allen, Catlin, Carter, Frary, Hawks, Hoyt, Sheldon, Stebbins, and Wells families. C. Alice Baker gave twelve dollars for the Catlin stone, but other amounts came from distant places like Philadelphia, Indiana, and New York. And the PVMA expected to add more names for the families of Alexander, Brooks, Corse, Field, French, Hinsdale, Hurst, Kellogg, Mattoon, Nims, Pomroy, Warner, and Williams. The last tablet was sponsored by Marshall Field, founder of the famous Chicago department store. Afterward, the group adjourned to dinner "served by attentive and pretty waiters" during which a lecture was given on the colonial "drinking habit," which must have made for stimulating antiquarian discussion.

But the purpose of the monument was clear. The tablets were links between generations, demonstrating the bonds of family and the perpetuity of memory. As the Reverend Lyman Whiting said, "Our lives are fuller and stronger when the story of those gone before us comes into our conversation, and we recount the benefits their lives and deeds have won for us." The inscribed stones were visual textbooks that would educate and remind onlookers of the past.

The mania for memorialization was not over. The next year the PVMA singled out one Deerfield captive for a special honor—Eunice Williams, the wife of Rev. John Williams. Eunice already had one memorial, her headstone in the Old Burying Ground. That inscription read:

Here lyeth the body of / Mrs. Eunice / Williams the virtuous / and desirable / consort of the Rev. Mr. John / Williams, & daughter to ye Rev. / Mr. Eleazer and Mrs. Esther Mather / of Northampton. She was born / Aug. 2, 1664. and fell by the / rage of ye Barbarous Enemy / March 1st, 1703–04.

But George Sheldon and the leaders of the PVMA decided to honor Eunice with another monument. They had thought about erecting one in the Old Burying Ground, but that seemed duplicative and might overshadow her original gravestone. Instead, they decided to place the monument a few miles from Deerfield, on the very spot where she was killed after the raid, during the forced march of the captives to Canada.

The dedication ceremony, attended by fifteen hundred people, was the biggest event sponsored by the fledgling PVMA. The printed program heralded the ceremony to follow: "On this occasion a memorial stone will be dedicated on the spot where Mrs. Eunice Williams was slain by her Indian Captor, March 1, 1703-04." The stone featured her brutal and bloody death, quoting the words of her husband, from *The Redeemed Captive*, carved for all to see: "THE CRUEL AND BLOODTHIRSTY / SAVAGE WHO TOOK HER, SLEW HER / WITH HIS HATCHETT AT ONE STROKE." The dedication was an elaborate event. The program listed a President of the Day, Chief Marshal, six assistant marshals, a fourteen-part agenda, including a hymn, prayer, dedicatory address, dirge, march to Larabee's Grove, basket collection of donations, music, a report of the committee transferring the memorial and land to the Association, acceptance of the trust by George Sheldon, president of the association, singing, a historical address, more music, a poem, and miscellaneous speakers, of which Daniel Slade, former owner of the Old Indian Door, was but one. That this entire program occurred in one afternoon testifies to the antiquarian enthusiasm of the participnats.

Why dedicate a monument to Eunice alone, but not any others slain during the march? Reverend Hazen answered that in his dedicatory address. Unlike others who had perished, the exact spot of Eunice's murder was known and could therefore be marked. He hoped that people would stop and read the monument and then be inspired to learn more about the past.

The minister imagined Eunice's last moments, describing how survivors from town had discovered her body on this spot and "reverently carried her back to Deerfield." Here, it seems, they buried her with her own slain infants and her neighbors. Hazen said that it was vital to "cherish the memory of those who suffered and died for us, for our country, in the cause of the advancement of true liberty." As far as Hazen was concerned, there were not *enough* of these memorials to the past, "of the sacrifices and the deaths by which our blessings have been won for us." Thus, this ceremony was about more than honoring a single Puritan woman a hundred and eighty years after her death. The memorial sanctified—indeed, deified—Eunice Williams and proclaimed the superiority of the white, Christian, Anglo-Saxon Puritans who had settled this valley, who had conquered and displaced the New England Indians, and reinforced the values they held dear.

However, in his odd remarks, Rev. John F. Moors did let *local* Indians off the hook for the massacre. "It was not the New England Indians," he said, "avenging the loss of favorite hunting grounds, or avenging the terrible massacre of their comrades at Turner's Falls 28 years before, that led to the attack on Deerfield." Moors was adamant: "The New England Indians had nothing to do with it." He named the real culprits:

> It was Indians *from Canada* who did this diabolical act, led by a Frenchman and accompanied by a large force of French soldiers who directed and controlled the whole enterprise. The inhuman cruelties [of] the massacre in cold blood of helpless children and defenseless women, the use of the hatchet and tomahawk to be rid of troublesome prisoners, may be in large measure laid to the Indians.

Moors hit home the major theme of the dedication—the supposed savagery of Natives. But, given their savage natures, they could not fully be blamed. The real fault, he argued, lay with the French officers, soldiers, and Catholic priests who directed them. Moors, in his naïveté, failed to understand the nuanced and complex relationship between the Natives and the French. The French were not the Indians' masters, and the Indians were not their slaves.

True Stories

Memorials were one thing—they could be seen, even touched. But there had to be more than just visual history planted in the Old Burying Ground or locked away in Memorial Hall. George Sheldon and the PVMA realized that to advance the mission of perpetuating the history, moral values, and superiority of their ancestors, they had to do more than erect monuments and markers. Creating Memorial Hall and erecting the Eunice Williams monument were crucial steps, but without a program of active research, writing, lectures, and publications, the early history of Deerfield might be lost.

So they turned to the written word to educate readers about the history of the town—and, in some ways, perpetuate its myths of colonists and Indians. PVMA meetings featured countless lectures and presentations, and the association began publishing research papers and pamphlets. In addition, the group started to publish *Proceedings of the Pocumtuck Valley Memorial Association*, a series of thick, hardbound volumes that documented all the activities of the PVMA, including ceremonies, meetings, lectures, and more. This collected material ranged from antiquarian minutiae to important and hitherto unknown discoveries. Sheldon undertook a number of research projects personally and inspired his disciples to do the same.

Although Sheldon was a polymath, passionate about many subjects, his true obsession was the colonial Indian wars, especially the 1675 Battle of Bloody Brook and the Deerfield Massacre of 1704. The principal published eyewitness accounts from the raid had been preserved in the narratives of John Williams and, later, his son Stephen. Joseph Kellogg left a very short handwritten manuscript entitled "When I Was Carried to Canada," written about forty years after the raid (although this only focused on his experiences in captivity, not the raid itself). No other captives had ever published memoirs about their experiences on the night of February 29, 1704, the march, or their captivity in Canada. The details of the story had been a mystery for generations, especially the fates of those, in particular the young girls, who never came back.

In today's world of the internet and instant information, it is remarkable that no one really knew the full story of 1704, beyond the Williams and some other accounts, until the late nineteenth century—almost two hundred years later. No one had followed the captives and their descendants to Canada. C. Alice Baker, a talented protégée and cousin of George Sheldon, took up the quest to learn more about the events of February 29, 1704. In December 1888, accompanied by her friend Emma Lewis Coleman, another antiquarian who later wrote a book about Deerfield, Baker went to Canada, the first of several trips, to research not just captives taken from Deerfield, but also those taken from all of New England.

Baker did what no American historian had ever done. She dug into government and church archives. She pored through the old French archives and asked "gracious priests" and "interested nuns" for guidance. She visited burying grounds to locate unrecorded gravestones. She drank water from the well of the homestead of Josiah Rising and Abigail Nims, two Deerfield captives who had married and built a life in French Canada. She ate apples from their orchard, and transplanted two small evergreen trees from Nims's Canadian home to her Deerfield birthplace. She stood before the grave of Therese Stebens, formerly Thankful Stebbins. She met with descendants. She pursued Indian oral traditions. Then she published a limited, privately printed edition of her book *True Story of New England Captives Carried to Canada During the Old French and Indian Wars*. In the preface she wrote: "As often as I have read in the annals of the early settlers of New England the pathetic words 'Carried captive to Canada whence they came not back' I have longed to know the fate of the captives." After Baker's death, Coleman expanded on her work and published a two-volume study, *New England Captives Carried to Canada Between 1677 and 1760 During the French and Indian Wars*. It was a landmark study that remains indispensable to historians today.

This pioneering work would soon be eclipsed by one by the ever-energetic George Sheldon. A formidable presence with his stern Yankee visage and flowing, snowy-white beard, Sheldon had *lived* Deerfield's history—he *remembered* watching the Indian House of his ancestor, Ensign Sheldon, being torn down. He was a human encyclopedia, and he knew more about Deerfield than anyone alive. He had long been at work on his own landmark study—in many ways it was his life's work. Finally, in 1895 and 1896, he published his magnum opus, *A History of Deerfield, Massachusetts*, in two thick volumes bound in handsome crimson cloth. Written in the classic, nineteenth-century antiquarian style, they are a massive collections of facts, names, dates, and more. Sheldon gathered original documents, transcribed primary sources, conducted oral history interviews, collected material that had never been assembled in one place before, and calculated intricate genealogies. Many of his discoveries would have been lost if he had not preserved them, as today many of those sources have since vanished.

Sheldon's *History* was not a literary masterpiece, nor was it intended to be. It was an enormous compilation of facts connected by an explanatory narrative. Even today, historians rely on it as an invaluable source. In addition to the *History*, he wrote numerous other articles and publications. Sheldon dominated his subject. Instrumental in the founding of PVMA, he appeared in a Thomas Edison silent film; posed for iconic photos by Deerfield's celebrated Allen sisters, who specialized in dreamy soft-focus portraits, nature photography, costumed Colonial Revival images, and more; and sat for a magnificent Augustus Vincent Tack oil portrait that today reposes at his stronghold, Memorial Hall. Through his scholarship, zeal, and single-minded dedication, Sheldon became a living legend, and a symbol of Deerfield, the spokesman for the values of his colonial forebears. As the nineteenth century came to a close, the story of the raid of 1704 had become fixed as the North Star of Deerfield's history. George Sheldon had won the narrative and now controlled for the next century how the story would be told in history, memory, and myth.

8

COLONIAL REVIVAL AND PATRIOTISM ENTHRONED

|||||||||||||||

At the turn of the twentieth century, another wave of memorialization commenced. This effort focused on Deerfield's town cemetery. On July 29, 1903, the PVMA convened a "field meeting" within the perimeter of the long vanished "old stockade." This meeting took place in conjunction with the forthcoming bicentennial of the Deerfield Massacre, probably because summer weather was more ideal for outdoor events than a February New England winter. A flag raising marked the center of the old fort, not far from the old town well and Civil War monument, so that "the people were both physically and in spirit at the very heart of Deerfield's most tragic event."

After a "basket picnic" with "coffee provided for all," the group headed west down Old Albany Road, toward the river. The agenda stated that "the Deerfield members of the Grand Army [Civil War veterans] will lead the march to the Old Burying Ground, where, at the grave of The Dead of 1704, there will be music and an address by Miss C. Alice Baker." The spot had only just acquired a new name. In 1703, it was simply called "the Burying place." By 1721 it was called "the Burying Yard." By 1803 no new dead were buried there. C. Alice Baker spoke about the tragic aftermath of the massacre:

Nothing was now left but to bury the dead, which was done.
Here, in one grave, equal in death, they lie together. Infants and

children of tender years, young men and maidens. Andrew, the Indian, Parthena, the slave, faithful unto death to her charge, Martin Smith freed from the sorrow and shame that beset his life, Benoni Stebbins, the hero, Samson Frary, the pioneer, the dauntless nine slain in the Meadow fight, and the rest of the 48 as if named, who fell that day all victims of horrid war.

The PVMA set a memorial stone atop an unusual feature in the landscape. In the southeast corner of the cemetery, not far from the gravestones of John and Eunice Williams, a spot of earth swelled to form a prominent mound. According to legend, it was here, in a mass grave, that the survivors had buried the bodies of the people who had been killed in 1704 during the raid and in the Meadows Fight.

George Sheldon echoed Baker's remarks, and said that all the victims were buried here together after the raid:

From the gray-haired man and matron to the babe of three weeks all were buried in one great grave. With these, whom his valor strove in vain to save, was laid all that was mortal of Sergeant Benjamin Wait. In the same grave lie four of Hadley's bravest sons, Samuel Boltwood, Robert Boltwood, Jonathan Ingram, and Nathaniel Warner. Here as a pledge and bond of union between Hadley and Deerfield their dust will be sacredly guarded.

Wait had been killed in the Meadows Fight, as had the four men from Hadley.

A common grave after a mass disaster was not unprecedented. In 1675, on the day after the Battle of Bloody Brook, the bodies of Colonel Lathrop, his men, and the teamsters from Deerfield were all buried together in one mass grave at the battle site. In Deerfield, unlike at Bloody Brook, no excavation was done to verify the legend (at least, none that is known). A photograph of the memorial, probably taken that day, shows how small and simple the stone was. It was as if the plain mound of earth alone spoke in simplicity for the dead.

A Silent Bicentennial

The next year, 1904, should have been a landmark one for Deerfield. It was the bicentennial of the 1704 raid—two hundred years had passed since that terrible night. It should have been a capstone year of commemorations, and one to celebrate the PVMA's impressive achievements to perpetuate the raid's memory. Strangely, the records of the organization are almost silent. On the national scene, nothing of significance could have distracted the people of Deerfield from a commemoration. President Theodore Roosevelt, in his third year in office after the 1901 assassination of President William McKinley, looked to an election campaign that fall. Although war had broken out between Russia and Japan, the United States was at peace. Nothing in the news should have prevented a major commemoration in Deerfield. And yet, from available evidence, it seems that nothing happened.

The previous summer, Deerfield had hosted Old Home Week, honoring the town's colonial heritage, but that celebration had little to do with 1704. A few casual mentions of the bicentennial appear in a PVMA *Proceedings* volume, but that is all. Perhaps in February 1904 an unusually large number of visitors thronged Memorial Hall to pay homage to the Old Indian Door and view the tablets. Perhaps a few hardy souls braved the winter weather and trekked to the Old Burying Ground to behold the gravestones of John and Eunice Williams and the mound. And perhaps someone even traveled a few miles from Deerfield to visit the Eunice Williams monument that marked the spot where she had been tomahawked to death. But the rest is silence.

Coinciding with the two hundredth anniversary year was the publication in 1904 of an important children's book, *The Boy Captive of Old Deerfield*, by the best-selling author Mary P. Wells Smith. Her family was intrigued by local history, probably because Asa Childs was a regular visitor to her father and recalled his time of serving at the Deerfield garrison during later raids. Smith's father used to point from their house in Greenfield Meadows and show where the captives had camped on their first night. As Wells remembered, "My father told me Asa stories in my childhood. It is interesting to realize that only two lifetimes take us back to the old Indian days."

Since the 1870s, Smith had been a successful and popular children's writer. She was a New Englander by birth, and *The Boy Captive of Old Deerfield* signaled her return to her roots, and an ambitious plan to write a series of novels setting young people in the context of American colonial history. Issued by the prestigious publisher Little, Brown & Company in Boston, *Boy Captive* was the inaugural volume in a new project that Wells named "The Old Deerfield Series" that would include four volumes. Inspired by the captivity tale of young Stephen Williams, son of Rev. John Williams, Wells followed up in 1905 with the next Deerfield volume in her series, *The Boy Captive in Canada*. She dedicated the book to C. Alice Baker, who had done pioneering research on the captives. The last two books in the series expanded beyond the 1704 raid to *Boys of the Border* and *Boys and Girls of Seventy-Seven*. Smith launched another collection of books called "The Young Puritans Series," which included the titles *The Young Puritans of Old Hadley*; *The Young Puritans in King Philips War*; *The Young Puritans in Captivity*; and *The Young and Old Puritans of Hatfield*.

By the time she finished, Wells had created a whole line of books featuring the exciting adventures of children in seventeenth- and eighteenth-century New England. Several generations of young Americans came to know the memory and myth of the Deerfield Massacre and Indian captivity through Smith's popular books, which remain in print today. In 1927, when Little, Brown published an illustrated promotional pamphlet celebrating Wells's success, she had just turned eighty-seven and was still going strong. Wells herself must have chosen the photograph on the pamphlet's front wrapper. It was not what one might expect—a flattering portrait of the author. It was a photograph of the tomahawk-scarred Old Indian Door.

Perhaps to ride the coattails of Mary P. Wells Smith, Deerfield resident Matilda Hyde, proprietor of the Olde Deerfield Doll House on Memorial Street, across the street from Memorial Hall, produced a series of colorful paper cutout dolls based on the 1704 raid. Each doll came with its own story and clothes, with a stand-up folder serving as a backdrop for play, with John Williams's house on one side for the Puritan child dolls, and a wigwam on the other, for the captive and Native dolls. Hyde sold this novelty—as well as Stephen and Eunice Williams figural cookie cutters—from her tearoom and shop.

By this point, tourists flocked to Deerfield to learn more about its colonial past. To satisfy the demand, Emma Lewis Coleman published, in 1907, the first tourist guide to the town: *A Historic and Present Day Guide to Old Deerfield*, in just 116 economical pages. Coleman opened with the most useful of information: how to get there. There were several train and trolley options, but, in the spirit of the modern age, she also offered a selection of automobile routes through the scenic countryside. Deerfield had once been a lonely outpost on the edge of the world; now a new highway system connected it with the surrounding area. That wasn't to say that driving in the countryside was easy: Some roads were just fine ("good macadam and dirt road rolling"), but others were less so ("road mostly fair, dirt, some pieces poor, winding; 15-20% grades up and down . . . drivers should exercise care"). In 1907, the U.S. road system was largely undeveloped and many roads were just dirt, and the macadam process was only in its infancy; many roads were mapped, though, because bicycles were so popular. Coleman recommended that in some places tourists should hire horses to traverse the country roads—sometimes old ways were the best.

The destination, however, was worth the journey. Deerfield's 2,111 residents stood ready to welcome tourists, who were in the thrall of the Colonial Revival craze and also the town's burgeoning arts and crafts movement. Thirteen pages of Coleman's book covered the town's history, but the majority of it featured specific homes, churches, and buildings in town. The PVMA received special notice:

Besides the room of tablets [Memorial Hall], there is in
the Hall an old-time kitchen, an Indian Room, devoted to
Indian relics . . . a library of over sixteen thousand titles and
unnumbered manuscripts . . . a domestic room . . . a Bedroom
and a Military Room . . .

But most important to Coleman were the stores that sold souvenirs and local handiworks. These included the work of rug-makers,
basket-weavers, metalworkers, and photographers, especially the
Allen sisters. Netted fringes and bedspreads made from old patterns
were highlighted ("bearing such quaint names as 'Moonshine Stitch'
and 'Matrimony Stitch'"), while the Blue and White Society offered
exquisite embroideries. Mrs. Childs's establishment next to the post
office sold bayberry candles. An advertisement in Coleman's book featured a logo of a Native with feathers and war paint representing the
Pocumtuck Basket-Makers.

But what brought people most of all was not the town's thriving
arts and crafts movement, but a single object that held immense sway
over the public imagination: the Old Indian Door. A charming piece of
random, vintage ephemera exemplifies the appeal. It is a high-quality,
platinum-silver-finish photo postcard of the door, circa the early 1900s.
The reverse bears no date or address, no stamp or postal cancellation,
just a handwritten message from a father to his son, so it must have been
mailed inside a sealed envelope:

Dear Edmund. This is a picture of an old wooden door—
studded with nails. It was in a house that the Indians attacked
nearly two hundred years ago in a little town called Deerfield.
If you look closely you will see where the Indians hacked at it
with their tomahawks. Daddy will read [to] you about it when
we are all home again. Are you being a good boy and how is
brother and . . . and Grandma and Grandpa. I wish I could go
in swimming with you. Goodbye. Daddy * a kiss for you.

The Impending Fate

In 1909, Hadley, Massachusetts—Deerfield's sister town twenty miles south—celebrated its two hundred and fiftieth anniversary. This four-day festival was one of the first local history parades, although it certainly foreshadowed more to come. Hadley went all out for four days straight—August 1 through 4. Events included the expected prayers and speeches, as well as horse races, baseball games, and trolley excursions. The last day featured a "street pageant," which was divided into five divisions: floats depicting Hadley's history; floats depicting the history of nearby towns; floats illustrating old-fashioned methods of travel; floats celebrating modern Hadley and its industries; and decorated carriages and modern automobiles.

An audience of ten thousand had been expected, but more than twenty-five thousand people turned up. The participants worked hard to produce elaborate floats. Each was drawn by mules or horses and operated as a kind of rolling *tableau vivant*. The eleven floats devoted to Hadley history led the parade, beginning with a float depicting the purchase of the land from Native Americans. Two floats depicted the early colonial history of "The French and Indian War," and another carried the theme "Opposing Races/Red Man or White?" One told the tale of "The Hadley Witch" of 1680, who had miraculously survived her hanging, and two floats illustrated a Colonial Revival theme, including "Ye old-time kitchen" and, from the American Revolution, "Burgoyne Presents Sword." The last was a Civil War float, "Spirit of '61." None of the floats presented any history more recent.

Following the Hadley floats were those of her sister towns. Hatfield and South Hadley were praised for their beautiful contributions. Deerfield's honored a darker theme: the massacre. Horses pulled a large float—sixteen feet long, eight feet wide—divided into two sections. The first part was a three-dimensional tableau of the front parlor of the Williams house on the *day before the raid*. Four wood posts supported a canvas roof stretched across a frame. A carefully lettered sign along the side read: "JOHN WILLIAMS & FAMILY, FEBRUARY 28, 1704." According to a description, the furnishings were all authentic:

The living-room had its appropriate furnishings for the period. The ancient color of the ceiling and walls, the brick fireplace, with its goose-necked andirons, and burning logs were prominent features. The "Betty lamp" hung on the wooden crane hinged to the manteltree, and furnished the only movable light for the family. Other heirlooms included a child's quaint high chair belonging to the early part of 1700. Powder horns and an ancient pistol fashioned after the one used by Rev. John Williams when the attack was made by the Indians, hung on the chimney-breast. Old silhouettes, crooked-neck squashes, dried apples, etc., were suspended from the ceiling and wall. The family Bible lay on the table, with ink-stand, quill pens, sand-box, wafers and writing paper 187 years old. A small brass-nailed trunk containing the papers of the minister, a spinning wheel, a cradle in which was the six-weeks old baby, an old churn, quaint chairs and stools made up the furnishings of the room.

This level of obsessive detail and antiquarian accuracy shouldn't have been surprising—the float was designed by George Sheldon, Deerfield's venerable historian. Sheldon even presented to the town a wooden gavel that had been carved from a preserved beam cut from his Deerfield lot some two centuries ago. But one person was strangely absent from the scene: the reverend himself. The central figure of the drama was represented only by a small portrait of him hanging beside the chimney.

Several people populated the interior of the float. A young woman sat in a chair beside a large, spinning wheel. She was probably meant to be young Eunice Williams, John's daughter. Behind her stood a Black woman working a butter churn. She was dressed differently than Eunice, in a kerchief and patterned blouse with the sleeves rolled up, and was meant to represent Parthena, Williams's enslaved woman. Behind her a woman sat at a drop-leaf table, mending clothes, probably meant to be the reverend's wife Eunice. Behind her a young boy sat on a stool and appeared to be using a knife to shave kindling from a stick. This was likely young Stephen Williams.

On the outside, a railing representing a low, pointed palisade fence surrounded the wagon, evoking the tall fence that was supposed to protect the Williams home and others from a raid but failed to do so because of the massive snowdrifts that enabled the attackers to scale the fence with ease. A sign attached to the fence read DEERFIELD in large letters and the front edge of the float was emblazoned with a foreboding warning, only two hundred years too late: THE IMPENDING FATE.

At the rear of the float stood several trees (or large limbs that represented a wooded area). The foliage was thickly bunched, but just through the branches, the face of a young man was visible. He represented the Natives waiting in ambush, ready to attack the peaceful group gathered in the minister's home.

Inside, the unsuspecting family awaited their "impending fate." For them, what was yet to come was still unknown, but for the audience it was all too clear. Not everyone appreciated the effort. The commemorative book published after the event criticized the float with a stunning understatement: "Old Deerfield presented an almost uncomfortable suggestion of the fate which impended over the early settlers."

Still, the float was an elaborate and altogether evocative display of myth, not history. It might have been as close to the real thing as George Sheldon could provide, but the serene depiction of a family awaiting slaughter in a parade of otherwise joyous celebration was not the truth. The first stirrings of historic preservation—which became an important element of the Colonial Revival movement—began with the effort to preserve the Old Indian House in Deerfield in 1847, and the effort to preserve Mount Vernon, George Washington's home, in 1853. In 1880, George Sheldon installed an iconic colonial kitchen in Memorial Hall, and then a classic schoolroom. From its founding, the PVMA was a nerve center of the heritage movement.

The Colonial Revival was a movement to preserve and advance traditional American values, culture, and patriotism during a time of disruption and social change in the late nineteenth and early twentieth centuries, by venerating the spirit, history, and material culture of colonial America from the 1620s through the Revolutionary War era. The

United States was in transition. There was another America outside
the borders of small towns like Deerfield. The migration from farms
to cities raised the age-old Jeffersonian dilemma: Was America to be
a pastoral, rural nation of farmers and tradesmen or an industrialized
urban nation of factories and workers? And who would those workers
be? The 1880s saw an influx of European immigration, especially from
Eastern Europe, places like Russia and Poland. The Connecticut River
Valley, including Deerfield, experienced a surge in Polish immigration
in the latter nineteenth and early twentieth centuries. Many Americans
treated the immigrants as unwashed, uncultured, and unwelcome—
unpatriotic foreign invaders who did not belong here, imported socialism, and undermined the traditional values of an older America.

The Revival, of which the Hadley parade was just one part, was
about a lot more than collecting antiques. Old Yankee values, some
people feared, were under siege. The Colonial Revival offered an
answer and a solution. With its nostalgia for a simpler time, it was
a resistance movement against the complexities and challenges of the
modern world, a rebellion against changing times. It was an attempt
to preserve traditional American values through the preservation and
presentation of the material culture of an earlier time. It was a reaction
against a complex and ugly world, which the colonial past was both
a refuge from and a bulwark against. The Revival was a masked effort to codify anti-immigration laws, promote the rise of the eugenics
movement of the time, solidify a white-European hegemony, and erase
Indians from history and even their own stories.

"New Attack on Deerfield," the *Springfield Daily Republican*
warned on Sunday, March 13, 1910. Two hundred and six years after
the raid of 1704, Indians had returned to attack the town again—
but only on camera for a silent movie produced by the Thomas Edison Company. As the newspaper continued, the only danger was
from "Moving Picture Red Skins." The film, titled *Ononko's Vow: A
Colonial Tale*, connected the Bloody Brook Massacre of 1675 to the
Deerfield raid of 1704 through a storyline that linked two families—
one white and the other Indian—over time. This was the very first

costumed attempt to reenact the raid, and is a rare survival from the dawn of cinema; 75 percent of all silent films have been lost.

The catalyst for the project was Herbert Streeter, a live-music and entertainment entrepreneur who owned the first movie theater in Greenfield. Streeter wrote the treatment for the film and pitched the Edison company to make it. The movie business was still in its infancy. In Paris, Auguste and Louis Lumière had produced the first "motion picture" just sixteen years earlier, in 1894. At the same time across the Atlantic, the Black Maria— Thomas Edison's film studio—had opened. Among its first films was a Native American–themed montage filmed September 24, 1894, entitled *Sioux Ghost Dance*. Also filmed on that day was another Native American picture, *Buffalo Dance*. The actors were employees of Buffalo Bill's Wild West Show, and it was the first time real Native Americans were filmed on camera. By the time Edison's studio shut down in 1918, it had made almost twelve hundred films, most of them shorts.

The improbable plot of *Ononko's Vow* was pure fiction. The main characters included a Narragansett Indian chief, Ungacook (probably an alliterative reference to Cooper's Chingachgook); his son Ononko; Ruth Smith, a young Puritan girl; her father, Jonathan Smith; and her beloved soldier and romantic interest, Ebenezer Dow.

At Bloody Brook, Ungacook saves Jonathan Smith from certain death, but the chief later dies in Smith's house from wounds he received in the fight. Before he expires Ungacook makes his young son, Ononko, swear an oath to always be a loyal friend to the Smith family. Twenty-six years later, the boy Ononko is now a man and a chief in his own right. On the Puritan side of the story, Jonathan Smith, a white-haired old man living in Deerfield on the day before the 1704 massacre, promises Ruth in marriage to Ebenezer Dow. During the attack, Dow volunteers to run for help and, like John Sheldon, Jr., jumps from a second-floor window to summon reinforcements. Attacking Natives chop through the front door, kill the men, and seize Ruth Smith to take her to Canada as a captive.

Jonathan Smith survives the raid and is rescued by the trader and military leader Pynchon. Smith reunites with Ononko, who vows to save Ruth. He follows her trail and catches up to the raiding party just as the

Indians are about to torture and kill her with their tomahawks. Ononko then offers to trade his life for Ruth's, invoking the "ancient right" of an Indian chief. He proclaims: "I am Ononko. Take me and set the white maiden free." The timely arrival of Ebenezer Dow and reinforcements interrupts his torture and imminent death. The young chief escorts Ruth and Ebenezer back to the edge of civilization, or, at least, to a ridge overlooking Deerfield. Ruth begs Ononko to stay, but he refuses: "You belong to the East. I go to the West." Before they part, however, he gives his blanket to Ruth to cherish as a remembrance of him. Streeter titled this last scene, "Ononko's Chivalry."

The *Republican* reported that audiences loved history films with one caveat: if the movies left out "the dry parts" and stuck with "hair-raising thrills." If audiences wanted excitement, that meant scenes of "Indians with their hatchets, tomahawks, bows and arrows, war paint and feathers." That was just the thing to make a crowd "sit up and give attention." How exciting it was, the article claimed, to sit in a safe and modern theater and watch a band of "bloodthirsty savages" creep "closer and closer" to attack as the "wily Indian, with cruel features and ready tomahawk, is approaching nearer and nearer to scalp." Paradoxically, the article cautioned that audiences might find strict historical accuracy uncomfortably real, because that would "take away from the romantic charm of a film." What they wanted—then as now—was escapist entertainment, easy to watch and not hard to take. What early twentieth-century audience wanted to see the two young children of Reverend Williams murdered on his own doorstep? Who would pay to see the brutal torture of captives, or children suffocating to death in cellars? As the Springfield newspaper concluded, "close adherence to the truth of life and history would take away all the romantic charm and leave the story without interest."

The arrival in Deerfield of the cast and crew from New York in late February 1910 created a local sensation. The production attracted immediate press coverage in local papers. Crowds of three to four hundred people assembled, curious about this new art form and eager to watch "history" (as a motion picture) being made. Filming began "on location" in Deerfield the first week in March, and involved about forty actors,

LEFT: This woodcut from the 1833 edition of *The Redeemed Captive* is the first artistic depiction of the Sheldon House under attack on February 29, 1704.

RIGHT: Fire and confusion at the climax of the raid.

BELOW: Deerfield laid waste as individual dramas play out within the palisade.

RIGHT: The Sheldon House under siege while the impregnable front door frustrates every effort to break it down.

RIGHT: The Old Indian Door framed by architectural fragments from the Sheldon House.

BELOW: Bird's-eye view of an isolated Deerfield in flames.

LEFT: Mohican Etow Oh Koam raises a classic war club, one of the deadliest weapons on the New England frontier. He was one of the "Four Indian Kings" who sailed to England in 1710 to meet Queen Anne, six years after the Deerfield Massacre, to solicit her help to fight French Canadians and to stop Jesuit missionaries from converting Indians to Catholicism. Their visit caused a public sensation and inspired artists to paint and engrave their portraits.

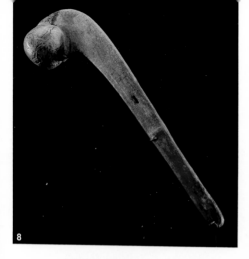

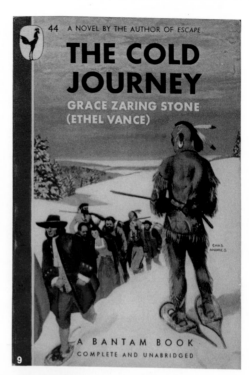

ABOVE: Beautiful but dangerous, an elegant New England war club of the type used during the Deerfield raid.

RIGHT: A pulp fiction novel depicting captives on the march under the watch of a snowshoe-clad Native wearing the secret weapon that gave the French and Indian raiders an advantage.

LEFT: Exhausted Deerfield captives on their three-hundred-mile trek to New France.

BELOW: The prisoners part ways as their captors divide them into smaller groups for the long winter journey to Canada.

LEFT: Jean-Baptiste Hertel de Rouville (1668–1722), the influential French officer who led the raid on Deerfield.

BELOW LEFT: Commemorative gifts—a bullet pouch, gorget, tobacco pouch, and wool sash—that Eunice Williams presented to her brother Stephen Williams during a reunion. Eunice returned to New England at least four times to visit her English family.

BELOW RIGHT: By tradition, snowshoes worn by John Sheldon during one of his dangerous journeys north to Canada to negotiate the release of some of the Deerfield captives.

RIGHT: Ash splint storage basket made by 26-year-old Marie Saraphine (Sophie) Watso, acknowledged as her Indian cousin by 21-year-old Catherine Williams during Watso's visit to Deerfield. Williams inscribed it: "Basket given me September 1837/By Sophie one of the Sr. Francis Indians/Connected with the Williams family."

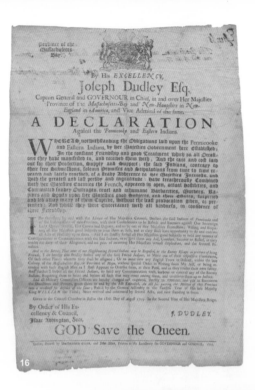

LEFT: Queen Anne's War comes to North America. Massachusetts governor Joseph Dudley's declaration of war against the French and the "Pennicooke and Eastern Indians" of New England dated August 18, 1703.

BELOW: Neck "halter" in the style of those used to restrain the Deerfield captives.

RIGHT: Oil portrait of the Rev. John Williams, likely painted in Boston at the height of his celebrity soon after his triumphant return from captivity in 1707. It was lost for hundreds of years, and rediscovered only recently at a local auction near Deerfield.

LEFT: Oil portrait of the Rev. Stephen Williams, who survived the massacre, was redeemed from captivity and, like his father John, became a minister. He did not return to Deerfield, a "melancholy place for me."

BELOW: Monument marking the approximate spot where Eunice Williams was slain by tomahawk on the captives' march the day after the raid.

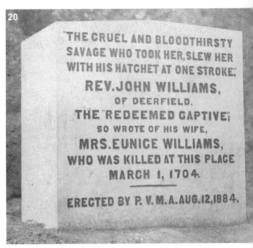

THE CRUEL AND BLOODTHIRSTY SAVAGE WHO TOOK HER, SLEW HER WITH HIS HATCHET AT ONE STROKE: REV. JOHN WILLIAMS, OF DEERFIELD. THE 'REDEEMED CAPTIVE; SO WROTE OF HIS WIFE, MRS. EUNICE WILLIAMS, WHO WAS KILLED AT THIS PLACE MARCH 1, 1704.

ERECTED BY P. V. M. A. AUG. 12, 1884.

ABOVE: The first photograph, ca. 1860–1870, of the gravestone of Eunice Williams. "Here lyeth the Body of Mrs. Eunice Williams the Vertous & desirable Consort of the Revrd Mr. John Williams . . . She was Born Augt 2 1664. And fell by the rage of ye Barbarous Enemy."

BELOW: The first photograph of the gravestone of John Williams, from a pair of stereo cards of his and Eunice's stones made by Benjamin Popkins, the man who decades earlier took one of two early daguerreotypes of the Old Indian House before its demolition. "Here lyes ye Body of the Revd Mr John Williams the Beloved and Faithfull Pastor of this place."

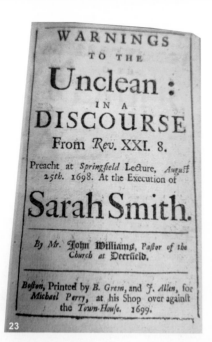

23

ABOVE: In 1699, the year after Sarah Smith was hanged, John Williams published the merciless sermon in which he had called for her execution.

BELOW RIGHT: Stone monument marking the location of the John Sheldon House, the famed "Old Indian House" that survived the Deerfield Massacre.

BELOW: Program for the Deerfield Pageant of 1916, the last year the celebration was ever held.

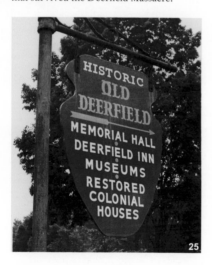

24

ABOVE: Vintage mid-20th century wood roadside sign documenting the growth of "Old Deerfield" as a popular tourist attraction. The arrowhead-shaped sign evokes an Indian theme but does not mention the 1704 attack.

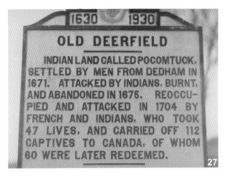

LEFT: A metal highway sign from 1930 alerts drivers that Old Deerfield, where 47 townspeople were killed and 112 taken captive in 1704, is nearby.

BELOW: George Sheldon (1818–1916), Deerfield's antiquarian in chief, dominant historian, memory keeper, mythmaker, and founder of Memorial Hall, in a portrait painted by Augustus Vincent Tack in 1905.

ABOVE: Memorial boulder and plaque honoring Godfrey Nims, whose family suffered terribly during the raid.

RIGHT: The cenotaphic chamber of ancestor worship inside Memorial Hall at the Pocumtuck Valley Memorial Association. White tablets resembling burial crypts bear the names of the captives and the dead from the Deerfield Massacre.

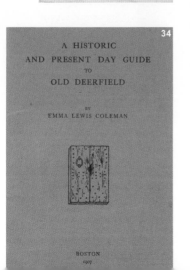

ABOVE: Another war, another roster of men at arms. A patriotic billboard erected on Deerfield's town commons, the site of the old palisade of 1704, listing the names of local men in uniform more than two centuries later during the Great War. The memorial highlights Tom Ashley, descendant of the storied Ashley family, teacher at the Deerfield Academy, and U.S. Marine killed in action.

LEFT: An advertising poster promoting the Deerfield pageant of 1913, the first of three ceremonial events commemorating Deerfield's history on the eve of World War I.

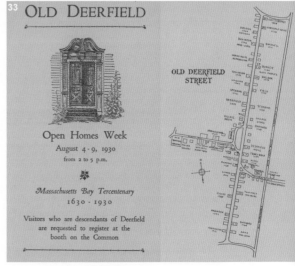

ABOVE: During the Massachusetts tercentenary in 1930, Deerfield's "Open Homes Week" in August of that year confirmed that the town had become a popular tourist attraction.

LEFT: Emma Lewis Coleman's important early guidebook to Deerfield encouraged automobile travel to the charming colonial town and helped make it a tourist destination.

LEFT: A historical anachronism: a bizarre postal cover (ca. 1938) celebrates National Air-Mail Week by commemorating the Bloody Brook Massacre of 1675.

RIGHT: Mass grave for the dead of 1704, topped with the memorial stone placed by the Pocumtuck Valley Memorial Association.

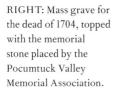

LEFT: "Edge of the Settlement." A still photo from the Edison Company silent film *Ononko's Vow.* The Indian chief parts forever from the white colonists— and the woman—he has served. "I go west," he says, foreshadowing Indian removal policy to come.

LEFT: "Ononko searching for Jonathan Smith after the Massacre." An Edison still photo from the film *Ononko's Vow*.

BELOW LEFT: Memorial Hall of the Pocumtuck Valley Memorial Association, the original home of the Deerfield Academy, designed by architect Asher Benjamin and dedicated in 1799.

RIGHT: A photograph by the Allen sisters, taken during a Deerfield pageant, of a little girl portraying Eunice Williams atop the shoulder of her white "Mohawk" captor.

BELOW: "Preparing for the Attack on Old Deerfield." An Indian encampment two miles from town just before the raid in an Edison still photo from *Ononko's Vow*.

being a good boy and how is brother and Nannie and Grandma and Granpa— I hope I could go in swimming with you— Love— Daddy

CORRESPONDENCE — ADDRESS ONLY

Dear Edmund. This is a picture of a old wooden door- studded with nails. It was in a house that the Indians attacked near two hundred years ago at a little town called Deerfield. If you look closely you can see where the Indians hacked at it with their tomahawks— Daddy will read you about it when we are all home again— love you

ABOVE AND LEFT: Vintage postcard of the Old Indian Door, inscribed on the verso with a charming inscription from "Daddy."

LEFT: The Bloody Brook Massacre reenacted for *Ononko's Vow*.

BELOW: Admission ticket to the Indian House Memorial and Pocumtuck Valley Memorial Association's Memorial Hall where the "cut and gashed" Indian Door was enshrined. Marketing the massacre became an important element in promoting early-20th-century tourism to Deerfield.

Old Deerfield Massacre Ticket

In February of 1704 the frontier town of Deerfield (est. 1673) was attacked by the French and Indians. Much of the town was destroyed and many of the inhabitants were taken captive. One of the houses most valiantly defended was the Ensign John Sheldon house just inside the stockade.

Romantic associations surrounding the Sheldon house and its cut and gashed door made it one of the earliest tourist attractions in the Connecticut River Valley. It became known as the Old Indian House.

With this ticket you can see the Indian House Memorial and Memorial Hall (where the historic Door is displayed). Marked on the ticket is also the Old Burying Ground where the victims of the Massacre were buried in a common grave.

	Adults	$2.00
Pocumtuck Valley Memorial Association	Student	$1.50
Indian House Memorial Association	Children	$1.00
	Ask about Family Rates	

LEFT: The replica of the Old Indian House, built by William Gass.

ABOVE: During its 250th anniversary parade in 1907, the neighboring town of Hatfield honored Deerfield by including a float commemorating the massacre and the "impending fate" that awaited the Williams family.

RIGHT: During a summer pageant, oxcarts depart Deerfield on the road to Bloody Brook.

BELOW: Carts depart for Bloody Brook in September 1675 on the road to the massacre.

LEFT: Reenactment scene of John Williams being redeemed from captivity at a Deerfield pageant.

BELOW LEFT: "Little captives of 1704," a tableau of paper cutout dolls sold at the Old Deerfield Doll House in the early 20th century.

ABOVE RIGHT: Woven raffia basket depicting the Old Indian House made by Sarah Cowles, a member of the Pocumtuck Basket Makers, circa 1903.

BELOW: Early-20th-century souvenir spoon made in Greenfield, Massachusetts, picturing the Old Indian House.

LEFT: Nostalgic sign painted in 1923 for the Old Deerfield Doll House, a tearoom and gift shop operated by Matilda Hyde on Memorial Street. Hyde produced a set of colorful cutout paper dolls with a Deerfield Massacre theme, as shown on the previous page.

BELOW: Improbable hero: John Williams immortalized as a toy in 1995, two hundred and ninety-one years after his death, as a modern-day action figure, sold along with a Mohawk warrior.

ABOVE: On February 28, 1954, the 250th anniversary of the raid, eight-year-old Molly Harlow renews the assault on the Old Indian Door in Memorial Hall.

BELOW: Puritan dolls from the Old Deerfield House "dressed to represent real characters in the history of the Deerfield Massacre of 1704."

LEFT: Henry Flynt, founder of Historic Deerfield, captured in an 18th century–style oil painting with two of his favorite things: a rare 17th-century Gerrit Onckelbag silver covered cup and the 18th-century Allen House, his residence in Deerfield.

BELOW: The title of Henry Flynt's first book is self-explanatory. He wanted Deerfield to promote patriotism and serve as a bulwark against communism during the Cold War.

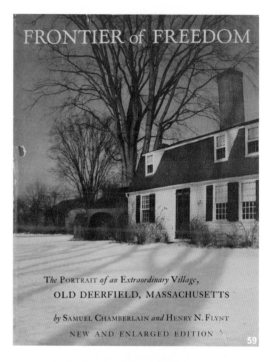

FRONTIER of FREEDOM

The PORTRAIT of an Extraordinary Village,
OLD DEERFIELD, MASSACHUSETTS

by SAMUEL CHAMBERLAIN and HENRY N. FLYNT
NEW AND ENLARGED EDITION

BELOW: A replica of the Old Indian House built on Deerfield's Main Street and dedicated in 1930.

half of them performers from Edison's Bedford Park studio, with extras recruited from Deerfield and surrounding areas. Interior scenes were filmed back at the studio, but outdoor scenes were shot around town, including on The Street, the slope of Pine Hill, and on Mount Pocumtuck, east of Memorial Hall. The production team spent four or five days on location, employed two cameras, and shot about one thousand feet of film, at an impressive cost of two thousand dollars.

Not surprising for the time, white actors played all the Native parts. "Redface" had been used as early as the Boston Tea Party, when colonists masqueraded as Natives. This early whitewashing in film, or, more aptly, red-washing, of painting actors in dark makeup, was de rigueur for the time. Even if professional Native actors had existed, they wouldn't have been hired. Whites were hired to impersonate them instead. Their faces were heavily made up to darken their skin tone, while their "noses were made crooked by means of a colored putty-like substance." Other early films also employed this practice. Two years after *Ononko's Vow*, Thomas Ince directed *The Indian Massacre*, later released as *The Heart of an Indian*, in which white actors were cast to portray Natives. Francis Ford (John Ford's brother) played the male lead, the Indian chief. In *Iola's Promise*, released the same year and directed by D. W. Griffith, Mary Pickford appeared in brown greasepaint and a black wig to play the main character, a Native. Griffith preferred casting Pickford in these roles because she "had a good face for Indians on account of her high cheekbones." Although some directors, like Ince, favored a more sympathetic portrayal of Native Americans, others, like Griffith, who would produce *The Birth of a Nation* five years later, depicted Natives as bloodthirsty, irredeemable savages.

For *Ononko's Vow* the cold weather in Deerfield was perfect for filming winter scenes. Untrodden white snow four feet deep blanketed the ground, creating an uncanny verisimilitude. The crew recreated the original palisade by planting three-foot-high pasteboard faux logs in the drifts, fostering the illusion that the rest of the palisade was buried below the snow—as it might have appeared in 1704. The director, Frank McGlynn, Sr., used a megaphone to shout directions to the cast while the cameras rolled. *Begin the attack, move faster, slow down, now closer again.* Battle casualties fell dead on cue at predesignated spots. McGlynn, a lawyer turned silent-film actor, knew what he was doing. Born in 1866, one year after the end of the Civil War and the assassination of Abraham Lincoln, he enjoyed a career that lasted half a century. Just five years after directing *Ononko's Vow*, he played Lincoln in a 1915 Edison silent film, and later he gained fame for his frequent portrayals of Lincoln in plays, sound films, and most notably, the 1935 Shirley Temple movie *The Littlest Rebel*. Three of McGlynn's young children, the oldest four and five years old, played captive villagers. Their father told them to do their best to look terrified. Watching them on-screen 114 years later, one would say they played their parts well.

Filming *Ononko's Vow* was not all smooth sailing. A few mishaps disrupted the production. An actor was almost shot in the head with wadding from a premature musket discharge fired by an enthusiastic extra. McGlynn stopped filming to remind the cast of the common-sense rule: do not point their muskets directly at one another. In the middle of another scene, a railroad train rolled by in the background and filming had to be delayed until the train had passed. No one had thought to check the railroad schedule in advance.

With winter filming completed, the cast and crew planned to come back during the summer to shoot the Bloody Brook scenes. Because that battle occurred in September, they had to wait until there were leaves on the trees and the streams flowed freely without ice. The Edison team returned and completed *Ononko's Vow* in late July 1910. One thousand spectators gathered at Whately Glen to watch the reenactment of the massacre. Auto parties came from distant towns. An electric commuter train offered the short ride from Greenfield. And a bus from South Deerfield brought more people. Thirty-two actors and sixty local extras played the parts of the Natives, soldiers, and teamsters.

The drama unfolded in three acts. First, the wagon train approached the ambush site and halted at the brook where the soldiers laid down their arms, to pick the "dear and deadly" grapes. Second, the action shifted to

Indians concealing themselves for the ambush. Finally, without warning, Indians lurking in the thicket attacked and massacred Captain Lathrop's command. Through the entire winter and summer filming of the movie, the actors played their parts with enthusiasm, speaking and shouting, even though this was, of course, a silent film, and not a word they spoke would be recorded. That did not stop them from vocalizing their parts. The Indians whooped in triumph, shouted "come on!" during an attack, and when a Native seized the heroine, Ruth Smith, "she screamed and begged aloud for mercy." Wounded men groaned in agony. To a modern, sophisticated audience, the acting in *Ononko's Vow* comes off as wooden, stiff, and unconvincing—even comical. But this was the dawn of the motion picture age, before the art had established its conventions and techniques. Crude equipment, erratic film speed, and exaggerated gestures and facial expressions were all hallmarks of the early, melodramatic silent films.

Ononko's Vow received wide, prerelease publicity in several film publications, including the *Edison Kinetogram* of September 15, 1910. The front cover carried a desolate, winter-scene photo of Ononko standing in the snow amid bare tree branches, arms folded, wrapped in an Indian blanket, gazing into the distance. A three-page article by Herbert Streeter introduced the film as "a pretty love tale." Released on September 30, the film premiered in Greenfield during the first week of October, at Washington Hall and at Herbert Streeter's small Bijou Theatre on Main Street. As it was a silent film, without synchronized sound, occasional title cards appeared on-screen to orient the audience. Live music substituted for recorded dialogue, which would not exist until 1927.

The local audience was thrilled to see the venerable George Sheldon appear on screen at the beginning and end of *Ononko's Vow*. The film opens with ninety-two-year-old Sheldon greeting a modern young couple, tourists who have come to Deerfield. He directs them to the Bloody Brook monument a few miles away, and then serves as the film's "narrator" of the historical story, which the young couple imagines for themselves. Sheldon appears again at the end, as though giving his benediction to the project. This is the only film footage of George Sheldon known to exist. An article about the movie paid homage to this legendary figure: "Our honored historian closes his tale for Sheldon will always keep alive the story of 'Old Deerfield' and our heroes."

The film drew enthusiastic reviews. A sampling of them from across the country confirms that the film was a hit. The *Burlington Daily News* (October 8, 1910) declared that the film "should be seen by everyone" and that it was "one of the best productions ever made." The *Public Opinion* in Chambersburg, Pennsylvania, (October 11) praised it as "one of the most elaborate Indian pictures ever put on the screen." The *Press and Sun-Bulletin* in Binghamton, New York, (October 20) was even more effusive: "There are many thrilling scenes, and the story is so vividly told that you can almost hear the war whoop of the Indians, the crackling flames of the burning buildings and the shrieks of those who are suffering at the hands of the Indians."

Promotional items and souvenirs were also produced. Streeter and Edison even published a set of picture postcards based on a number of different still photographs made during the production. This set included images of the ox carts departing Deerfield in 1675, the Bloody Brook Massacre, the Sheldon House with dead bodies scattered about after the 1704 raid, and of course, Ononko himself. No doubt Streeter sold these at the premiere and at subsequent screenings. He also marketed the movie with promotional gimmicks, including the sale of souvenir tomahawks at screenings. An advertisement stated that such items were "all the rage," and more than that, they were *authentic*—"the real thing!!" Carved by Hiram J. Wood in South Deerfield, the objects were made from "a big elm tree cut on the Bloody Brook Battle Ground." The large tree, which had grown on the edge of the stream, had been felled to build a new cement bridge. Customers were warned that supply was limited and tomahawks would be sold only at the Bijou Theatre on October 6, 7, and 8. The purchase price was ten cents.

Ononko's Vow was a product of its time, riddled with historical errors and egregious Native racial stereotypes that would never survive modern scrutiny. White men impersonating Indians with preposterous red makeup, elaborate cheekbones, prosthetic noses, and shaggy black wigs? Surviving records indicate that not one Native was cast in the film. Instead, the movie stereotyped Indians as "savages" driven by bloodlust, and described the events of 1675 and 1704 as "massacres." Of course, the two principal Native characters were the exception. Ungacook and Ononko were "good Indians," happy to serve the white man and vouchsafe his protection. They represented the "noble savage" trope, self-sacrificing even to their own deaths. At the climax of the film, Ononko gives Ruth his blanket (to save the unprepared white girl from dying of hypothermia)—because he has nothing left to give her. She possesses everything that belonged to him— his clothes, his lands, and perhaps even his heart. As she turns to leave with her white fiancé, Ebenezer Dow, Ononko moves to follow her. It's a split second, but isn't that what history is made of? Obviously the producers thought so, but the Edison *Kinetogram* banished the thought of a forbidden romance between an Indian chief and a white Puritan maiden: "Perhaps because in the breast of the handsome savage some gentle thought of the girl he has saved has entered; but his nobility of character permits him to entertain the thought only for a fleeting moment."

The movie might have a different ending today, with Ruth abandoning the stolid Ebenezer, fleeing Deerfield, and running away with romantic and willing Ononko. Hollywood is all about happy endings, so often lacking in history.

The Deerfield Pageants

Perhaps inspired by the celebration in Hadley three years earlier or, more likely, by the exciting motion picture filmed in town earlier that year, Deerfield produced its own commemoration in 1910. This event took the form of a "pageant" that was so successful that two other pageants followed in 1913 and 1916. For a brief window of time, these became regular events during which townspeople would gather to reenact a series of milestone episodes in Deerfield's history. Before the era of film, television, and radio these pageants were the drive-in movies of their day. The live pageants were large-scale outdoor reenactments that took place in a large field behind the Allen house in the very center of Deerfield.

The pageants were equal parts costume party, folk art, community the-ater, and historical reenactment. The first historical pageant in America took place in Philadelphia, the cradle of liberty, in 1908. The point of pageants was to create an immediate connection between the actor, the character, and the audience: After all, many of the actors played their own ancestors, cre-ating a bond with the past in which they could comprehend and value their ancestors' strengths and sacrifices. But more than that, these pageants were also public and visual demonstrations of community solidarity.

It was also a great way to teach about the past—or a mythical past, as New Englanders wished it had been. Pageantry was about dramatic presentation, not perfect historical accuracy (though inaccuracy might have been anathema to George Sheldon). These performances—with local buy-in—were dramatic public education, especially for the young. Every person—especially today—has heard the plaintive cry from school students that history is *boring*. This was a way to dress it up and make it exciting. Besides, if the next generation didn't care about his-tory or where they came from, what would happen to it? This must have nagged at the nonagenarian George Sheldon.

So how did pageantry begin in Deerfield? The romantic answer is a fictional retelling imagined by Mary Master Needham in her 1912 book *Folk Festivals*. The book begins in Deerfield, where a young girl named Pollie complains to her mother and refuses to attend any more public history events:

> I'm tired and sick of the whole performance of these
> anniversaries and holidays. I want to do something myself—not
> just sit around and bask in the fact that a hundred and fifty or
> two hundred years ago I had a few ancestors who did something,
> or else were "done for" themselves in that everlasting massacre
> of ours. We'll never hear the end of that massacre.

Only when a friend suggests to Pollie that they *act out* that history *for themselves* does the skeptic change her mind. Passive book history is one thing; active history quite another.

Charming as this story is, fictional "Pollie" probably did not start the pageant craze in Deerfield. The more capitalistic version is that Margaret MacLaren Eager, the famous "pageant master," directed a play in nearby Greenfield in February 1910. She had already organized pageants across New England, in Northampton, Bennington, Salem, and also in Saratoga, New York, and other towns. According to the *Greenfield Gazette and Courier*, she had approached Deerfield's Improvement Society about hosting a pageant in town that summer. It might have been just what the town needed. George Sheldon was in his nineties—although going strong, like an immortal Father Christmas. C. Alice Baker had died just months earlier, on May 22, 1909. Who could carry on the torch of history? Eager's answer was: everyone. And people would pay to see it.

Men, women, and children—many of them descendants of the very people who had lived through the events they reenacted—dressed for their roles in semi-authentic period costumes. These theatrical performances were amateur shows and featured handmade costumes sewn locally, so little attention was paid to scrupulous historical accuracy. The presence of George Sheldon must have ensured that no one veered too far into inaccuracy, although these were certainly modern interpretations.

Deerfield rode the cutting edge of modernity. According to the *Greenfield Gazette and Courier* of July 16, 1910: "The out of door historical pageant is a novelty about here," the newspaper boasted, and "Deerfield is thus very much abreast of the times."

1910 Pageant

The pageant of 1910 unfolded over three days—July 14, 15, and 16—at 8:00 p.m. on Thursday and 4 p.m. on Friday and Saturday. The site was the grounds behind the Allen homestead in Deerfield, which had a natural rolling slope into a wide field. The grounds themselves were a perfect stage. As the *Greenfield Gazette and Courier* raved: "With Deerfield mountain as a background and the sky and the moon and the stars overhead, no more beautiful setting could be imagined."

Bleachers were installed, and individual seats were sold as for any theater performance. New to the era, however, was the appearance of

the automobile, and these were welcome to "drive up" as well and park
on either side of the pageant grounds. Evening performances were no
problem: When it got dark, car lights were turned on, aided by two cal-
cium lights ("limelights") at the rear.

The Allen sisters were local antiquarians, preservationists, and photographers who devoted themselves to telling Deerfield's history. They specialized in taking photographs that documented the "Colonial Revival"
era, a nostalgic time in the early 1900s when a craze for early American
furniture, dress, customs, decorations, textiles, pewter, silver tankards and
candlesticks, and more swept the country, especially in the New England
states. Prices for a seat at the pageant ranged from fifty cents to one dollar.

The show featured an extended scene portraying the events at Bloody
Brook in 1675. As a sqeamish Needham explained, it was sanitized:

> No history of Deerfield—no visit to Deerfield—Deerfield itself
> is not complete without "the massacre." Therefore, it was fair
> to assume that no historical pageant would be complete without
> it. But how could a massacre be made vivid without being
> offensive? It spoke much for the "poetry" of those in charge of
> the pageant that the only evidence of the massacre itself was in a
> fusillade of rifle shots, fired in the near-by woods. We had seen
> Captain Lathrop and his men start with the carts; we knew to
> what they were going; and when the shots came the impressive
> silence bespoke a recognition of the waste and the tragedy of that
> pioneer time and of those who gave their blood for us.

The massacre of 1704 was a key part of the 1910 pageant.

The next scene involved Captain Appleton protecting women
and children, followed by Hannah Beaman's bravery in protecting
her school flock from the Natives attacking. Several scenes depicted
1704, according to Needham:

> We saw the savages as they surprised the sleeping town and
> each claimed a captive. We saw John Williams, the pastor, as

he was led out of the "Old Indian House" by an Indian. We
admired him and wondered at him when we saw how erect and
unafraid he seemed. But it was not so with Dame Williams.
Slowly, as if she were falling in her grief and terror, she was
dragged along by her captor. She turned back often to look at
their five children; at little Stephen who had not forgotten his
silver buttons and buckles, and at small Eunice who, touching
some chord in her captor's heart was carried in his arms. After
her came maidens and youths, some solemn, some shrinking,
many terrified, as they started on their long three hundred mile
march to Canada. We watched them in silence as they climbed
the hill and were swallowed up in the gloom of the woods.

Then the scene shifted to Canada, where an adult Eunice had transitioned into the Native community:

Here was Eunice Williams, a child no longer. She was dressed in
Indian garb . . . and neither prayer nor threat could ever procure
her ransom. She married an Indian and died—an Indian!

The rest of the program depicted John Williams's return from captivity, and quaint scenes of a colonial wedding, erecting the Revolutionary War Liberty Pole, and a trifling "Parson Ashley's Tea Party."

Three hundred people performed in 1910. According to the
Springfield Daily Republican: "Garrets have been ransacked for colonial costumes and old-fashioned finery. Silver buckles have been
polished, wigs powdered, and not a flintlock, smoothbore or musket in the old town but has been brought out of its resting place and
pressed into service." Not only were many performers playing their
actual ancestors, but they were probably wearing their clothes and
carrying their weapons!

The Deerfield pageant of 1910 was an immense success. As many as
twelve hundred paying customers attended. Margaret Eager took home
a third of the profits: $393.

1913 Pageant

The second Deerfield pageant was held over four days in August 1913. Once again, the performances took place on the ground of the Allen homestead. The run of show illustrated the history of Deerfield from its ancient beginnings to its present day, beginning with a performance of "Old Pocumtuck Indian Legends," before energetically opening with six separate episodes. The first episode focused on Native history, "The Pocumtuck Indians attacked by the Iroquois," but soon moved on to Deerfield's colonial past with "The coming of the First Settler, Samuel Hinsdale" in 1669. The third episode depicted the events of 1675 at Bloody Brook, while the fourth focused on 1694 and "Alarm at the Dame School" when Hannah Beaman and her flock of students barely escaped Indian capture. The raid of February 29, 1704, was not performed, but instead the program showcased a sequence on "The day after the Deerfield Massacre," when the "Captives [were] taken to Canada." The fifth episode highlighted the return of Reverend Williams in 1706, while the sixth episode was set in 1774 with skits on the Liberty Pole and Parson Ashley's Tea Party.

1916 Pageant

The pageant of 1916 was more elaborate and sophisticated than those of 1910 or 1913. Once again it was held on the Allen farmstead over a course of four days, August 11 to 15. But now ten organizing committees with almost fifty members aspired to professionalize the pageant. The program declared: "In producing its third community pageant Deerfield is proving itself a leader in one of the greatest dramatic movements of the age, Community Drama, a drama in which the townspeople are the cast, the hero and the audience all in one."

The pageant of 1916 was an elaborate concoction of commemoration and historical myth, meant to surpass its predecessors. While the pageants of 1910 and 1913 had focused on "the vicissitudes of the little frontier town," the pageant of 1916 would focus on Deerfield's Puritan heritage. The program wrapper pictured a rapturous Puritan minister, arms aloft with Bible in hand. It might as well have been John Williams—or John

Williams as he was mythologized. But the pageant got off track by announcing it would "celebrate the genius of William Shakespeare" on the three hundredth anniversary of his death.

Now the action moved on to New England. This scene opened in Pocumtuck Valley, in the seventeenth century, with an "Indian warrior" surveying his lands from the vista of Pocumtuck Rock. Then the scene shifted to "The Feast of Corn," in which the Native tribe celebrated a successful harvest and gave "thanks to the Great Spirit" for the plenty. The ceremony was interrupted, however, by a visitor, William Pynchon. The visitor "purchased" surplus corn with "bright colored blankets, beads, and wampum" so that the grain could stave off famine in the settler towns of the Connecticut Valley.

But all was not well: in a spirit of foreshadowing—good for the settlers, bad for the Natives—"the Spirit of Vision approaches [the Indians] and points towards the trees from which emerges the Pioneer Spirit. Deerfield, Greenfield, Conway, Shelburne, and Gill enter followed by Agriculture, Industry, and War." In a melancholy moment the Indians "turn and look sadly back over their beloved valley then kneel to kiss the ground and rising continue their slow march until they pass from sight." This narrative played into the popular stereotype of the vanishing red man who quits the stage and defers obediently to a "superior" white civilization. The scene ends in sanctimonious triumph: "Deerfield led by the Pioneer Spirit comes over the hill and takes her place upon the Great Rock," displacing the Natives. So where Indians had stood in the opening scene now stood the white settler, master over land that he now claimed.

A reenactment of Bloody Brook followed, but this time, the murders did not take place on stage: "As the last cart disappears behind the trees the sound of firing is heard combined with the yells of the Indians."

The raid of February 29, 1704, was glossed over. The attack was not portrayed in the pageant. Only a short scene of captives being led away by the Indians and the French was performed on the green. This scene shifted to a "council fire" long after the raid, attended by Governor Belcher and meant to mark peace after the long period of Indian wars. Four different "tribes" marched before the governor: "Each tribe as it arrives passes before him with bowed head," symbolizing their submission. "Joseph Kellogg, who had survived the 1704 raid, then gave a remarkably conciliatory welcome to the assembled tribes."

> Good friends and brethren, this (holding up a string of wampum) is to wipe away all tears from your eyes. (Then holding out another.) This is to open your throats that you may speak with freedom. (Then a third.) This is to comfort you under all your difficulties.

What sort of historical séance was this? A survivor of the Deerfield raid offering comfort for the *Natives'* hardships? Offering sympathy and to wipe away the tears of those who had *perpetrated* the "massacre" of colonists who were now enshrined in the marble tablets at Memorial Hall? Adding to this new version of history was the appearance of Stephen Williams, the reverend's son, inviting the assembled tribes to a service in the meetinghouse, preaching Isaiah 2:4 about "beating swords into plowshares," and declaring: "nation shall not lift up sword against nation, neither shall they learn war any more." For the fiction of the pageant, the "Indian Wars" of New England, and all of North America, were long over, having been concluded peacefully and honorably—on both sides. Or so the pageant claimed.

What stands out about the 1916 pageant is how, over two centuries, Deerfield had transformed and mythologized its tragic history into an entertainment event. Its colonial past was celebrated as a tourist attraction—as long as the bloody and violent bits were left out. They were inconvenient in a narrative that now eulogized the defeated Natives. The very descendants of the victims of Bloody Brook and 1704 not only watched from the audience but participated as characters—both white and Native—in mythological pageantry. Deerfield recreated and rewrote its history as a ritual that people paid money to see. It was the continued celebration and recreation of a defeat—or was it? Deerfield had prevailed in the end. Perhaps the pageants were an act of claiming the event as its own. Reenactment was thus an act of appropriation.

The 1916 pageant turned out to be the last. Margaret Eager died in January 1918; she did not live to see her nephew Samuel return from fighting in the Great War. Had she been planning a fourth pageant for the next summer? The summer of 1919 would have coincided with the three-year cycle. The 1916 pageant had been a financial success: One thousand dollars had gone to fix the town's water supply. But perhaps there had just been too much pageantry. Helen Gerrett, a longtime Deerfield resident who witnessed these pageants as a child, declared: "Three pageants was one too many." The year 1919 was tumultuous. The United States had been bloodied in the Great World War in 1917 and 1918, and by the postwar influenza pandemic.

As My Mother Tells It

In 1922, a chance encounter led to the return of another Williams descendant to Deerfield. A young nurse worked to care for the famous painter Abbott Handerson Thayer, in Dublin, New Hampshire. Her name was Elizabeth Sadoques, and she was one of the first American Indian registered nurses in America. Thayer's assistant, who had been born in Deerfield, wrote excitedly to her mother, who still lived there: "The nurse we have is a pureblood Indian and has [an] ancestor named Eunice Williams who was taken capture [*sic*] from Deerfield." She continued that Sadoques was "very interesting"—"she is a charmer from the word go and very refined."

In the 1880s, the Sadoques family had left Odanak, the site of the St. Francis mission in Quebec. Israel and Mary Sadoques resettled in Keene, New Hampshire, where Israel made handwoven baskets and operated a tannery. They had eight children, six of whom were daughters: Mary, Ida, Margaret, Agnes, Maude, and the youngest, Elizabeth. While other daughters became bookkeepers or managers of millinery stores in Keene, the youngest Sadoques set out to New York, where she trained as a nurse and graduated in 1919.

Upon receiving the letter from her daughter, Mary Williams Field

Fuller realized that she and the young nurse were actually cousins. Their common ancestor was Robert Williams of Roxbury, the Reverend John Williams's grandfather. Excited and intrigued, she begged Sadoques to come to Deerfield from her home in New Hampshire. By this time, Thayer had died (in May 1921), and so she was available for a visit. On February 28, 1922 (the night before the anniversary of the 1704 attack), Elizabeth Sadoques gave a speech at the annual meeting of the Pocumtuck Valley Memorial Association in Deerfield's Town Hall. She titled her talk "History and Traditions of Eunice Williams and Her Descendants." Her narrative must have kept the Deerfield audience spellbound.

"I will tell a tradition that has existed in my family for two centuries," she began. "I will tell it exactly as my mother tells it and which was told [to] her by her mother." Sadoques began at the time of the first settlers, when "strange men" (the white colonists) appeared. She turned to what her audience wanted to hear, a tale preserved by a Native tradition of oral history and storytelling:

> Many years ago, when there existed a great number of wars between the French and English, a number of captives were brought to Canada from the land of the . . . English settlers. Counted among them were two small children, a brother and sister, who were brought to the camp-fires of the Abenaki. The boy was given up but the little girl was adopted into the tribe and grew up as an Indian child later marrying an Indian brave.

The two captive children were none other than Stephen Williams, who had returned to New England, and Eunice Williams, who did not.

The family's origins and the desire to find their roots had been as important in 1837 as it was now. The Eunice who visited in 1837 (the granddaughter of Reverend Williams's daughter) was actually Sadoques's great-great-great-grandmother. As Sadoques related to the Deerfield audience, Eunice Williams was remembered "perfectly" by her granddaughter, who had been intrigued about her grandmother's visits to New England before she died. These visits had spurred her own in 1837.

But one thing confused Elizabeth Sadoques in 1922. Although Deerfield was very interested in her story about Eunice, there was little enthusiasm for the Indian part of it. George Sheldon had all but ignored the 1837 visit, and it merited no more than the briefest of mentions in his history of Deerfield. The scrupulous Sheldon even got the date wrong—perhaps an indication of just how little he thought it mattered. Or perhaps he believed that the visit was a mythmaking expedition, in line with the *Hampshire Gazette*'s claim that the Abenaki visitors were not really descended from Eunice Williams.

The Sadoques visit was a breakthrough. It was the first time that the PVMA had invited an Indian to address its membership. This could have been a turning point that led to a deeper participation of several Indian tribes in the narrative that George Sheldon and the PVMA had heretofore controlled, one that recognized that Indian voices had much to contribute to the story. It could have helped dispel the myth of the "vanishing race" that had been erased from history. Contrary to George Sheldon's controlling narrative, the Indians had never gone away. They were still here. It would be a long time before Deerfield was ready to recognize that.

The Elm and the Phoenix

Perhaps the old cliché "absence makes the heart grow fonder" was never so true as it was in Deerfield. The loss of the Old Indian House had been felt keenly for generations. The town seal even depicted it. In 1930, the Old Indian House rose phoenixlike once more. The firm of William Gass and Sons ("Specialists in Rustic Transformations") built a life-size replica from scratch. Gass had been a student of Deerfield Academy and then joined the family construction business. He had a knack not only for restoring old colonial houses, but for understanding them—their dimensions, their features, their quirks and characteristics. He was the perfect person to remake history.

The house had been the subject of many artistic images, but only two photographs of the original structure existed. One was a daguerreotype taken by Greenfield resident Benjamin Popkins. Popkins was not the best photographer, for he chose an angle that allowed a large elm tree to obscure a clear view of the house. Popkins later sold the single, unique image to Judge Francis M. Thompson, who donated it to the PVMA in 1898. The other image was also a daguerreotype, taken by William North, who produced a much clearer and better result. The *Greenfield Gazette and Courier* reported on May 11, 1842, that "Mr. North, the Daguerreotype artist, has taken a most perfect likeness of the Old Indian House in Deerfield. Even the prints of the axe can be seen upon the door." North's image was copied by J. L. Lovell, who printed and sold cabinet cards (photographic prints measuring about five by seven inches and affixed to a sturdy cardboard mount) with the house's history printed on the card.

Because another building—the white frame house built by the Hoyts in 1848—still occupied the original site, the replica of the Old Indian House could not be built on its original historic location, near the back of the Brick Church. But a suitable lot farther north up The Street was vacant, so Gass chose that. But he did not construct a replica of the Old Indian Door. The massive elm tree, a "witness tree to the massacre" that had stood in front of the original Old Indian House, had been cut down. Most of its lumber was sawn into planks for a nearby barn. Gass salvaged enough of it to craft his front door.

The house was completed and officially opened in 1930, in time for the Massachusetts tercentenary. Gass issued a commemorative booklet, including the following poem:

As the well-loved forms of respected men
By the skill of the sculptor live again,
So, in this replica, phoenixwise,
The Indian House is before our eyes.
The tree whose shadows have danced before
The original lives in the new "old door."
The crane in the fireplace seems to say,
"See how folks lived in that far-gone day

When mothers spun or sat to sew
And the babies played in the fire's red glow,
When life was vivid and men were men."
In this house the old times breathe again,
The joys they loved and their wild fears, too.
In this reproduction live anew.

George Sheldon's wife Jennie praised Gass's "conscientious" work as "a remarkably accurate reproduction." But the replica of the Old Indian House was as much about its accumulated myths as it was about reconstructing history. But perhaps that did not matter. The building became the center of a thriving arts and crafts scene. Mrs. Gertrude Ashley— secretary of the Pocumtuck basket-makers—was the first guardian.

Gass visited President Calvin Coolidge at his personal office in Northampton in 1928, told him about his New Indian House project, and asked Coolidge if he would provide a horseshoe from his farm to replace the original, preserved in the PVMA Memorial Hall, that had hung above the front door in 1704. This was not a generic symbol for good luck. According to folklore, witches could not pass under iron. Coolidge showed up unannounced, did not tour the house, presented the horseshoe without fanfare, left immediately, got into his car, and drove away. It hangs there today and, as best as can be told, no witch has passed under it since.

In August 1930, Deerfield hosted an "Open Homes Week." From 2 to 5:00 p.m. on every day from August 4 to 9, visitors were invited to visit and inspect thirty-one different historic houses in the town. The program was "in honor of the Massachusetts Bay Tercentenary 1630 to 1930," and was but one part of a much larger celebration throughout the state. The newest house in town, "Indian House Reproduction," was listed in the fold-over brochure as being "open daily." The house was the heart of Deerfield's thriving industries trade, and special products such as rugs, netting, basketry, ironwork, and photography were noted in the promotional brochure. "Visitors who are descendants of Deerfield are requested to register at the booth on the

Common," said the program. So the spirit of the Old Indian House, reincarnated in Gass's facsimile, served the local economy while simultaneously reminding every visitor to Deerfield of the raid of 1704.

The renewed interest in Deerfield and its history inspired another generation of authors. Grace Zaring Stone was one of them. Her stories originated from places she visited, such as the West Indies (1929's *The Heaven and Earth of Doña Elena*) and China (1930's *The Bitter Tea of General Yen*). She moved to Stonington, Connecticut, and lived about one hundred miles from Deerfield. In 1934, she published *The Cold Journey*, a fictional account of the raid on Deerfield (called Redfield in her book). It met with exceptional praise: *Kirkus Reviews* complimented Stone for expanding the narrative to the captives' experiences in Quebec, which was "rarely touched upon in the annals of our history." The novel received rave reviews:

> Her Americans, with their fanatical piety and simple beliefs
> are creatures of flesh and blood, and stand out against the
> background of Indian shadows and French subtleties. To make
> realism romantic without a touch of sentimentality is a difficult
> task. Miss Stone has given us a vigorous novel, which will
> enhance her reputation.

Early editions featured blasé landscape artwork in soothing blue and snow tones on the dust jacket, but later editions ratcheted up the excitement with a lurid pulp fiction–style cover and sensational taglines: "The Red Man owned her completely. . . he wanted her ALIVE!" The cover depicted captives on the march under the watch of a snowshoe-clad Native cradling a musket. It is obvious that the lead captive, dressed in a long black coat with big silver pewter buttons and wearing a vest, white collar, and broad-brimmed black hat, represents John Williams.

In 1934, the Improved Order of Red Men, one of the nation's oldest white fraternal orders, threw a party at Red Men's Hall, their headquarters in South Deerfield, the former Bloody Brook. The admission ticket depicted in profile an Indian chief wearing a feathered headdress, armed with a bow and tomahawk, but no real Indians attended the party. If anyone noticed the irony of all this, it was not recorded.

Appropriation of Indian iconography became commonplace in American pop culture through place-names, movies, television programs, comics, summer camps, professional sports, commercial products, theme restaurants, tourism, souvenirs, advertising art, children's toys, and more. A few were based directly on the Deerfield story, others inspired by familiar themes. In a historical anachronism, a bizarre souvenir postal cover from 1938 celebrated National Air-Mail Week by commemorating the Bloody Brook Massacre. The cover pictured Indians on horseback armed with long lances tipped with pennants, mounting a cavalry charge against colonists on the other side of a stream. It was a fantasy scene out of the Wild West.

Indian captivity remained a popular theme. Walter Edmonds wrote *Drums Along the Mohawk,* which inspired the 1939 motion picture starring Henry Fonda and was set in the American Revolution, more than seventy years after the Deerfield raid. Edmonds followed up with a captivity novel, *In the Hands of the Senecas,* which was reprinted in 1949 as a pulp fiction paperback under the title *The Captive Woman.* The cover depicts a blond white woman wearing a low-cut blouse with shredded short sleeves and bound at the wrists. Behind her two bare-chested Indians debate her fate. "Would they be tortured—sold—or forced to marry?" asks the lurid cover copy. Indian captivity literature enjoyed a long life, from Mary Rowlandson and John Williams to the 1956 film *The Searchers,* directed by John Ford and starring John Wayne.

9

NEW INTERPRETATIONS AND A "MASSACRE" REIMAGINED

|||||||||||||||

The year 1936 might have been the most significant one in Deerfield's history since the massacre of 1704. It began, as many great obsessions do, with an unremarkable incident. Henry and Helen Flynt deposited their young son safely for enrollment at the prestigious Deerfield Academy. Henry was a lawyer and Helen an heiress to an Ohio steel manufacturing fortune. For the next four years, they visited Deerfield frequently and grew close to the academy's legendary headmaster, Frank Boyden. Henry Flynt had been born in Monson, Massachusetts, about forty miles south of Deerfield, and had come to Deerfield as a young boy, he recalled, "looking for Indian artifacts." Boyden and the Flynts cherished the small-town ideal that Deerfield so perfectly encapsulated with its mile-long Street lined with examples of early American architecture. Many of the houses dated to the 1700s, and looked it, needing tender care and preservation. Henry and Helen shared a belief in American greatness, patriotism, and exceptionalism that the headmaster instilled in all his pupils. What, they began to wonder, could they do to help preserve these values and the founding principles of America? It would be a Colonial Revival on a grand scale.

By 1939, the Flynts had taken their first tentative steps. Inspired by Colonial Williamsburg and Henry Francis du Pont's Winterthur, they considered preserving Deerfield's historic homes, and perhaps constructing replicas of others. Correspondence passed between the Flynts and Williamsburg as to how best to preserve the town, but World War II put a temporary stop to the plans. After the war, the Flynts and Williamsburg parted ways, possibly over the fact that the Flynt wealth was in no way comparable to the Rockefeller money that was funding Williamsburg. In fact, by 1969, when Deerfield boasted about twenty thousand visitors a year, its rival in Virginia drew fourteen thousand people in a *day*. In 1942, the Flynts purchased their first historic house in Deerfield (the Manning house), followed two years later by the so-called "pink house," named for its old, rose-colored paint. A year later, the Flynts made three major purchases: the Deerfield Inn, the Ashley house, and the Allen house—all major coups. Frank Boyden, convinced that the Flynts' growing interest was good for the local economy, the academy, and Deerfield, acted as their principal advisor and egged on their passion.

Buying the Allen house was necessary for a pressing reason beyond the need for historic preservation: apparently "there was a possibility that a Greenfield liquor dealer would buy it," the Flynts wrote to Boyden, and "you felt the purchaser might not be a good influence for the Academy and its boys and we agreed." Historic preservation was just one motivation for the Flynts in general: Some of these houses, once repaired and refurbished, were used by the academy as classrooms, faculty housing, or student dormitories. This was a boon to both the Flynts and Boyden: The academy got more facilities and the town got spruced up. Henry and Helen turned to a special person to assist them: Elizabeth Fuller—the woman who had excitedly written to her mother in 1921 about Elizabeth Sadoques and her Deerfield connection. Fuller served as director of research and development for the large-scale project, while William Gass, who had rebuilt the Old Indian House, worked as the chief contractor.

As the Flynts refined their master plan for Deerfield, they ruled out competing with the grand, massive scale of the Rockefellers' Williamsburg. That would have overwhelmed the landscape of the small town, and anyway, they could never have afforded the expense. Yes, the Flynts possessed significant wealth, but they could not match the resources of the Rockefellers or the Du Ponts. Henry and Helen decided to furnish and decorate their historic houses and build an important collection of early American furniture, pewter, silver, ceramics, paintings, prints, textiles, and other decorative arts they acquired from private dealers and auction houses.

By the 1950s, world affairs had overshadowed Deerfield just as they had centuries earlier, in the late 1600s and early 1700s. The post–World War II Cold War and Soviet domination of Eastern Europe made preserving Deerfield all the more important to Henry and Helen Flynt. They believed that the Soviet Union and Communism posed an existential threat to the United States. To the Flynts, Deerfield represented "the spirit of free enterprise, the spirit of New England, the spirit which needs to go out into the nation now." More than ever, they were convinced that America needed to harken back to its frontier ideals in order to succeed in this new conflict. Deerfield provided just one—although perhaps the best—example of how to survive, and even triumph. "Is it not possible to sum up the strength of this Republic, its vigor and idealism and enterprise, in a single American community?" Henry asked.

In his patriotic enthusiasm, Flynt sponsored research into Deerfield's Revolutionary War liberty pole, its history and exact location. When that was determined, he funded a replacement pole and a replica of the patriot Taunton flag that spelled out the word LIBERTY. As he wrote, "If the aspirations, ideals and struggles of the American people could be summed up in one word, that word is emblazoned on the Taunton flag." It was a symbol of resistance: not only by the colonists to the global politics of British tyranny in their times, but by Americans to the Soviet oppression and totalitarianism of the postwar era.

The Flynts turned their attention to another symbol of freedom and the values of the founding generation—the Pocumtuck Valley Memorial Association. Horrified to learn that the PVMA's Memorial Hall had been unheated since 1799 (limiting tourism and endangering the collection of artifacts, books, documents, and more), Henry immediately started a new campaign to combat this travesty:

> Memorial Hall had never had heat. This makes the treasures
> inaccessible to students or visitors for most of the year and has

had a bad effect on many of the items located there. One of the
first things in spreading the gospel of courage and the spirit of
enterprise and of use in overcoming the rampant Communistic
or Socialistic ideas is to hold forth this shield or banner of
Deerfield courage throughout the year.

In 1952, Henry Flynt co-authored a book titled *Frontier of Freedom*
(eventually the title would be updated to the more neutral *Historic Deerfield:
Houses and Interiors*). The original title implied—in its use of the singular,
rather than the plural—that there was now only one frontier against the
Soviet Union—the United States of America, and maybe Deerfield itself.
The book placed Deerfield and its values as the singular locus and the only
frontier that mattered. Flynt even spoke to one remaining piece of living
history from the 1704 raid: the giant sycamore tree in the common. This
now-gargantuan tree "was already a well-established inhabitant when the
first settlers from Dedham arrived on the site of this 'Frontier of Freedom.'"
It was this freedom and liberty to create new lives without oppression that
made America so special and so powerful. As Flynt continued, "The free
individual is our answer to Marxism, to the siren song of collectivism, to the
stifled churches and carefully concealed People's Paradises behind the Iron
Curtain." If Flynt considered that the English appropriation of Native lands
was in some ways similar to Soviet methods, he did not mention it.

In 1952, the Flynts established a foundation to support their dual mission to combine historic preservation and patriotism.

The Flynts were once described as the "fairy godparents" who adopted Deerfield. Indeed, without their patronage, Historic Deerfield
would not exist today. Always granting wishes, they hired William Gass
to make those wishes come true. His job was to take decrepit homes
and turn them into colonial treasure boxes. But Gass was not a trained
preservationist. He was self-taught, and often relied more on gut feeling
for what *felt* right than what actually *was* right. In restoring the Dwight
house, for example, Gass added a nineteenth-century slate roof rather
than a period roof from the previous century simply because he thought
the slate looked nicer and would last longer. Such decisions would dismay

preservationists today. The massive kitchen that Gass installed in the Dwight house was another piece of historical revisionism, and based on the Dwight Stowell house in New Salem. There was a massive oak lintel, complete with lug pole and trammel bar, accessorized with bake ovens, kettles, and a smoke oven, as well as various utensils of different metals (copper, brass, tin, and iron) and ceramic pottery pieces. Massive brick chimneys cluttered with kitchenware *looked* authentic, but they were a far cry from earlier wood-paneled versions. Our vision of what an authentic colonial kitchen should look like often stems from these carefully created, but inaccurate, stereotypes: "the huge kitchen fireplace, with its pewter-laden mantel, the old flintlock hung above, strings of peppers and onions overhead and the family of our forebears gathered about it in the ruddy glow of hickory and birch," wrote Walter Dyer in *The Lure of the Antique* some forty years earlier, in 1910. Colonial kitchens would have been cramped and multifunctional workspaces, with far fewer cooking implements and serving-ware, and likely as not a bed tucked to the side to benefit from the fire's warmth. These inaccurate reconstructions were a vital part of Deerfield's own self-fashioning and mythmaking. Later, as the Flynts matured in sophistication, they transcended Gass's vision and insisted on absolute historical accuracy that satisfied scrupulous and modern museum standards.

But simple reconstruction was not enough—Henry and Helen Flynt wanted total immersion. Beyond the brick fireplaces, Deerfield's historic houses were illuminated with purposely dim interiors—historic mood lighting. Not just to see the past, but to inhabit it. As Henry Flynt wrote,

> It is not long before you become imbued with a perfectly
> human desire to see how these people lived in the early days.
> You want to sit in their chairs, sleep in their beds, cover your
> sofas with 18th century materials, and, one must then have a
> *bourette* or damask or equally fine hangings at the windows.

Modern furnishings would not do. They could never compare with the originals. Thus the Flynts went on a buying spree for antiques that lasted the rest of their lives. They prioritized the purchase of heirlooms linked to Deerfield, especially those which could be linked to individual families and houses. "We have been able to locate and have purchased and placed in the Allen House quite a number of pieces of furniture that have been there at various times," Flynt wrote in triumph in 1946. The Flynts had excellent taste and pursued the best pieces connected to Deerfield or the Connecticut River Valley.

This is not to say that the Flynts were universally accepted in Deerfield. The descendants of some of the original families turned up their noses at these outsiders with their presumptuous plans. By 1952, this divide had become unpleasantly obvious, when Henry Flynt wrote to Frank Boyden that he and his wife felt "we were not wanted in Deerfield anymore." If they couldn't work with Deerfield Academy and other locals to promote their overwhelming passion for the town's preservation, then they would have to strike out on their own, which is exactly what they did. After consulting their children, whose patrimony stood to be decreased by this venture, the Flynts created the Heritage Foundation (not to be confused with the Washington, D.C., think tank), which was renamed Historic Deerfield in 1971.

The name spoke to the Flynts' hope: a focus on a shared colonial "heritage" that was the key to triumphing in this new battle for world domination. The lessons of the American frontier would serve as a bulwark against contamination from the outside world, just as the earlier Colonial Revival movement had done. The enemy was no longer here, skulking in the woods, waiting with tomahawk and knife in hand to kill and then scalp the unsuspecting farmer. Now a different enemy threatened American values, traditions, and way of life. The danger now was an ideological invasion of alien ideas, backed by nuclear weapons. It was still a foreign enemy, and it could still be defeated. But this was more than an effort for restoration, it was a reconstruction; it was active mythmaking. As *Antiques* magazine stated in September 1956, the Flynts had "re-created" Deerfield.

This project was not always about historical accuracy, as much as what the past was supposed to be. "Though the visitor has the impression of being transported to the eighteenth century," *Antiques* stated, "the village has none of the new rawness it must have had then." Rather, the prestigious publication concluded, "it has mellowed and ripened," as if the town were some exotic flower in bloom. As one woman said, "Deerfield looks like a lovely place to be homesick for." It was myth—not the reality—that attracted people.

The late 1940s and early 1950s were the dawn of a new era in America. At a time when new technologies like the atomic bomb caused panic, it was calming to retreat into the historic past. Deerfield was not alone in embracing early American history, or wanting to preserve—or even enhance—it. The National Trust for Historic Preservation was created through an act of Congress, signed into law by President Harry Truman in 1949. Soon other museums devoted to early America began opening throughout New England: Old Sturbridge Village opened in 1946, followed by Plimouth Plantation and Vermont's Shelbourne Museum in 1947. According to Alice Winchester, editor of *Antiques*, these institutions "did influence each other in what they bought and how they used their collections. They had fun *and* felt they were contributing something useful to society." In 1962, Deerfield was granted a high accolade: It was declared a National Historic Landmark. But all of these things coincided with social and political changes in America, and in the world. Deerfield was holding on to the past in the face of a very uncertain future. It was "a precious island in the flow of time."

It was no surprise when *National Geographic* finally published in July 1969 a coveted cover story that "made" the town, written by one of its star contributors, Bart McDowell, titled "Deerfield Keeps a Truce with Time." McDowell produced a seminal article that annointed Deerfield as a quintessential American historic village. Indeed, this became the single most influential article ever published about Deerfield. The piece made Rev. John Williams the hero of the story and the "Deerfield Massacre" famous. McDowell's vivid prose transported readers to the terrifying night of February 29, 1704, through the eyes of the English colonists. It was not meant to be an exhaustive, nuanced, in-depth study of the raid. This early but sophisticated travel journalism shifted effortlessly between Deerfield's storied past and its vital present. McDowell wove headmaster Frank Boyden, local farmer Frank Yazwinski, Deerfield Academy, the Bement School, students, and local children into his character-driven narrative. He celebrated what Henry and Helen Flynt had done for Deerfield, and he ratified for several million readers the significance of their achievement.

In addition to preserving historic houses and collecting fine antiques, the Flynts were keen to maintain the overall aesthetic appearance of The Street. They had street-level telephone poles, phone lines, and electrical power lines removed and those utilities buried underground to preserve the pristine colonial appearance of The Street. They objected to any commercial development in town such as shops, gas stations, or restaurants (aside from their own Deerfield Inn). But their sensibilities could not control commercial development just outside of town along Routes 5 and 10, which ran parallel to The Street.

Two mid-twentieth-century roadside-themed restaurants capitalized on their proximity to Deerfield. The Stockade, on Routes 5 and 10 in South Deerfield, with its long, two-story, fort-like, big brown wood building and massive stone chimney, evoked the Old Indian House on steroids. Not to be confused with the more modest "Ye Stockade Shop and Tea Room," which operated in Old Deerfield around 1910, this Stockade traded on the Deerfield Massacre. The caption on the back of a souvenir photo postcard blended fact and fiction and read: "Purchased from the Pocumtuck Indians. For 50 years the French and the Abenaqui Indians from Canada attacked Deerfield. In 1704, during a severe raid, 110 settlers were taken captive to Canada. Within the stockade houses were burned and 50 settlers massacred."

The Gables Food Shop, opened in 1946 and reopened in a new, expanded location on Routes 5 and 10 in 1955, relished "massacre kitsch." The oversize menu featured long, overwrought, dramatic accounts of the Bloody Brook and Deerfield Massacres, including historical quotations and even poetry. A foldover panel pictured woodcuts of a hatchet-wielding Indian attacking a settler defending an ox cart, and another of a colonist and an Indian grappling in a death struggle. A souvenir postcard boasted that the Gables was a "mirror of colonial America" and promised customers "leisurely dining" while entertaining them with tales of early American bloodbaths.

If these restaurants, long shuttered, were still in business today, they might carry in their gift shops one of the most fetching Deerfield Massacre souvenirs ever made—a John Williams action figure. Created in 1995 as part of the "American Heroes: True Stories of Strength and Courage" series, the Williams figure, armed with a flintlock pistol and musket, is packaged in a blister pack with another figure, a Mohawk Indian raising a tomahawk and gripping a scalping knife. Williams stands ready to fire his pistol at the Indian's chest, and the Mohawk is poised to strike Williams with his tomahawk. "MOHAWK CAPTURES JOHN WILLIAMS" screams a blood-red sticker on the box, and between the figures sits a booklet titled "Deerfield Massacre." What John Williams would have said about his effigy, we can only guess.

The Return of the Native

February 2004 marked the three hundredth anniversary of the Deerfield Massacre. The tercentenary was marked with special exhibitions and events, which portrayed the raid from both sides of history and emphasized its diverse and multicultural background. For too long the narrative had been one-sided, based largely on John Williams's *The Redeemed Captive* and George Sheldon's *History*. The voices of Native Americans had gone unheard, because for a long time no one wanted to hear what they had to say and also because they created no written records of their own about the attack. Theirs was a rich oral tradition, with stories passed down from generation to generation. Over time, stories can change, be altered, forgotten, or even lost— this is memory and mythmaking at its strongest, and its weakest. It is often said that the winners write the history, and the "winners" of this storytelling contest were the white colonists. They and their descendants controlled the narrative through letters, books, memorials, and mythmaking. Yes, the English might have lost the battle in February 1704, but they won the long war of historical memory.

Those myths and legends became ones of courage, perseverance, inspiration, and, ultimately, the triumph of a superior civilization.

The vocabulary used to describe the past is telling. To the white colonists who lived through the raid, Deerfield had not experienced a massacre. They called it an "attack," an "assault," a "raid," a "sack," or a "destruction." One early account described it as "mischief." The survivors, despite all they had suffered, never spoke of the "Deerfield Massacre." That word, "massacre," does not appear once in John Williams's *Redeemed Captive*. It was not until the one hundredth anniversary, in 1804, that Rev. John Taylor called the raid a "massacre," in his centenary sermon. In that text, the word "massacre" appears no fewer than five times. Examples include "those who fell in the general massacre" and "in this hour of darkness, and massacre." The term entered popular use in the nineteenth century, especially after the "massacre" of George Armstrong Custer and his 7th Cavalry at the Little Bighorn on, of all days, July 4, 1876, the centennial of the founding of the United States. (In a historical curiosity, a soldier from Deerfield served on the burial party sent to the battle site, where he collected several arrows that he pulled from the bodies of the dead.) The massacre-centric cenotaphs installed in Memorial Hall, the cult of the Indian door, and the replica of the Old Indian House, where the proprietors sold "Deerfield Massacre" tickets, legitimized the word and erased Indians as "savages" and a "vanished race." By the time of the bicentennial in 1904, influential historians such as George Sheldon and Emma Coleman all referred to the events of February 29, 1704, as the Deerfield "Massacre."

Thus, three centuries later, an event that might have been no more than a dusty footnote in history was publicly commemorated and debated. A five-part radio program entitled *Captive Lands, Captive Hearts* aired in February 2004, followed by commemorative events in Deerfield on February 28 and 29 featuring reenactors, fireplace cooking lessons, and candle-making, with more activities held at the Old Indian House, all attended by a crowd of three thousand visitors. A few hundred reenactors converged on Deerfield to recreate scenes from the raid and the Meadows Fight. These activities combined antiquarian enthusiasm, as in the Colonial Revival, with scrupulous scholarly reinterpretation. Later, that April, a peace tree from the Kanienkehaka (Mohawk) homelands in Quebec was planted on Arbor Day. Scholarly conferences offered academic histories, and Deerfield even hosted the world premiere of an opera written for the occasion, *The Captivation of Eunice Williams*. Donald Friary, emeritus executive director of Historic Deerfield, led an eight-day journey that followed the route that the captives took on their forced march to Canada. The previous year, photographer Allison Williams Bell had followed the route on a snowy winter day and produced for the three hundredth anniversary a photo essay documenting the geographic locations mentioned by John and Stephen Williams, and how they look today.

The Native point of view was now highlighted. No longer were Native descendants sidelined as exotic curiosities. Instead, they were valued as partners in telling the story, with valuable contributions to make. An archaeological dig was funded by UMass Amherst to examine the remains of a seventeenth-century fortification built by the Pocumtucks. In 2003, two of Elizabeth Sadoques's relatives visited, to add their stories to that of their relatives from 1922. Claudia Chicklas, a daughter, and Lynn Murphy, a granddaughter, added their own observations to a new exhibit at the PVMA. Titled "Remembering 1704: Context and Commemoration of the Deerfield Raid," it opened in February 2004 and ran for more than a year, until May 2005. It was the first collaborative effort of the PVMA and Historic Deerfield and included thirteen prestigious advisors from diverse backgrounds.

The goal of the exhibition was twofold and tied into different ideas about history, memory, and myth. The first goal was to "help visitors better understand the context of the raid in its time," and to see the motives of all sides involved. The second goal was to "trace the ways in which the raid has been commemorated since," thus revealing myth-making that had unfolded over centuries. How the past shapes the present is not an objective and neutral process; rather, it is a contentious and subjective progression influenced by pressures of the time.

As expected, the museum exhibition at Historic Deerfield's giant, open-storage museum and conference center, the Flynt Center of Early New England Life, featured rare and precious items. John Williams's Geneva

Bible was displayed—Puritans favored Calvin's text to what they considered the less rigorous King James version. Ensign Sheldon's snowshoes on which he marched to Canada to seek the captives' release were featured, as was a delicate two-handled silver cup owned by Hannah Beaman, the brave schoolteacher who managed to save her pupils from an ambush. Inscribed in script "H * Beaman" on its base, it was likely a posthumous gift to the Deerfield community to keep her memory alive. As Beaman had no children, the cup would have been used in church ceremonies for the community. Also on display was a tiny scrap of linen fabric, possibly from a man's shirt. Its ocher color was reputedly a bloodstain from one of the victims of the 1704 raid. Philip Zea, president of Historic Deerfield, called it "Deerfield's shroud of Turin." And, of course, the Old Indian Door starred in the commemoration.

But these were all artifacts associated with colonists. What about Native objects? In 2004, the gifts given by Eunice and her husband Arosen were correctly identified for the first time. The significance of these objects had been lost; they had simply been labeled "Indian objects, 18th century" at the PVMA. Now the four pieces—the sash, tobacco pouch, bullet pouch, and gorget—were labeled correctly and their family connections made clear. To many, including Rosemarie Belisle, Societé d'Histoire d'Oka (Oka Historical Society in Quebec), displaying and orally authenticating them were an important part of history, not myth. As she noted, "The capacity to understand [Arosen's gifts] as tokens of friendship shows how he has come a long way from being simply 'the Indian who married Mr. Williams's sister.'" Lynn Murphy, the granddaughter of Elizabeth Sadoques, fashioned a basket to match the one that her Native ancestor Sophie Watso had made and presented to Catherine Williams in 1837. Today it rests beside its elder sister in the PVMA collections.

Still, not everyone was happy with the anniversary programs. Of the 196 visitor responses, 157 were positive, 11 neutral, and 8 negative. While the overwhelming majority appreciated balanced storytelling, one visitor wrote: "Enough with the political correctness." Many linked the display to recent events, comparing the 1704 raid to the 9/11 attacks, which had occurred just a few years earlier. A review in an academic journal complained:

"Although Remembering 1704 does listen to the voices of those groups who have traditionally been ignored when telling the story of 1704, the exhibition swings a bit too heavily toward the Native perspective on the raid." Given, however, that Indian viewpoints had been obscured to the point of exclusion for three hundred years, it was hard to see how they could have been overemphasized now for audiences keen to learn more.

The PVMA also revisited the message of Memorial Hall. In an exhibition entitled "Covering Up History: Rethinking Memorials" they concealed with fabric screens and de-colonized several of the marble tablets memorializing the dead of 1704. The old, cenotaphic stones embedded in the walls contained stereotypical nineteenth-century antipathy to the Indians. By the twentieth century, it was time to change that. For example, the tablet honoring Frank and Parthena (misspelled as Pathena on the original) had referred to them as the "negro servants of the Rev. John Williams," to conceal the embarrassing fact that Williams was a slave owner. Now a fabric screen rightly listed them as "African slaves," their true and involuntary status. The text of the main tablet was also revised and reprinted on a fabric screen. The original had been inscribed as follows:

ERECTED A.D. MDCCCLXXXII, / BY THE / POCUMTUCK VALLEY MEMORIAL ASSOCIATION: / IN HONOR OF THE PIONEERS / OF THIS VALLEY, BY WHOSE COURAGE / AND ENERGY, FAITH AND FORTITUDE / THE SAVAGE WAS EXPELLED / AND THE WILDERNESS SUBDUED; / AND TO PERPETUATE THE REMEMBRANCE / OF THE SUFFERINGS AT DEERFIELD, / FEB. 29, 1703-4, / WHEN BEFORE THE BREAK OF DAY, 340 FRENCH AND INDIANS, / UNDER THE SIEUR HERTEL DE ROUVILLE, / SWARMING IN OVER THE PALISADES ON THE DRIFTED SNOW, / SURPRISED AND SACKED THE SLEEPING TOWN, / AND KILLED OR CAPTURED / THE GREATER PART OF ITS INHABITANTS.

Additional tablets had added bloody details:

RECORDED IN LOVE AND REVERENCE BY THEIR
KINDRED; / ARE THE NAMES AND AGES OF THOSE /
WHO LOST THEIR LIVES IN THE ASSAULT, / OR WERE
SLAIN ON THE MEADOWS, / IN THE HEROIC ATTEMPT
TO RESCUE THE CAPTIVES, / OR WHO DIED ON
THE HURRIED RETREAT TO CANADA, / VICTIMS TO
STARVATION OR THE TOMAHAWK.

Below is the new, revised text:

REVISED A.D. MMIV, / BY THE / POCUMTUCK VALLEY
/ MEMORIAL ASSOCIATION: / COMMEMORATING THE
ENGLISH SETTLERS / OF THIS VALLEY, WHO DROVE
/ THE POCUMTUCKS / FROM THEIR HOMELAND / IN
ORDER TO SET UP / AN ENGLISH SETTLEMENT; / AND TO
PERPETUATE THE REMEMBRANCE / OF THE SUFFERINGS
AT DEERFIELD, / FEB. 29, 1704, / WHEN BEFORE THE
BREAK OF DAY, ABOUT 300 FRENCH AND NATIVE
ALLIES, / UNDER THE SIEUR HERTEL DE ROUVILLE, /
SURPRISED AND ATTACKED THE TOWN, / AND KILLED
OR CAPTURED / ABOUT HALF OF ITS INHABITANTS. /

The updated text revised a few facts and figures, reducing the esti-
mated number of attackers from 340 to 300 and recalculating that about
half the town, rather than "the greater part," had been killed or taken
captive. More significantly, no longer were the colonists "pioneers of
the valley" extolled for expelling or exterminating Native Americans
from their land ("the savage was expelled"). Now they were settlers
who "drove the Pocumtucks from their homeland."

Even more egregious, to modern readers, was the Field family tablet.
The original had been carved as follows:

SARAH FIELD, 2. / MARY, HER MOTHER, 28, / WIFE OF
JOHN, / WITH CHILDREN, / MARY, 6, AND JOHN, 3, /

were captured. / Mary, adopted by an Indian, / WAS NAMED
WALAHOWEY. / She married a savage, / and became one.

In contrast, the new cloth screen read:

SARAH FIELD, 2. / MARY, HER MOTHER, 28, / WIFE OF
JOHN, / with children, / MARY, 6, AND JOHN, 3, / were
captured. / Mary, adopted by a / Kanien'kehaka (Mohawk) /
WAS NAMED WALAHOWEY / (WELAHAWI). / She married
a Kanien'kehaka / and adopted the culture, / customs and
language of her / new community in Kahnawake.

The old language "she married a savage, and became one" was now replaced with a nuanced text to explain Mary's new life in a Native community.
In addition, the PVMA added a new tablet to the room to honor the Indians.

But one of the most attended activities occurred later that year, on
July 17, when Native descendants joined with their American counterparts in a welcoming procession. The marchers started just shy of
Pine Hill in the North Meadows, where the raiders of 1704 had camped
and planned their attack. Just after 10 a.m., they marched down Deerfield's Street before a large audience. Five separate groups carried ban-
ners denoting the different communities of the massacre: Wobanakiak
(Abenaki and Pennacook), Kanienkehaka (Mohawk), Wendat (Huron),
English, and French. Real descendants and historical reenactors walked
together. At the very end of the procession were two final groups, the
American Friends Service Committee and Traprock Peace Center, who
carried a final message to onlookers: "Justice and Peace in Our Time."
The procession ended at the Deerfield Common, which would have been
at the center of the palisade fort, and where a commemorative flame was
lit. This fire burned just a few feet from the boulders marking where
the houses of John Williams, Benoni Stebbins, and Ensign John Sheldon
once stood, and had experienced fire of another kind.

Three musical dance troupes from communities who had sent raiders to Deerfield in 1704 gave performances: Thunderhawk Dancers (Mo-

hawks from Kahnawake), Mikwôbait Dancers (Abenakis from Odanak), and Andicha n'de Wendat (Hurons from Wendake). Now, instead of guns and tomahawks, the dancers performed with drums and bright costumes to standing-room-only crowds. Line Descombes, the leader of the group from Wendake, was a descendant of the Wendat chief, Tsohahisen, who had participated in the 1704 raid. Descendants of this Huron family had not visited Deerfield since the raid three hundred years ago. On Sunday, activities began with an interfaith service held at Deerfield's Brick Church Meeting House, where the Reverend John Fessenden had given his sermon during the visit of Eunice Williams's Abenaki descendants in 1837. The focus of the service was the remembrance of all those—Native, French, and English—who had died in the wars of the frontier. The church was aglow with the flickering light of candles. It echoed with shared songs and prayers.

The three hundredth anniversary was not the end of such efforts. Every four years, on leap day, Deerfield continues to commemorate 1704. Every year, the Dublin Seminar, a prestigious, annual weekend-long scholarly symposium dedicated to the history and material culture of New England, publishes a book-length record of its proceedings. In July 2023 the seminar convened in Deerfield. The theme of the conference was "Indigenous Histories in New England: Pastkeepers and Pastkeeping." The symposium featured twenty-six diverse speakers on seven panels including "Confronting Colonization at a Commemorative Moment: Reflections on Plymouth 400"; "Indigenous Histories in New England Museums"; "New Stories for Familiar Histories"; "Relocation, Resistance, & Resilience"; "Archives and Identity"; and "Land and Indigenous Values."

The panels covered the emergence of ethnohistory, bringing in Native perspectives that had been excluded, colonial mythology, the stereotype of the vanishing race, how museums represent Native peoples, ownership of the past, the spiritual dimension of objects, the legitimacy of oral history and inherited stories, and decolonizing Deerfield's Memorial Hall.

Events like this, plus the inclusion of indigenous people in public spaces—as scholars, authors, curators, museum professionals, teachers, and speakers—ensures that in the future, a Native perspective will always inform in the interpretation of Deerfield's history. It is their story too.

EPILOGUE:
THE GHOST OF A TOWN

If you go there today, you will find little evidence of the Deerfield Massacre. Not a single home or structure from 1704 survives. The ghost of Old Deerfield is invisible. Any traces—charred wood corner posts, burned-out cellars, rusted black-iron door locks and hinges, melted lead bullets, even splintered fragments of the palisade fort—lie buried deep down below another Deerfield: the pristine, present-day, beautifully restored Revolutionary War–era storybook town that sits atop the site of the massacre. On the surface, on the front lawn of the town common, huge boulders bearing bronze plaques mark the places where John Williams, John Sheldon, and Benoni Stebbins once lived. Nearby stands the only living witness to what happened that night: a colossal, majestic, three-hundred-and-fifty-year-old sycamore tree of tremendous girth. Up The Street, toward the north end of town, the original point of attack, you will find a faithful, century-old replica of Ensign Sheldon's "Old Indian House."

On Memorial Street, you will see the big, red brick Memorial Hall, headquarters of the Pocumtuck Valley Memorial Association, a century-and-a-half-old museum of colonial New England life. There you will find the principal relic of the Deerfield Massacre, the Old Indian Door, enshrined in a special chamber devoted to its veneration and preservation. If you run your hands along the deep cuts, grooves, and gouges made more than three hundred years ago (which you must not do—centuries of thoughtless caresses have worn down the sharp edges of the cuts) you can imagine the thud of hatchets striking wood. The hole that the Indians chopped through the door still beckons curious eyes. This tomahawk-scarred door is a portal to the Deerfield Massacre.

At a recent commemoration of the raid on a cold February weekend in 2021, visitors watched costumed French and Indian warriors fire flintlock muskets at the English in a reenactment of the Meadows Fight within earshot of the resting place of John and Eunice Williams. The visitors also attended a comprehensive presentation by eight historical interpreters dressed, equipped, and armed as the raiders of 1704: Indian warriors, French Canadian militiamen, and French officers, one representing Jean-Baptiste Hertel de Rouville, the commander of the raid. Standing together on stage, these eight reenactors were formidable by themselves. But imagine them multiplied forty times, to their full strength of more than three hundred on February 29, 1704, and one could see how the people of Deerfield did not stand a chance on the night of the raid. Throughout the day, more armed reenactors strolled up and down The Street, and chatted with tourists inside the replica of the Old Indian House—their quarters for the weekend.

On February 28 a few hardy visitors stayed up past midnight to part the curtain between past and present and retrace the steps. It was February 29 now. They hiked the icy back roads between the town and the river. Moon shadows illuminated the silver and dark frozen puddles that crackled beneath their feet as they followed a road to the North Meadows, where they held a vigil under the inky black starlit sky. They looked up at Orion and the Big Dipper in the heavens, and listened to the mournful sound of coyotes crying in the fields. It was the same sky, but on that night it had glowed bright orange once the town was aflame.

The French and Indians passed through here twice, once before dawn on their way to town to launch the raid, and then after sunrise on their retreat with the captives in tow and ambushing the pursuing colonists. No monument marks the spot. On this night, the horizontal, robot-like steel arms of four huge, hundred-foot-tall industrial electrical towers loomed over the ground of the Meadows Fight.

From here the visitors walked back to The Street and followed the route of the raiders south through town. They stopped at the Deerfield Inn to warm themselves and sit by the hearth in the cozy front parlor, where they stacked more logs on the roaring fire. They peered outside through a frosty windowpane at the empty street outside. From this vantage point, just through this window, they could have seen it all: the entire war party of several hundred French and Indians advancing en masse to breach the palisade. They left the inn and walked south to the town common, until they arrived where they imagined it must have started, the place where the Indians scaled the snowdrift, dropped into the fort, and unlocked the north gate. They turned right on the common and paused to linger where three houses once stood close together—the John Sheldon House, the Asa Stebbins House, and the John Williams House. Tonight the common was deserted.

The visitors moved on to their final destination—the Old Burying Ground. There, from a distance, they saw the grass-carpeted mound topped with a simple, rectangular stone carved with the date "1704" that marks the mass grave of those killed in the attack. Or does it? Recently, ground-penetrating radar revealed that no human remains lie beneath the mound. The bones of the dead of 1704 have vanished.

They searched for the two tall gravestones that they knew stood beside a large tree. These were easy to find in the light of day, but darkness had transformed the black ground into a minefield of hard to see and easy to trip over markers. A flashlight beam pinpointed the spot. They made a pilgrimage to the resting places of John and Eunice Williams. They read the carved inscriptions. They lingered there a long time. Then they reached out and touched the stones.

If you walk down to the river on a night like this and get close to the water, you will hear it before you see it, the sound of the current lapping against its banks. This is the same riverine music that filled the ears of the colonists three hundred years ago, and before that, the Native Pocumtuck people who had occupied these lands for several thousand years. Over the centuries, melting snow and ice, torrential summer rains, and rising floodwaters have reshaped the contours of the riverbanks many times. The geography is ever-changing. Today it is impossible to pinpoint the exact spot where the French and Indians and the Deerfield captives crossed the river on their way north. But the same waters still flow, just as they did on the morning of February 29, 1704, when the captives crossed over to the other side on their perilous journey to a strange and hostile land, not knowing when, if ever, they would return.

ACKNOWLEDGMENTS

||||||||||||||

I thank my editor, Colin Harrison, Vice President and Editor in Chief of Scribner, for nurturing this book through the Covid interregnum that disrupted the publishing industry. Colin is an extraordinary editor with the talent to see a manuscript simultaneously through two points of view—the editor's and the author's. A distinguished author in his own right, Colin understood from the start where I hoped to take the book and helped me stay on that path with invaluable advice and sound judgment calls. One of the most memorable pleasures of working together was a marathon dinner in New York at the Century where we mapped out on a sheet of paper the final architecture of the book. As a fellow collector with a shared passion for material culture, Colin understood the importance of artifacts, documents, artworks, objects, images, and ephemera in the narrative.

Colin's right hand, Assistant Editor Emily Polson, always kept the trains running. In countless ways, she made this a better book, and I thank her for it. Emily valued the extra dimension that art can add to a book, something that is often overlooked.

Thanks to Scribner's Senior Art Director, Jaya Miceli, for designing a beautiful and exciting dust jacket, which was perfect from the start and captured the heart of the book.

I thank Paul Samuelson, Scribner's Deputy Director of Publicity, for performing as many conjuring tricks as the witches of Salem to bring attention to my book.

And my sincere thanks to Senior Production Editor Mark LaFlaur and the entire Scribner production team for molding *The Deerfield Massacre* into the tangible object that you hold in your hands. Without them, there would be no book.

My friend and agent Richard Abate loves American history as much as I do, and over many years and several books he has shared in my obsessions with Abraham Lincoln, the Civil War, African American history, John F. Kennedy, Dr. Martin Luther King, Jr., early America, and more. We've had lots of good times, but never so much fun as we did on set during the filming in Savannah of the Apple TV+ *Manhunt* series. My entertainment lawyer, James Gregorio, has been with me all the way on our book and film projects.

I owe much to my professors at the University of Chicago: John Hope Franklin introduced me to the American South from the 1600s to Reconstruction and to the richness of African American history; Edward M. Cook, Jr., and Willi Paul Adams guided me through colonial America and the Revolution; Arthur Mann, expert on American social movements and my unofficial tour guide, introduced me to the romance of New England; and Mark Kishlansky inspired my passion for a vast, early America when he assigned a junior year colloquium paper on alternative explanations for the Salem witchcraft hysteria.

At Historic Deerfield, President John Davis extended every possible courtesy to help me with the book, providing access to HD's vast collections and offering additional support with generous enthusiasm. Historic Deerfield preserves the most beautiful street in America, and much else, with its unsurpassed historic houses, collections, Flynt Center, scholarship, and other educational programs. Jesse Vanek, Vice President for Development and Communications, was a cheerleader for the project from the start. Penny Leveritt, Visual Resources Manager, supplied every image that I requested. Anne Lanning, Senior Vice President, arranged private visits to every historic house I wanted to see. Librarian Jeanne Solensky made all the resources of the Memorial Libraries available to me in the tradition of her great predecessors David Bosse and David Proper.

Phil Zea, former president of Historic Deerfield, gave me a tour of the overlooked, bloody ground of the Meadows Fight, and then placed in my hands a rare, centuries-old wooden ball-headed war club. One swing of it conveyed in an instant how deadly it was, in a way that viewing it behind its Plexiglas museum display case could never suggest. The war club is now my weapon of choice. Phil was kind enough to invite me to stay in my old fellowship room at the historic Allen House when I visited Deerfield for the most recent 2021 commemoration of the events of 1704.

At the Deerfield Inn, thanks to innkeeper Laurie McDonald for her unsurpassed hospitality. She is an unfailingly welcoming and gracious host.

In the heart of Deerfield, at the Pocumtuck Valley Memorial Association, Executive Director Tim Neumann and Curator Ray Ratigan offered invaluable assistance by answering innumerable queries—often on short notice—and by sharing dozens of images of treasures from the PVMA collections. At the front desk, every visitor receives a cheerful welcome from Assistant Manager Katharine Wilby, a member of Deerfield's historic Hoyt family. Kay is a descendant of David Hoyt, who survived the massacre but died in the subsequent Meadows Fight. Her ancestors bought the Old Indian House in 1744, and later one of them tore it down. Thankfully, PVMA does not hold Kay responsible for this crime. During delightful front porch dinners at the Deerfield Inn and drinks in the Beehive Parlor (named for its vintage, bright yellow wallpaper depicting dozens of beehives) Tim Neumann gave me a priceless education in Deerfield lore. And through exhibits, websites, and public events, he has been a pioneer in restoring proper credit to the Indians who had hitherto been erased from the history of 1704. It is their story too. He has done the same for overlooked African Americans from Deerfield's past. Whenever I asked, Tim dropped everything to help me with this book. One day, we spent an hour pondering the meaning of the hex signs etched onto the iron inner latch of the Old Indian Door, and interpreting the pattern of decorative nails hammered into its exterior. On one quiet afternoon, standing by ourselves in the 1704 room at Memorial Hall, we imagined we could still hear the sound of the tomahawks and hatchets. No visit to Deerfield is complete without a pilgrimage to my favorite stand-alone museum in America, the Pocumtuck Valley Memorial Association and its Memorial Hall. There is so much to see here that any visitor risks slipping into an ecstatic antiquarian frenzy that can overwhelm the senses.

I thank my first readers, Michael F. Bishop and my wife, Jeannette Nolen-Swanson, for their helpful comments on the first draft. Michael, author and former Executive Director of the International Churchill Society and the Abraham Lincoln Bicentennial Commission, is a frequent book reviewer for the *Wall Street Journal*, and has been an early and keen reader of several of my books. Jeannette, former Social Science Editor at *Encyclopaedia Britannica*, covered law, economics, finance, psychology, architecture, and historic preservation. She has an uncanny talent for spotting errors, and she caught a number of them. As a practicing psychologist with a master's degree in historic preservation, Jeannette also offered insights that saved this author from cracking up while struggling to finish a book on deadline. James Rosen and I read each other's books before they are published. An insightful journalist and author of several books on the zeitgeist of the Nixon and Reagan eras, James gave close scrutiny to my manuscript.

Thanks to Jon Peede, former Chairman of the National Endowment for the Humanities, for helpful conversations on how to think about Deerfield and its place in early America. And I thank my friend the late Charles Blackwell, Ambassador of the Chickasaw Nation to the United States, for illuminating conversations about the unforgivable erasure of Indians (the word he always preferred) from the American story, and for fun discussions about the fine points of tomahawks, war clubs, pottery, and baskets. I thank Margaret Bruchac, an expert on Abenaki culture and traditions and Associate Professor at the University of Pennsylvania, for a wonderful conversation about Deerfield after the 2023 Dublin Seminar. Through her books and articles, including an eye-opening piece on George Sheldon's efforts to erase "vanishing Indians" from the story, she has honored forgotten voices and allowed them to speak.

I thank Erica Munkwitz, extraordinary historian of the British Empire, for invaluable research assistance and suggestions on how to think about this book, and for locating a number of elusive images.

Thanks to Karen Needles for providing first-rate, high-resolution scans of dozens of Deerfield documents, images, and artifacts from my personal collection. Karen shares my Abraham Lincoln obsession, and has discovered hundreds of Civil War, Lincoln, and other important documents in the bowels of the National Archives. I thank Dan McCarthy for contributing a number of important photographs for the book. Harry Newman at the Old Print Shop provided the rare engraving of one of the "Four Indian Kings" holding a war club. I have enjoyed endless conversations with Gary Eyler of the Old Colony Shop about early American historical documents, material culture, and the history of Deerfield.

I came to Deerfield for the first time many years ago when I received a Historic Deerfield Fellowship in Early American History and Decorative Arts (as it was styled then) to study furniture, paintings, silver, architecture, landscapes, ceramics, textiles, gravestones, historic preservation, and, of course, the massacre of 1704. Every summer for more than sixty years, since 1956, Historic Deerfield has invited a small group of college students to join an intensive immersion course of study in early American material culture. The fellows have produced a legacy of several hundred research papers. Education Director J. Ritchie Garrison and tutor Tom Michie ran the fellowship program during my summer, and their passion, humor, and contagious love of history benefit our class to this day. A cadre of volunteer docents gives guided tours of Deerfield's historic houses, and I have fond memories of the unforgettable Helen Gerrett, Hazel Prey, and Priscilla March.

Don Friary, former longtime executive director of Historic Deerfield, and his wife, Grace, former head of communications, were larger-than-life, omnipresent figures to our class that summer. Thanks to Don's terrifying performance attired as a Puritan minister delivering a fire-and-brimstone sermon in an age of unshakeable superstition and dread of the supernatural, witchcraft became the unofficial theme of our fellowship year. Little did we know that not long before our year, Don had conducted a candlelit séance for the summer fellows in the dining room of his residence at the Dickinson House, a two-hundred-and-fifty-year-old mansion that sits upon a hill overlooking the street down which French and Indian raiders advanced on the night of the massacre. A shadowy spirit manifested herself, knocked one fellow out of his chair, drove the rest of the fellows screaming out of the room, and, when they returned, flipped the heavy dining room table upside down. Perhaps it was the restless soul of the unfortunate Sarah Smith. To this day, all the participants swear that it happened. Some swear to never talk about it again. Decades later, whenever my classmate Ellen Snyder-Grenier and I encounter each other, we flash the secret hex sign that we concocted to protect our class from New England's ghosts and witches.

During Don's superb tenure under Henry and Helen Flynt and beyond, he commanded supernatural powers to transform Historic Deerfield from good to great. Over the years many of us have benefitted from the wise counsel of Don and Grace Friary. Don is an expert on 1704, and he has led several tours that retraced the route that the captives followed on their three-hundred-mile trek to New France.

This book is a personal journey. I have returned to Deerfield many times for research, writing, commemorations, celebrations, anniversaries, memorial services, and reunions. The fellowship alumni are a close-knit group, and we enjoy friendships that reach across time and generations. It is impossible to name them all, but I relish good times and fond memories with: Alexandra Deutsch, Ellen Snyder-Grenier, Thomas Jayne, Tim Neumann, Bill Alpert, Alvin Riggs, Peter Rippe, Robert Grant Irving, David Dangremond, Phil Zea, Peter Hirtle, Kevin Sweeney, Leigh Keno, Richard Candee, Jay Cantor, Lee Magnuson, Bill Myhre, Thomas Michie, Marla Miller, Philippe Halbert, and John Botello.

I must include the unofficial godfather of generations of Deerfield Summer Fellows: Joseph Peter Spang III. Peter *was* Deerfield. As the first employee of the Flynts and their first curator, he was present at the creation, and until his passing in 2020 he possessed an infallible memory of the founding era and everything that followed. Peter was a human encyclopedia of all things Deerfield, and he corresponded with many of us for decades. At our most recent reunion, in the summer of 2023, it was obvious how much we loved and missed him. My proudest moment during my fellowship year was when I won the tongue-in-cheek Peter Spang Prize, awarded to the Deerfield Fellow "most susceptible to antiquarian distraction."

Once, during an after-dark tour of the silver collection that Peter gave the fellows, I asked why Boston tankards had smooth surfaces but Philadelphia tankards were decorated with thin concentric bands. The epitome of wry Yankee humor, Peter responded with typical wit. "Why?" he said. "WHY?" As though the answer should be obvious to any thinking person. "To give one confidence that one's tankard would not burst asunder when filled with ale!"

As we approach America's 2026 semiquincentennial, the 250th anniversary of the founding of the United States, thanks to everyone, past and present, who helped breathe life into what Conrad Aiken called a "ghost of a town . . . the most beautiful ghost of its kind."

I end these acknowledgments with a personal plea. If this book does nothing else, I hope that it leads to my Holy Grail. To paraphrase John F. Kennedy, let the word go forth: I will pay any price, bear any burden, to add to my research library a complete copy of the urtext, the 1707 first edition of John Williams's *The Redeemed Captive*, the origin tale where this story began.

James L. Swanson
Deerfield, Massachusetts
July 15, 2023

APPENDIX:
LIST OF HISTORICAL CHARACTERS

|||||||||||||||||

The Reverend John Williams, Deerfield's Puritan minister after 1686. A larger-than-life, passionate leader of his people and the biggest prize captured in the Deerfield Massacre, who by personal example inspired his worshippers to endure their long ordeal and test of their faith. He led them safely home, united in purpose and as heroic symbols of their age. His best-selling book *The Redeemed Captive* chronicled the raid, his suffering, and his redemption. Celebrated as one of the greatest heroes of a lost, pre-Revolutionary America, long before the United States even existed, Williams returned to his shattered town, reclaimed his pulpit, and preached for the next quarter century. Until the day he died, he longed for the homecoming of his lost, little girl Eunice.

Eunice Williams, wife of John and equal partner in his leadership of their tight-knit community, slain by tomahawk during the forced march to Canada.

The Williams children, including two young sons (one a newborn babe) slain in front of John's eyes on the night of the raid; seven-year-old captive Eunice, who was adopted by Indians, never to return from her captivity; and son Stephen, who lived with the Indians, learned their language and customs, resisted all efforts to convert and adopt him, and returned home to serve as an expert scout and guide who then followed his father into the ministry and wrote a book about his experience.

Frank and Parthena, an enslaved couple owned by John Williams. Slavery was legal in early Massachusetts, as it was in other Northeastern states at that time, including New York. Williams united the couple in marriage, and they were among the very few Black people who lived in pre–Revolutionary War Deerfield. Parthena was murdered by Indians during the first few minutes of the raid, alongside the two youngest children of Reverend Williams. Frank was taken captive and on the first night of the march of the captives to Canada he was, as described by John Williams, murdered by some drunken Indians who had killed his wife earlier that day.

Jean-Baptiste Hertel de Rouville, the courtly French officer, and son of a famous frontier officer, who commanded the attack along with his brothers and extended family (one of whom was killed in the raid) and all motivated by honor, rank, status, and fame.

Individual captives on the march to Canada—especially several women—who proved too weak to continue the journey and, after Reverend Williams comforted and prayed with them, were slain. Williams left behind a written account of the horrors he had witnessed. This is a tale of blood and madness, and is very much a women's story too.

The raiders, French-Canadian fighters and Indian warriors from several tribes. The French were not the masters of their Indian allies, but equal partners. They practiced a style of warfare unique to the English colonies in which opposing sides did not fight in the classical European style with flags, drums, elegant uniforms, and firing lines of massed troops arrayed in neat formations. Instead, the Indian "skulking" way of war that dominated the New England frontier depended on stealth, lying in wait, surprise, ambush, and sudden raids in the middle of the night. The names of most of the Indian raiders have been lost, but their individual tribes and characteristics are known, as are the names of many of their leaders.

Increase and Cotton Mather, the legendary New England Puritan ministers who interpreted the massacre as a sign of God's disfavor, but who later turned Williams and the Deerfield captives into a cause célèbre and who upon Williams's return mythologized him into one of the greatest heroes in early America.

Four young men, Thomas Baker, John Nims, Martin Kellogg, and Joseph Petty, who made a daring escape from their captivity, outfoxed the manhunt for them, and undertook a harrowing, month-long winter trek on foot and by canoe back to Deerfield, until one day they staggered into town—starving, bedraggled, and exhausted—to the astonishment of their neighbors.

The Canadian Jesuit Catholic leaders who tempted their prisoners to renounce their religion and convert to Catholicism under threat of death and who failed many times to bribe John Williams with promises of gold and freedom if only he abandoned his faith and his congregation. He vowed he would die first before renouncing his God and betraying his people.

The unredeemed captives—mostly young boys and girls—who never came home, were absorbed into Native communities, and vanished from history.

Ensign John Sheldon, fearless wilderness adventurer and a hardened veteran of frontier warfare whose home fell during the raid and who led not one but three heroic missions deep into enemy territory to free the captives, including his own family. Later the Sheldon House and its tomahawk-scarred "Old Indian Door" became holy relics of New England's historic mission, its "errand into the wilderness"; in the 1840s, pleas to save his house led to the first organized but failed historic preservation campaign in America.

Colonel Samuel Partridge, militia commander of western Massachusetts, venerable and canny Indian fighter on the New England frontier for decades who gave the misguided and deadly advice that it was too deep into the winter to expect a raid on Deerfield in February 1704.

The Deerfield menfolk and garrison soldiers who survived the raid but made a heedless pursuit (against the counsel of Captain Wells) to rescue their friends and families and catch up with the French and Indian raiders a few miles outside of town, only to be ambushed in the meadows where they fought a brave, suicidal, and failed battle.

Captain Jonathan Wells, commander of the Deerfield garrison the night of the attack who watched helplessly as some of his men were slaughtered during the "Meadows Fight."

Benoni Stebbins, the plucky, stubborn farmer whose fortified house and its occupants—men, women, and children—fought off with furious volleys of musketry for several hours every attempt by up to three hundred French and Indians to chop down the front door with axes and tomahawks, or set the house ablaze and burn the defenders alive. The occupants shot down every raider who approached (many defenders fired their muskets forty to fifty times), including one of the French officers who led the raid.

Fitz-John Winthrop, governor of Connecticut, who strained under the never-ending raids, killings, and kidnappings across New England that plagued his tenure, and who fretted about how to protect Deerfield from a major attack.

Joseph Dudley, Massachusetts governor who never abandoned his efforts to use force or negotiation—paying ransom money, trading prisoners, or even planning a military invasion of Canada—to rescue the Deerfield hostages.

Baptiste, a notorious French privateer and English prisoner, who became a pawn in the negotiations between the English and French governors over the fate of the Deerfield captives.

French Governor General Vaudreuil of Canada, who believed that it was an "absolute necessity that we were to embroil" his Native allies with the New England colonists and that "the English and the Indians must be kept irreconcilable enemies," and ordered the attack on Deerfield, only to see it backfire on him when his superiors in France learned of the brutality of the massacre.

Arosen, the Native who married Eunice Williams, John's daughter who had been taken captive as a child, raised as an Indian, abandoned her religion, forgot her English language, and never came home to Deer-field. Her mysterious fate haunted John Williams until his end of days. Eunice's many descendants still live in Canada today.

Deerfield pre-1704, the people and the place, emerge as a collective character in the narrative. The texture of daily life in this remote, late seventeenth- and early eighteenth-century farming community por-trays Deerfield as it was in the days preceding Bloody Brook in 1675 and the raid in 1704. This was not a wealthy, elite town like some that dotted the Atlantic coast. Instead, it was home to simple, hard-working neighbors with close ties to networks of family and friends. Understanding what the townspeople had built makes it easier to comprehend what they lost.

CHAPTER NOTES

‖‖‖‖‖‖‖‖‖‖

Prologue

For coverage of the founding of the town of Pocumtuck (soon renamed Deerfield), see George Sheldon's monumental two-volume work *A History of Deerfield, Massachusetts* (Deerfield: Press of E.A. Hall & Co., 1895–96), at pages 1–80. (Hereinafter cited as "Sheldon.") I used the best facsimile edition, reprinted in 1983 by the Pocumtuck Valley Memorial Association, which preserves the original layout and pagination. For an essential corrective to Sheldon's worldview, see Margaret M. Bruchac, "Revisiting Pocumtuck History in Deerfield: George Sheldon's Vanishing Indian Act." *Historical Journal of Massachusetts,* volume 39 (1–2), Summer 2011, pages 31–77.

Part I A HISTORY OF SUPERSTITION, VIOLENCE AND MASSACRE

Chapter 1: "Dear and Deadly Grapes"

For the quotation from William Bradford's *Of Plimoth Plantation,* see *Plymouth Colony: Narratives of English Settlement and Native Resistance from the Mayflower to King Philip's War,* edited by Lisa Brooks and Kelly Wisecup (New York: Library of America, 2022), at page 315. The passage is familiar to several generations of Americans because the *Wall Street Journal* has, for decades, reprinted an excerpt from Bradford to celebrate Thanksgiving. *Plymouth Colony* is an invaluable, 1,265-page volume that collects more than fifty essential sources on the English settlement of North America.

Alden Vaughan's *New England Frontier: Puritans and Indians, 1620–1675* (New York: Little, Brown, 1965) establishes the context for relations between English colonists and the Native population decades before Deerfield existed, including the Pequot War of 1637, the first serious military conflict between Puritans and Indians.

Richard Melvoin's *New England Outpost: War and Society in Colonial Deerfield* (New York: W. W. Norton, 1989), hereinafter cited as "Melvoin," profiles the creation of the town Pocumtuck, later Deerfield, and life there prior to its fate in King Philip's War in 1675, on pages 71–91.

For George Sheldon's overall coverage of King Philip's War, see Sheldon, pages 81–178; for attacks on Deerfield, pages 93–100; and for the slaughter at Bloody Brook, pages 100–111.

George Madison Bodge's comprehensive *Soldiers in King Philip's War* (Boston: 1896) remains an invaluable account. For a long time, Douglas Edwards Leach's *Flintlock and Tomahawk: New England in King Philip's War* (New York: W. W. Norton, 1958) was the classic, modern work on the subject, but it gave scant coverage to Deerfield, on pages 86–89. Recent rewarding scholarship has devoted much needed additional attention to the conflict. But, as in Leach, Deerfield and Bloody Brook do not figure prominently in it. These titles include Lisa Brooks, *Our Beloved Kin: A New History of King Philip's War* (New Haven: Yale University Press, 2018); Jill Lepore, *The Name of War: King Philip's War and the Origins of American Identity* (New York: Random House, 1998); Eric B. Schultz and Michael J. Tougias, *King Philip's War: The History and Legacy of America's Forgotten Conflict* (Woodstock, Vt.: Countryman Press, 1999); Edward Lodi, *Who When Where in King Philip's War* (Middleborough, Mass.: Rock Village Publishing, 2015). Schultz and Tougias are an exception and provide excellent coverage of attacks on Deerfield and the Bloody Brook fight, and they revisit many of the historic sites of the war. The best short introduction to the conflict is Gabriele Esposito's *King Philip's War 1675–76* (New York: Osprey Publishing, 2020). Heavily illustrated with paintings, maps, weapons, photographs, and more, it is superb.

For the death of Deerfield in the aftermath of King Philip's War, see Melvoin, 124–28; for the resurgence of the town between 1680 and 1688 after it was abandoned in the aftermath of that war, Melvoin, 131–51; and for Deerfield's flowering in the fifteen years between 1689 and the 1704 massacre, Melvoin, 152–81.

For more on Rev. John Williams, see George Sheldon's *Heredity and Early Environment of John Williams "The Redeemed Captive"* (Boston: W. B. Clarke Co., 1905).

For excellent coverage of the first American proxy war between England and France, see Michael G. Laramie's *King William's War: The First Contest for North America, 1689–1697* (Yardley, Pa.: Wetstholme, 2017).

For the history of violence in Deerfield in the 1680s and 1690s, from the end of King Philip's War to the massacre of 1704, see Sheldon at pages 243–91 and Melvoin at 182–204.

Also see Howard Peckham's *The Colonial Wars 1689–1762* (Chicago: University of Chicago Press, 1964) for coverage of King William's War (pages 25–56) and Queen Anne's War (pages 57–76).

John Williams published his merciless lecture against Sarah Smith in 1699, the year after she was hanged, in a pamphlet titled: *Warnings to the Unclean: In a Discourse . . . Preacht at Springfield Lecture, August 25th 1698. At the Execution of Sarah Smith. By Mr. John Williams, Pastor of the Church at Deerfield.*

The letter from Northampton Rev. Solomon Stoddard to Governor Dudley proposing the purchase of "suitable dogs" to hunt and attack the enemy is in Sheldon, pages 290–291. There is no record that Dudley acquired such Indian-hunting hounds, but that does not call into doubt that many New Englanders shared Stoddard's commonly held sentiment that the Natives did not deserve to be treated as human beings.

Stoddard was right to say that Indians did not fight in the conventional European way. To understand their effective and deadly methods, see Wayne Lee's *The Cutting-Off Way: Indigenous Warfare in Eastern North America, 1500–1800* (Chapel Hill: University of North Carolina Press, 2023), Steven C. Eames's *Rustic Warriors: Warfare and the Provincial Soldier on the New England Frontier, 1689–1748* (New York: New York University Press, 2011), Patrick Malone's *The Skulking Way of War: Technology and Tactics Among the New England Indians* (Lanham, Md.: Madison Books, 2000), and Rene Chartrand's *Raiders from New France: North American Forest Warfare Tactics, 17th–18th Centuries* (New York: Osprey Publishing, 2019). The latter is an excellent, heavily illustrated introduction to the subject.

Chapter 2: Blood in the Snow: February 29, 1704

It was George Sheldon who, writing almost two centuries after the massacre, evoked the zeitgeist of this "age of superstition" when people told stories of "Indian horrors, of ghosts or of the fearful pranks of witches and wizards." See Sheldon, pages 281–82.

The Salem witchcraft hysteria remains the most written about, notorious episode in colonial America, and the outbreak was not limited to Salem. What happened in 1692 was about a lot more than the fear of witchcraft in Salem. Several excellent books offer multiple contexts and explanations for the culture of dread that possessed the public mind and triggered the hysteria: Stacy Schiff, *The Witches: Salem, 1692* (New York: Little, Brown, 2015); Mary Beth Norton, *In the Devil's Snare: The Salem Witchcraft Crisis of 1692* (New York: Knopf, 2002); John Putnam Demos, *Entertaining Satan: Witchcraft and the Culture of Early New England* (New York: Oxford, 1982); Richard Godbeer, *The Devil's Dominion: Magic and Religion in Early New England* (New York: Cambridge University Press, 1992); Paul Boyer and Stephen Nissenbaum, *Salem Possessed: The Social Origins of Witchcraft* (Cambridge: Harvard University Press, 1974). The 1992 Dublin Seminar for New England Folklife looked beyond Salem to explore Native American shamans in New England, black arts and black magic in African religion, the spiritual beliefs of American slaves, witchcraft and sex, witchcraft in Canada, magical healers, and the occult in eighteenth-century New England. For this collection of provocative essays, see Peter Benes, ed., *Wonders of the Invisible World: 1600–1900* (Boston: Boston University Press, 1995).

Rev. Solomon Stoddard's comments about the "ominous sounds" previous to February 29, 1704, appear in Sheldon, page 282.

The origins, context, narrative, aftermath, memory, legend, and myths of the Deerfield Massacre became Sheldon's lifetime obsession. It is no surprise that he devoted a good part of his history of Deerfield to it. For his account, see Sheldon, 283–384.

The ultimate source text for the Deerfield Massacre is *The Redeemed Captive* by Rev. John Williams, the man who was there on the ground on February 29, 1704, who survived the bloody violence and his long captivity, and who came home to tell the tale. Williams was one of a handful of witnesses who wrote anything at all about the experience, and his was the longest and most comprehensive work. His 1707 account is one of the two or three best Indian captivity narratives ever written.

Epaphras Hoyt's *Antiquarian Researches: Comprising a History of the Indian Wars in the Country Bordering the Connecticut River and Part Adjacent* (Greenfield, Mass.: Ansel Phelps, 1824) covers 1704 on pages 183–96.

Also see Elihu Hoyt's *A Brief Sketch of the First Settlement of Deerfield, Mass.* (Greenfield, Mass.: James P. Fogg, 1833), which covers "a few of the events which took place there in early times by one of descendants of the first settlers of the town."

For excellent coverage of the events leading up to the attack on Deerfield, and the raid itself, see *The Francis Parkman Reader: Selected and Edited with an Introduction and Notes by Samuel Eliot Morison* (Cambridge: Da Capo Press, 1998). The *Reader* includes two excellent chapters on Queen Anne's War (pages 360–70) and the sack of Deerfield (pages 371–90). Parkman, a nineteenth-century literary giant and one of the great American historians, was introduced to a wider, modern audience by Morison, another legendary historian.

Michael G. Laramie's *Queen Anne's War: The Second Contest for North America 1702–1713* (Yardley, Pa.: Westholme, 2021) is an excellent account of the European conflict that led to war in New England and to the Deerfield Massacre, and he treats the event on pages 73–81.

For an excellent summary of the historical prologue to the raid, its conduct, and its consequences, see Melvoin, 211–26.

The spring 2004 special issue of *Historic Deerfield* magazine *Rediscovering 1704*, provides an excellent overview of the raid.

In his compelling book *The Unredeemed Captive: A Family Story from Early America* (New York: Knopf, 1994) (hereinafter cited as "Demos"), John Demos resurrected the story of Eunice Williams, the young daughter of Rev. John Williams who was captured on February 29, lived out the rest of her life with Indians in Canada, and was never redeemed. To her father and to all of New England, Eunice became a living but forever lost symbol of the enduring pain that Deerfield had suffered. The heart of Demos's book is not the raid itself, but its long aftermath. His brief account of February 29 appears on page 15–25.

The finest scholarly account of the Deerfield Massacre remains, of course, the two-volume set by Professors Evan Haefeli and Kevin Sweeney. *Captive and Captors: The 1704 French and Indian Raid on Deerfield* (Amherst: University of Massachusetts Press, 2003) is an expert, multicultural, and encylopedic study of, among other things, the origins of Deerfield; the diverse cultures of indigenous peoples; the history of New France; the North American proxy wars between the English and French empires; the pretext, context, and story of the raid and Indian captivity; and the aftermath and multiple consequences for those involved. Haefeli and Sweeney followed up with a second, companion volume, *Captive Histories: English, French, and Native Narratives of the Deerfield Raid* (Amherst: University of Massachusetts Press, 2006), a collection of invaluable source materials including English, French, Mohawk, and Abenaki narratives. I have learned much from Evan and Kevin, a fellow alumnus of the Historic Deerfield Fellowship Program.

Chapter 3: "Fell by the rage of ye Barbarous Enemy": On the March

John Williams's account in the *The Redeemed Captive* remains the principal source for his personal experiences during his three-hundred-mile journey into captivity, including the heartbreaking murder of his beloved wife Eunice; the slaughter of several other women, and children too; the killing of Parthena's husband, Frank; and numerous death threats to slay Williams and other captives by scalping them, striking them with tomahawks or war clubs, or burning them alive at the stake—all part his Job-like sufferings and test of faith.

For more on the march to Canada, see Melvoin at pages 234–37; Demos at pages 25–39; and Haefeli and Sweeney at pages 125–42.

Part II THE AFTERMATH: CAPTIVITY AND A TEST OF FAITH

Chapter 4: Tales of Captivity

John Williams is the principal source for the long Canadian captivity. Also see Melvoin at pages 237–44; Demos at pages 34–51; and Haefeli and Sweeney at pages 145–77.

Chapter 5: Redemption and Return to Zion

The Redeemed Captive is the principal source for the redemption and return of John Willams to New England, and then Deerfield. George Sheldon covers his return on pages 359–61, as do Demos on pages 49–55; Melvoin on pages 245–48; and Haefeli and Sweeney on pages 177–81.

Chapter 6: End of Days

The source for much of the information about John Williams during his post-captivity life—his behavior, personality, habits, interests, activities, travels, and more—is his 1729 eulogy, by Rev. Isaac Chauncy, which reviews Williams's life from his return in 1707 to his death in 1729. Estate inventories are the source for details about his earthly possessions. Details about his political and military missions to Canada appear in Sheldon on pages 373–84, in Melvoin at 251, and in Haefeli and Sweeney on pages 201–4. Demos covers the last days of John Williams at pages 171–76. Strangely, a full-length biography of John Williams has never been written.

Part III MEMORY, MYTH AND LEGEND

Chapter 7: Antiquarian Sanctification

It was not unusual for ministers to publish important sermons, and Reverend Taylor's survives. See *A Century Sermon, Preached at Deerfield, February 29, 1804: In Commemoration of the Destruction of the Town by the French and Indians. By the Rev. John Taylor, A.M. Minister of the Church in Deerfield* (Greenfield, Mass.: John Denio, 1804).

The celebrated visit to Deerfield in 1837 by a party of Indians is documented primarily in the nineteenth-century newspaper articles referenced in Chapter 7. Artifacts from this visit are preserved in the Memorial Hall of the Pocumtuck Valley Memorial Association.

The unusual sermon of Rev. Fessenden on the 1837 visit is worth reading in full. See John Fessenden, *A Sermon: Preached to the First Congregational Society in Deerfield, Mass., and in the Hearing of Several Indians of Both Sexes, Supposed to be Descendants of Eunice Williams, daughter of Rev. John Williams, First Minister of Deerfield*, August 27, 1837 (Greenfield, Mass.: Phelps and Ingersoll, 1837).

For Edward Everett's speech at Bloody Brook, see *Address Delivered at Bloody Brook, September 30, 1835, in Commemoration of the Fall of the "Flower of Essex" at That Spot, in King Philip's War* (Boston: Russell, Shattuck & Williams, 1835).

The effort to save the Old Indian House is documented in the files of the Pocumtuck Valley Memorial Association, period newspaper accounts, the original broadside circular advocating for its preservation, and folders of ephemera and correspondence.

The story of the Old Indian Door is documented in the files of the Pocumtuck Valley Memorial Association and includes the handwritten correspondence related to the sale of the precious artifact, its removal from Deerfield, the agonizing and often feckless effort to buy it back, its return to Deerfield, and its mishandling until it was secured in old Memorial Hall of the PVMA.

The erection of the monument to Eunice Williams on August 12,

1884, at the place where she was slain by tomahawk in 1704 is covered in *Pocumtuck Valley Memorial Association History and Proceedings*, Volume II, at pages 152–88.

The creation and dedication of the tablets in Memorial Hall in 1883 is covered in *Pocumtuck Valley Memorial Association History and Proceedings*, Volume II, at pages 96–104.

The complete text of the inscriptions carved on the set of cenotaphic tablets can be found in *Catalogue of the Relics and Curiosities in Memorial Hall, Deerfield, Mass., U.S.A. Collected by the Pocumtuck Valley Memorial Association* (Deerfield: Published by the Association, 1886), pages 59–63.

The laying of a memorial stone atop the mound in the Old Burying Ground on July 29, 1903 is covered at length in *Pocumtuck Valley Memorial Association History and Proceedings*, Volume IV, at pages 379–408.

Chapter 8: Colonial Revival and Patriotism Enthroned

The Colonial Revival in America (New York: W. W. Norton, 1985), edited by Alan Axelrod, contains fourteen insightful essays on the history, psychology, and enduring influence of antiquarianism, collecting and the revival upon art, architecture, city planning, decorative arts, interior design, and literature. Also see the 2004 Dublin Seminar for New England Folklife, *New England Collectors and Collections* (Boston University, 2006), edited by Peter Benes. Of special interest in that volume of essays is Donald R. Friary's "A Family Enterprise: Collecting Deerfield's Past," on pages 53–68.

I conducted a hands-on, personal examination of paper dolls, tin cookie cutters, artifacts, baskets, metalware, ironware, vintage photographs, postcards, broadsides, toy action figures, restaurant menus, ephemera, vintage books, and more that form a *tout ensemble* of Deerfield's myth and memory.

My description of the Deerfield Massacre float created for the 1907 parade celebrating Hatfield's two hundred and fiftieth anniversary is based on close inspection of what might be the sole surviving contemporary, oversize press photo of the float taken during the parade. The commemorative hardbound book published after the August 1–4 festivities also includes a description of the float on page 61, plus a small, hard to decipher, photo of it. The book is *Old Hadley Quarter Millennial Celebration 1909* (Springfield, Mass.: F.A. Bassette Company, 1909).

Mary Master Needham's *Folk Festivals: Their Growth and How to Give Them* (New York: B. W. Huebsch, 1912), published two years after the 1910 Deerfield pageant, described the details of the first event. The quotations from Needham appear on pages 3, 11, 12, 13, and 14 in her book. The illustrated paperbound programs for the 1910, 1913, and 1916 pageants provide detailed notes on each year's attractions. For more on the pageants, see the annual proceedings of the 2000 Dublin Seminar for New England Folklife, edited by Peter Benes, *New England Celebrates: Spectacle, Commemoration, and Festivity* (Boston: Boston University, 2002), which includes Angela Goebel Bain's article "Historical Pageantry in Old Deerfield: 1910, 1913, 1916" on pages 120–36.

My comments about *Ononko's Vow* are based on the period newspaper accounts referenced in chapter 8, the contents of a subject file folder in the Deerfield Libraries containing clippings and other printed materials, Edison still photographs depicting a number of scenes, and watching the silent film several times.

The lecture by Elizabeth M. Sadoques, "The History and Traditions of Eunice Williams and Her Descendants," was published in Volume VI of the *Pocumtuck Valley Memorial Association History and Proceedings* (1929), at page 128. Haefeli and Sweeney reprint the lecture with an introduction and annotations in their *Captive Histories* at page 255.

For more on Sadoques's visit to Deerfield, see the article "Abenaki Connections to 1704: The Sadoques Family and Deerfield," by Margaret Bruchac, on pages 21–24 of the *Rediscovering 1704* issue (spring 2004) of *Historic Deerfield* magazine. Haefeli and Sweeney reprinted an expanded version of Bruchac's essay with an introduction in *Captive Histories*, at page 262.

Chapter 9: New Interpretations and a "Massacre" Reimagined

Henry Flynt's comments about the Cold War and his passionate mission statement about the singular role of Deerfield as a patriotic bulwark against socialism, Marxism, and Communism appear in Samuel Chamberlain and Henry Flynt, *Frontier of Freedom: The Soul and Substance of America in One Extraordinary Village, Old Deerfield, Massachusetts* (New York: Hastings House, 1957), on pages 7–8. The archives of Historic Deerfield hold voluminous records pertaining to the Flynts' early involvement with the town of Deerfield, their creation of the foundation, and the establishment of its successor organization, Historic Deerfield.

The three hundredth anniversary of the Deerfield Massacre in February 2004 was well documented in the press and in publications from the Pocumtuck Valley Memorial Association and Historic Deerfield.

I attended in the 2023 Dublin Seminar and observed the proceedings firsthand.

Epilogue: The Ghost of a Town

I attended the February 2021 commemoration in Deerfield and witnessed or participated in everything that I describe in the epilogue. I joined the midnight walk through town, crossed the icy fields, and gazed up at the constellations. I sat in the front parlor of the Deerfield Inn and warmed myself by the fire. And I walked down to the banks and heard the river, then walked to the Old Burying Ground and found the gravestones of John and Eunice Williams, separated in life, united in death. I laid my hand upon the stones.

BIBLIOGRAPHY

||||||||||||||

A Note on Sources

The literature on early America is vast, and I do not attempt to catalog it here. The complete bibliography contains several thousand books and articles. Any attempt to cite them all, when I could never read them all, seemed pointless, and of little use to a general reader who wanted to learn more. The bibliography for this book is hardly exhaustive and, with few exceptions, a selective shelf list of titles from my own library, and the principal works I consulted while researching and writing *The Deerfield Massacre*. These are the sources that I either liked the most, found most helpful, or that I believed might prove most interesting to general readers who might use *The Deerfield Massacre* as the starting point to pursue the story in greater depth. To begin that pursuit, I suggest a handful of titles.

George Sheldon's thick, two-volume masterwork, *A History of Deerfield, Massachusetts,* remains an essential work. A nineteenth-century founder of the Pocumtuck Valley Memorial Association and unofficial historian in chief of Deerfield, Sheldon dominated the town's narrative for decades. He had his shortcomings. He erased Indians and Eastern European immigrants as important actors in the story, and perpetuated the myth of the "vanishing Indians" who had conveniently disappeared from history, while he excavated their burial places. But it is a mistake to dismiss Sheldon as an amateur, obsolete, antiquarian crank. His genius was that he recognized that history is more than the lives and deeds of the great and powerful. To Sheldon, history was more than tales of heroes, presidents, generals, or founders. It was also the story of ordinary people and the material culture of their everyday lives. He collected and preserved priceless material once dismissed as worthless, and gathered many historical documents that would otherwise have been lost. Today, George Sheldon has come into disfavor among professional historians, who have rightly taken him to task. Despite some faults in interpretation, regrettable omissions, and certain inevitable factual errors, Sheldon's work is still worth reading. For a modern perspective on George Sheldon's literary erasures of indigenous history, see Margaret M. Bruchac's "Revisiting Pocumtuck History in Deerfield: George Sheldon's Vanishing Indian Act" in the summer 2011 issue of the *Historical Journal of Massachusetts.*

After Sheldon's two-volume history, the Pocumtuck Valley Memorial Association published a series of volumes containing a treasure trove of articles, lectures, information, historical documents, transcripts, and more. Titled *Proceedings of the Pocumtuck Valley Memorial Association,* Volume I covered the years 1870 to 1879; Volume II the years 1880 to 1889; Volume III 1890 to 1898; Volume IV 1899 to 1904; Volume V 1905 to 1911; Volume VI 1912 to 1920; Volume VII 1921 to 1929; Vol VIII 1930 to 1938; plus single volumes from 1939 through 1942. During its run, the *PVMA Proceedings* published just over forty-eight hundred pages of research material. Each printed volume contains its own index, but the Historic Deerfield and PVMA Memorial Libraries contain an unpublished master subject matter index or finding aid to all the volumes.

For an excellent history on the early relations between English colonists and Natives prior to King Philip's War, see Alden T. Vaughan, *The New England Frontier: Puritans and Indians 1620–1675.*

King Philip's War hit Deerfield hard, and the disaster at Bloody Brook in September 1675 haunted the town for more than twenty-five years, until the attack in February 1704 eclipsed the earlier event. For more on that all too forgotten war, I like Douglas Edward Leach's classic study, *Flintlock and Tomahawk: New England in King Philip's War*. I also suggest *King Philip's War: The History and Legacy of America's Forgotten Conflict* by Eric B. Schultz and Michael Tougias; *In the Name of War: Kings Philip's War and the Origins of American Identity* by Jill Lepore; *Memory Lands: King Philip's War and the Place of Violence in the Northeast* by Christine M. DeLucia; and *Our Beloved Kin: A New History of King Philip's War* by Lisa Brooks. Brooks does an excellent job of restoring a Native perspective, too often overlooked, to the story. George Sheldon's *A History of Deerfield, Massachusetts* includes valuable material on King Philip's War. For the rest of the story, see Colin Calloway's excellent *After King Philip's War: Presence and Persistence in Indian New England*.

For more military history, see Howard H. Peckham's *The Colonial Wars 1689–1762*.

For coverage of Indian ambushes, raids, and attacks on Deerfield, including Bloody Brook and the 1704 Massacre, Richard Melvoin's *New England Outpost: War and Society in Colonial Deerfield* is excellent. George Sheldon's *History of Deerfield* includes comprehensive coverage of the violence preceding, during, and following the massacre.

For military tactics see Patrick M. Malone's *The Skulking Way of War: Technology and Tactics Among the New England Indians* and Steven C. Eames's *Rustic Warriors: Warfare and the Provincial Soldier on the New England Frontier, 1689–1748*.

Michael G. Laramie's *Queen Anne's War: The Second Contest for North America, 1702–1713*, covers the conflict in New England, the Deerfield Massacre, and the wider European war, and is the companion to Laramie's *King William's War: The First Contest for North America, 1689–1697*.

Osprey has published several excellent pictorial books—illustrated with many full-color paintings—on the military history of New England, including Gabrielle Esposito's *King Philip's War: America's Deadliest Conflict;* Michael Johnson's *Indian Tribes of the New England Frontier;* Rene Chartrand's *Colonial American Troops 1610–1774*, and also Chartrand's *Raiders from New France: North American Forest Tactics 17th–18th Centuries*. I recommend them all.

John Demos's award-winning *The Unredeemed Captive: A Family Story from Early American Life* remains a classic in the field. The title is a twist on the title of Rev. John Williams's own memoir, *The Redeemed Captive*. Demos tells the counter-tale of Eunice Williams, the child taken captive on February 29, 1704, and who never came home.

Evan Haefeli and Kevin Sweeney have written the classic two-volume scholarly work on the Deerfield raid. Their encyclopedic *Captors and Captives: The 1704 French and Indian Raid on Deerfield* remains the most comprehensive account for the context, backstory, motives, and aftermath of the attack, and their *Captive Histories: English, French and Native Narratives of the 1704 Deerfield Raid* collects valuable English, French, and Indian sources, and includes the best annotated version of *The Redeemed Captive* by Rev. John Williams. Their edited version deserves reprinting as a separate, stand-alone volume of Willams's captivity narrative.

For an introduction to the rich literature on Indian captivity narratives, see *Puritans Among the Indians: Accounts of Captivity and Redemption*, edited by Alden T. Vaughan and Edward W. Clark. For the pioneering work on the subject see Emma Lewis Coleman's two-volume *New England Captives Carried to Canada Between 1677 and 1760 During the French and Indian War*.

For a collection of more than twenty beautiful but stark contemporary color photographs taken by Allison Williams Bell of the snowy, frozen route that the Deerfield captives marched to Canada, see the Spring 2004 "Rediscovering 1704" issue of *Historic Deerfield* magazine.

For valuable books about Deerfield beyond the story of the massacre, see Emma Lewis Coleman's *A Historic and Present Day Guide to Old Deerfield*, Elizabeth Stillinger's *Historic Deerfield: A Portrait of Early America*, and Susan McGowan and Amelia Miller's *Family and Landscape: Deerfield Home Lots from 1671*.

Michael Batinski's *Pastkeepers in a Small Place* is in outstanding overview of Deerfield's place though several centuries of American history.

While James Deetz's classic *In Small Things Forgotten: The Archeology of Early American Life* is not about Deerfield per se, its pioneering insights about the value of material culture illuminate much about Deerfield. Alexander Nemerov's *The Forest: A Fable of America in the 1830s* looks at material culture and the natural world in fascinating and even eerie new ways applicable to all periods of American history, and is about a lot more than the 1830s.

C. Alice Baker and Emma L. Coleman's little book *Epitaphs in the Old Burying Ground at Deerfield Massachusetts* conjures, at least to me, the churchyard in James Joyce's "The Dead" in *Dubliners,* or the gravestones in Edgar Lee Masters's *Spoon River Anthology.*

Suzanne L. Flynt takes Deerfield into the twentieth century through her books *The Allen Sisters: Pictorial Photographers 1885–1920* and *Poetry in the Earth: The Arts and Crafts Movement in Deerfield, Massachusetts.*

For Henry Flynt's own account of why he founded Historic Deerfield, his origin tale appears in the book by Samuel Chamberlain and Henry N. Flynt, *Frontier of Freedom: The Soul and Substance of America in One Extraordinary Village, Old Deerfield, Massachusetts.* Their revised follow-up volume, *Historic Deerfield: Houses and Interiors,* appeared a few years later. A personal favorite of mine remains Henry Flynt's little-known essay, "To Collect or Not to Collect: Notes About Old Deerfield and Its Collections," a pamphlet printed privately from the 1963 Walpole Society *Note Book.* It is a revealing portrait of a collector's mind.

Bart McDowell's July 1969 *National Geographic* article, "Deerfield Keeps a Truce with Time," helped put Historic Deerfield on the map and was the first article I ever read about the town. For specialized coverage of Historic Deerfield's collections and architecture see the September 1956, October 1974, January 1982, and March 1985 issues of the magazine *Antiques.*

Although my book is not about the Salem witchcraft trials, those disruptive events reveal much about the zeitgeist of late-seventeenth-century New England. Several excellent studies explore the era when things supernatural and the wonders of the invisible world possessed popular culture. For further reading I suggest *Salem Possessed: The Social Dynamics of Witchcraft* by Paul Boyer and Stephen Nissenbaum; *Entertaining Satan: Witchcraft and the Culture of Early New England* by John Demos; *In the Devil's Snare: The Salem Witchcraft Crisis of 1692* by Mary Beth Norton; and *The Witches: Salem, 1692* by Stacy Schiff.

Beginning almost fifty years ago, the annual Dublin Seminar for New England Folklife has published its proceedings in an invaluable collection of thematic volumes. Anyone studying Deerfield will find several to be of special interest, including the 1976 and 1978 seminars, *Puritan Gravestone Art;* the 1989 seminar, *New England/ New France 1600 to 1850;* the 1992 seminar, *Wonders of the Invisible World: 1600–1900;* the 2000 seminar, *New England Celebrates: Spectacle, Commemoration, and Festivity;* and the 2006 seminar, *New England Collectors and Collections.* The 2023 seminar, which awaits publication, was held in Deerfield and will be valuable to anyone interested in the lasting Indian presence in New England for the last several thousand years.

For more, see Ned Blackhawk's *The Rediscovery of America: Native People and the Unmaking of America;* Pekka Hamalainen's *Indigenous Continent: The Epic Contest for North America;* and Caroline Dodds Pennock's *On Savage Shores: How Indigenous Americans Discovered Europe.*

Recent scholarship has explored "decolonizing" early American history to restore Native voices to the narrative. See Margaret M. Bruchac's *Savage Kin: Indigenous Informants and American Anthropologists* and Linda Tuhiwai Smith's *Decolonizing Methodologies: Research and Indigenous Peoples.* Also see *Indigenous Archeologies: A Reader on Decolonization,* edited by Margaret M. Bruchac, Siobhan Hart, and Martin Wobst.

Photographer Sandra Matthews produced a mesmerizing book with haunting images of contemporary buildings and monuments sitting atop traditional Indian homelands in her *Occupying Massachusetts: Layers of History on Indigenous Land.*

Finally, beyond the published sources, a walk through the Deerfield landscape tells stories through its outdoor spaces: The Street, river, meadows, geography, architecture, monuments, gravestones, and more. Anyone who wants to learn more about Deerfield would gain much from visiting the town after reading about it.

Bibliography

Abbott, Katharine M. *Old Paths and Legends of the New England Border: Connecticut, Deerfield, Berkshire.* New York: G. P. Putnam's Sons, 1907.

Alden, John R. *Pioneer America.* New York: Alfred A. Knopf, 1966.

[American Guide Series]. *Massachusetts: A Guide to Its Places and People.* Boston: Houghton Mifflin, 1937.

Antiques magazine. The Deerfield Issue, September 1956.

Antiques magazine. The Historic Deerfield Issue, March 1985.

Ashley, Gertrude Porter. *Memories of Old Deerfield by Gertrude Porter Ashley Custodian of the Indian House Memorial Inc.* Deerfield, Mass.: Published by the Author, 1934.

Atkinson, Jay. *Massacre on the Merrimack: Hannah Duston's Captivity and Revenge in Colonial America.* Guilford, Conn.: Rowman & Littlefield, 2015.

Axelrod, Alan, ed. *The Colonial Revival in America.* New York: W. W. Norton, 1985.

Baker, C. Alice, and Emma L. Coleman. *Epitaphs in the Old Burying Ground at Deerfield Massachusetts.* Westminster, Md.: Heritage Books, 2007. Reprint of original 1924 edition.

Baseler, Marilyn C. *"Asylum for Mankind": America 1607–1800.* Ithaca: Cornell University Press, 1998.

Batinski, Michael C. *Pastkeepers in a Small Place: Five Centuries in Deerfield, Massachusetts.* Amherst: University of Massachusetts Press, 2004.

Benes, Peter, ed. *Puritan Gravestone Art: The Dublin Seminar for New England Folklife Annual Proceedings 1976.* Dublin, N.H.: Boston University & the Dublin Seminar, 1976.

Benes, Peter, ed. *Puritan Gravestone Art II: The Dublin Seminar for*

New England Folklife Annual Proceedings 1978. Boston: Boston University, 1978.

Benes, Peter, ed. *New England/New France 1600–1850: The Dublin Seminar for New England Folklife Annual Proceedings 1989.* Boston: Boston University, 1992.

Benes, Peter, ed. *Wonders of the Invisible World: 1600–1900: The Dublin Seminar for New England Folklife Annual Proceedings 1992.* Boston: Boston University, 1995.

Benes, Peter, ed. *New England Celebrates: Spectacle, Commemoration, and Festivity: The Dublin Seminar for New England Folklife Annual Proceedings 2000.* Boston: Boston University, 2002.

Benes, Peter, ed. *New England Collectors and Collections: The Dublin Seminar for New England Folklife Annual Proceedings.* Boston: Boston University, 2006.

Blackhawk, Ned. *The Rediscovery of America: Native Peoples and the Unmaking of America.* New Haven: Yale University Press, 2003.

Boyer, Paul, and Stephen Nissenbaum. *Salem Possessed: The Social Origins of Witchcraft.* Cambridge: Harvard University Press, 1974.

Bremer, Francis J. *John Winthrop: America's Forgotten Founding Father.* New York: Oxford University Press, 2003.

Brooks, Lisa, and Kelly Wisecup, eds. *Plymouth Colony: Narratives of English Settlement and Native Resistance from the Mayflower to King Philip's War.* New York: Library of America, 2022.

Brown, Dona. *Inventing New England: Regional Tourism in the Nineteenth Century.* Washington, D.C.: Smithsonian Institution Press, 1995.

Bruchac, Margaret M. "Earthshapers and Placemakers: Algonkian Indian Stories and the Landscape." In C. Smith and H. M. Wobst, eds., *Indigenous Archaeologies: Decolonizing Theory and Practice.* London: Routledge, 2005, pp. 56–80.

Brumwell, Stephen. *White Devil: A True Story of War, Savagery, and Vengeance in Colonial America.* Boston: Da Capo Press, 2004.

Bunker, Nick. *Making Haste from Babylon: The Mayflower Pilgrims and Their World.* New York: Alfred A. Knopf, 2010.

Calder, Isabel M. *Colonial Captivities, Marches and Journeys*. New York: Macmillan, 1935.

Calloway, Colin G., ed. *After King Philip's War: Presence and Persistence in Indian New England*. Hanover, N.H.: University Press of New England, 1997.

Chamberlain, Samuel, and Henry N. Flynt. *Frontier of Freedom: The Soul and Substance of America Portrayed in One Extraordinary Village, Old Deerfield, Massachusetts*. New York: Hastings House, 1957. Revised and enlarged edition of *Frontiers of Freedom*, copyright 1965, 1957, & 1952 by Hastings House.

Chamberlain, Samuel, and Henry N. Flynt. *Historic Deerfield: Houses and Interiors*. Revised and enlarged edition of *Frontiers of Freedom*, copyright 1965, 1957, & 1952 by Hastings House.

Chapin, Bradley, ed. *Provincial America 1600–1763*. New York: The Free Press, 1966.

Chartrand, Rene. *Colonial American Troops 1610–1774 (1)*. Long Island, N.Y.: Osprey Publishing, 2002.

Chartrand, Rene. *Raiders from New France: North American Forest Tactics, 17th–18th Centuries*. New York: Osprey Publishing, 2019.

Chase, Theodore, and Laurel K. Gabel. *Gravestone Chronicles: Some Eighteenth-Century New England Carvers and Their Work*. Boston: New England Historic Genealogical Society, 1990.

Coleman, Emma Lewis. *A Historic and Present Day Guide to Old Deerfield*. Boston: Plimpton Press, 1907.

Coleman, Emma Lewis. *New England Captives Carried to Canada Between 1677 and 1760 During the French and Indian Wars*. 2 vols. Portland, Maine: The Southworth Press, 1925.

Colley, Linda. *Captives: The Story of Britain's Pursuit of Empire and How Its Soldiers and Civilians Were Held Captive by the Dream of Global Supremacy, 1600–1850*. New York: Pantheon Books, 2002.

Coontz, Stephanie. *The Way We Never Were: American Families and the Nostalgia Trip*. New York: Basic Books, 1992.

Crawford, Mary Caroline. *Social Life in New England*. New York: Grosset & Dunlap, 1914.

Cronon, William. *Changes in the Land: Indians, Colonists, and the Ecology of New England*. New York: Hill and Wang, 1983.

Cummings, Abbott Lowell. *The Framed Houses of Massachusetts Bay, 1625–1725*. Cambridge: Belknap Press, 1979.

Deetz, James. *In Small Things Forgotten: The Archeology of Early American Life*. New York: Anchor Books, 1977.

Deetz, James. "Material Culture and Worldview in Colonial Anglo-America." In *The Recovery of Meaning: Historical Archaeology in the Eastern United States*. Mark P. Leone and Parker B. Potter, Jr., eds. Washington, D.C.: Smithsonian Institution Press, 1988, pp. 219–233.

Demos, John. *A Little Commonwealth: Family Life in Plymouth Colony*. New York: Oxford University Press, 1970.

Demos, John. *The Unredeemed Captive: A Family Story from Early America*. New York: Alfred A. Knopf, 1994.

Demos, John. *Entertaining Satan: Witchcraft and the Culture of Early New England*. New York: Oxford University Press, 1982.

Demos, John. *Remarkable Providences: Readings in Early American History*. Boston: Northeastern University Press, 1991.

Donahue, Mary. *Massachusetts Officers and Soldiers 1702–1722: Queen Anne's War to Drummer's War*. Boston: Society of Colonial Wars, 1980.

Drake, Samuel. *The Border Wars of New England*. New York: Charles Scribner's Sons, 1897.

Drenth, Wienand, and Jonathon Riley. *The First Colonial Soldiers*. 2 vols. Eindhoven: Drenth Publishing, 2014–2015.

Eames, Steven C. *Rustic Warriors: Warfare and the Provincial Soldier on the New England Frontier, 1689–1748*. New York: New York University Press, 2011.

Esposito, Gabrielle. *King Philip's War: America's Deadliest Colonial Conflict*. New York: Osprey Publishing, 2020.

Fales, Dean A., Jr. *The Furniture of Historic Deerfield*. New York: E. P. Dutton, 1976.

Flynt, Suzanne L. *The Allen Sisters: Pictorial Photographers 1885–1920.* Deerfield: Pocumtuck Valley Memorial Association, 2002.

Flynt, Suzanne L. "The Old Indian House Door." In *The French and Indian Raid on Deerfield, Massachusetts, February 29, 1704.* Deerfield, Mass.: Historic Deerfield.

Flynt, Suzanne L. *Poetry to the Earth: The Arts & Crafts Movement in Deerfield.* Deerfield, Mass.: Pocumtuck Valley Memorial Association, 2012.

Flynt, Suzanne L., Susan McGowan, and Amelia F. Miller. *Gathered and Preserved: Memorial Hall, Pocumtuck Valley Memorial Association.* Deerfield, Mass.: PVMA, 1991.

Foster, Michael K., and William Cowan, eds. *In Search of New England's Native Past: Selected Essays of Gordon M. Day.* Amherst: University of Massachusetts Press, 1998.

Gaskill, Malcolm. *Between Two Worlds: How the English Became Americans.* New York: Basic Books, 2014.

Greene, Jack P. *Settlements to Society 1607 to 1763: A Documentary History of Colonial America.* New York: W. W. Norton, 1975.

Haefeli, Evan, and Kevin Sweeney. "Revisiting the Redeemed Captive: New Perspectives on the 1704 Attack on Deerfield." *William and Mary Quarterly* 52 (1): 3–46.

Haefeli, Evan, and Kevin Sweeney. *Captors and Captives: The 1704 French and Indian Raid on Deerfield.* Amherst: University of Massachusetts Press, 2003.

Haefeli, Evan, and Kevin Sweeney. *Captive Histories: English, French, and Native Narratives of the 1704 Deerfield Raid.* Amherst: University of Massachusetts Press, 2006.

Hamalainen, Pekka. *Indigenous Continent: The Epic Conquest for North America.* New York: Liveright, 2022.

Hardin, John Wesley. *Faded Memories: Songs of Deerfield.* Deerfield: Historic Deerfield, 1976. [A 33⅓ record album of original folk song inspired by the history of Deerfield.]

Hart, Siobhan M. *Colonialism, Community, and Heritage in Native New England.* Gainesville: University Press of Florida, 2019.

Historic Deerfield. *Rediscovering 1704: A Publication of Historic Deerfield* 4 (1) (Spring 2004).

Horwitz, Tony. *A Voyage Long and Strange: Rediscovering the New World.* New York: Henry Holt, 2008.

Howe, Margery Burnham. *Deerfield Embroidery: Traditional Patterns from Colonial Massachusetts.* New York: Charles Scribner's Sons, 1976.

Hoyt, Epaphras. *Antiquarian Researches: Comprising a History of the Indian Wars in the Country Bordering Connecticut River and Parts Adjacent.* Greenfield, Mass.: Ansel Phelps, 1824.

Hutchinson, Thomas. *The History of the Province of Massachusetts Bay.* 3 vols. London: M. Richardson, 1765–1828.

Jaffe, David. *A Nation of Goods: The Material Culture of Early America.* Philadelphia: University of Pennsylvania Press, 2010.

Johnson, Clifton, ed. *Historic Hadley Quarter Millennial Souvenir: Official Program for the Four Days of the Hadley Quarter-Millennial Celebration.* Northampton, Mass.: Souvenir Publishing Co., 1909.

Johnson, Clifton, ed. *Old Hadley Quarter Millennial Celebration 1909: Sunday Monday Tuesday and Wednesday—August 1, 2, 3 and 4, The Story of the Four Days with the Various Addresses and Numerous Illustrations.* Springfield, Mass.: F. A. Bassette Co., 1909.

Johnson, Michael. *Indian Tribes of the New England Frontier.* Long Island, N.Y.: Osprey Publishing, 2006.

Kimball, Everett. *The Public Life of Joseph Dudley.* London: Longman's, Green & Co., 1911.

Laramie, Michael G. *King William's War: The First Contest for North America, 1689–1697.* Yardley, Pa.: Westholme, 2017.

Laramie, Michael G. *Queen Anne's War: The Second Contest for North America, 1702–1713.* Yardley, Pa: Westholme, 2021.

Leach, Douglas Edward. *Flintlock and Tomahawk: New England in King Philip's War.* Woodstock, Vt.: Countryman Press, 2009.

Lincoln, Charles H., ed. *Narratives of the Indian Wars 1675–1699.* New York: Charles Scribner's Sons, 1913.

Lockridge, Kenneth A. *A New England Town, The First Hundred Years: Dedham, Massachusetts, 1636–1736.* New York: W. W. Norton, 1970.

Lopez, Amanda Rivera. "Exhibiting the Raid of 1704: A Changing Story of Politics, Place, and People." In *The French and Indian Raid on Deerfield, Massachusetts, February 29, 1704*. Deerfield, Mass.: Historic Deerfield, 2008.

Malone, Patrick M. *The Skulking Way of War: Technology and Tactics Among the New England Indians*. Lanham, Md.: Madison Books, 2000.

Matthews, Sandra. *Occupying Massachusetts: Layers of History on Indigenous Land*. Staunton, Va.: George F. Thompson, 2022.

McDowell, Bart. "Deerfield Keeps a Truce with Time." *National Geographic*, June 1969, pp. 780–809.

McGowan, Susan, and Amelia F. Miller. *Family & Landscape: Deerfield Home Lots from 1671*. Deerfield: Pocumtuck Valley Memorial Association, 1996.

McNamara, Martha J., and Georgia Barnhill. *New Views of New England: Studies in Material and Visual Culture, 1680–1830*. Boston: The Colonial Society of Massachusetts, 2012.

Melvoin, Richard I. *New England Outpost: War and Society in Colonial Deerfield*. New York: W. W. Norton, 1989.

Miller, Amelia, and A. R. Riggs, eds. *Romance, Remedies, and Revolution: The Journal of Dr. Elihu Ashley of Deerfield, Massachusetts, 1773–1775*. Amherst: University of Massachusetts Press, 2007.

Miller, Perry. *Errand into the Wilderness*. Cambridge: Belknap Press, 1956.

Morgan, Edmund S. *The Puritan Family: Religion & Domestic Relations in Seventeenth Century New England*. New York: Harper & Row, 1966.

Morgan, Edmund S. *The Puritan Dilemma: The Story of John Winthrop*. Boston: Little, Brown, 1958.

Morison, Samuel Eliot. *The Francis Parkman Reader: Selected and Edited with an Introduction and Notes by Samuel Eliot Morison*. Boston: Da Capo Press, 1998.

Needham, Mary Master. *Folk Festivals: Their Growth and How to Give Them*. New York: B. W. Huebsch, 1912.

Nemerov, Alexander. *The Forest: A Fable of America in the 1830s*. Princeton: Princeton University Press, 2023.

Newberry Library. *Narratives of Captivity Among the Indians of North America: A List of Books and Manuscripts on This Subject in the Edward E. Ayer Collection of the Newberry Library*. Chicago: The Newberry Library, 1912.

Nims, Godfrey. *Dedication of the Godfrey Nims Memorial, the eleventh reunion of the Nims Family Association, and held on the field day of the Pocumtuck Valley Memorial Association; Deerfield, Massachusetts, Thursday, August Thirteenth, Nineteen Hundred Fourteen*. Greenfield, Mass.: E. A. Hall & Co., 1914.

Norton, Mary Beth. *In the Devil's Snare: The Salem Witchcraft Crisis of 1692*. New York: Alfred A. Knopf, 2002.

Parrington, Vernon Louis. *The Colonial Mind 1620–1800*. New York: Harcourt, Brace and Co., 1927.

Paynter, Robert, and Elizabeth S. Chilton. "Deerfield Village and Nearby Sites: Ancient and Historical Archaeology in the Connecticut River Valley." In *Archaeology in America: An Encyclopedia*, Francis P. McManamon, ed. Westport, Conn.: Greenwood, 2009.

Peckham, Howard H. *The Colonial Wars 1689–1762*. Chicago: University of Chicago Press, 1964.

Penhallow, Samuel. *The History of the Wars of New England with the Eastern Indians*. Boston: T. Fleet, 1726.

Pennock, Caroline Dodds. *On Savage Shores: How Indigenous Americans Discovered Europe*. New York: Alfred A. Knopf, 2023.

Philbrick, Nathaniel. *Mayflower: A Story of Courage, Community, and War*. New York: Viking, 2006.

Pocumtuck Valley Memorial Association. *Catalogue of the Relics and Curiosities in Memorial Hall, Deerfield, Mass., U.S.A. Collected by the Pocumtuck Valley Memorial Association*. Deerfield: Published by the Association, 1886.

Pocumtuck Valley Memorial Association. *Catalogue of the Relics in Memorial Hall, Deerfield, Mass., U.S.A. Gathered and Preserved by the Pocumtuck Valley Memorial Association. Second Edition*. Deerfield: Published by the Association, 1908.

Pocumtuck Valley Memorial Association. *Catalogue of the Relics in Me-*

morial Hall, Deerfield, Mass., U.S.A. Gathered and Preserved by the Pocumtuck Valley Memorial Association. Third Edition. Deerfield: Published by the Association, 1920.

Rogers, Janet W. B., and Eric Widmer, eds. *The Transcendent Mirror: A Bicentennial Anthology for Deerfield.* Deerfield: Deerfield Academy Press, 1999.

Ross, John F. *War on the Run: The Epic Story of Robert Rogers and the Conquest of America's First Frontier.* New York: Bantam Books, 2009.

Rotman, Deborah. *Historical Archeology of Gendered Lives.* New York: Springer, 2009.

Russo, D. J. "The Deerfield Massacre of 1704 & Local Historical Writing in the United States." In *The Triumph of Culture: 18th Century Perspectives.* Paul Fritz and David Williams, eds. Toronto: A. M. Hakkert, 1972.

Saunt, Claudio. *Unworthy Republic: The Dispossession of Native Americans and the Road to Indian Territory.* New York: W. W. Norton, 2020.

Schiff, Stacy. *The Witches: Salem, 1692.* New York: Little, Brown, 2015.

Schultz, Eric B., and Michael J. Tougias. *King Philip's War: The History and Legacy of America's Forgotten Conflict.* Woodstock, Vt.: Countryman Press, 1999.

Sheldon, George. *A History of Deerfield, Massachusetts: The Times When and the People by Whom It was Settled, Unsettled and Resettled: With a Special Study of the Indian Wars of the Connecticut Valley.* 2 vols. Deerfield, Mass: E.A. Hall & Co., 1895, 1896.

Sheldon, George. *Heredity and Early Environment of John Williams "The Redeemed Captive."* Boston: W. B. Clarke Co., 1905.

Sheldon, George. *A Guide to the Museum of the Pocumtuck Valley Memorial Association. With original illustrations by Frances S. Allen and Mary E. Allen.* Deerfield: Pocumtuck Valley Memorial Association, 1908.

Sheldon, George, and J. M. Arms Sheldon. *The Rev. John Williams House.* Deerfield. Mass.: n.p., 1918.

Silliman, Stephen W. "Change and Continuity, Practice and Memory: Native American Persistence in Colonial New England." *American Antiquity* 74 (2) (2009): 211–230.

Silver, Peter. *Our Savage Neighbors: How Indian War Transformed Early America.* New York: W. W. Norton, 2008.

Simmons, William S. *Spirit of the New-England Tribes: Indian History and Folklore, 1620–1984.* Hanover, N.H.: University Press of New England, 1986.

Smith, Clara. *Narratives of Captivity Among the Indians of North America: A List of Books and Manuscripts on This Subject in the Edward E. Ayer Collection of the Newberry Library,* Supplement I. Chicago: Newberry Library, 1928.

Smith, Linda Tuhiwai. *Decolonizing Methodologies: Research and Indigenous Peoples.* London: Zed Books, 1993.

Stebbins, Henry R., Jr. *The Dead 1704: The Stebbins Family in Colonial New England 1634–1724.* Gales Ferry, Conn.: Husky Trail Press, n.d.

Stillinger, Elizabeth. *The Antiquers: The Lives and Careers, the Deals, the Finds, the Collections of the Men and Women Who Were Responsible for the Changing Taste in American Antiques, 1850–1930.* New York: Alfred A. Knopf, 1980.

Stillinger, Elizabeth. *Historic Deerfield: A Portrait of Early America.* New York: Dutton Studio Books, 1992.

Sword, Wiley. *President Washington's Indian War: The Struggle for the Old Northwest, 1790–1796.* Norman: University of Oklahoma Press, 1985.

Sylvester, Herbert Milton. *Indian Wars of New England.* 3 vols. Boston: W. B. Clarke Co., 1910.

Taylor, Alan. *American Colonies: The Settling of North America.* New York: Penguin Books, 2001.

Taylor, Alan. *Colonial America: A Very Short Introduction.* New York: Oxford University Press, 2013.

Taylor, John. *A Century Sermon, Preached at Deerfield, February 29, 1804: In Commemoration of the Destruction of the Town by the French and Indians.* Greenfield, Mass.: John Denio, 1804.

Vaughan, Alden T. *The New England Frontier: Puritans and Indians 1620–1675*. Boston: Little, Brown, 1965.

Vaughan, Alden T., and Edward W. Clark, eds. *Puritans Among the Indians: Accounts of Captivity and Redemption 1676–1724*. Cambridge, Mass.: Belknap Press, 1981.

Ward, Gerald W. R., and William N. Hosley, Jr. *The Great River: Art & Society of the Connecticut River Valley 1635–1820*. Hartford, Conn.: Wadsworth Atheneum, 1985.

Warren, James A. *God, War, and Providence: The Epic Struggle of Roger Williams and the Narragansett Indians Against the Puritans of New England*. New York: Scribner, 2018.

Weidensaul, Scott. *The First Frontier: The Forgotten History of Struggle, Savagery & Endurance in Early America*. Boston: Houghton Mifflin, 2012.

Wheelwright, Edward. *Memoir of Daniel Denison Slade, M.D.* Cambridge, Mass.: John Wilson and Son, 1900.

Woods, Marianne Berger. "Viewing Colonial America Through the Lens of Wallace Nutting." *American Art* 8 (2) (Spring 1994): 66–86.

ILLUSTRATION CREDITS

Interior

Author photo by Lisa Nipp

Photo Insert

10–11 Courtesy of Pocumtuck Valley Memorial Association's Memorial Hall Museum, Deerfield, Massachusetts

12 McCord Museum of Canadian History

13–17 Courtesy of Pocumtuck Valley Memorial Association's Memorial Hall Museum, Deerfield, Massachusetts

18 Courtesy of Historic Deerfield, Deerfield, Massachusetts

19 Courtesy of Pocumtuck Valley Memorial Association's Memorial Hall Museum, Deerfield, Massachusetts

20 Author's collection

21–22 Courtesy of Pocumtuck Valley Memorial Association's Memorial Hall Museum, Deerfield, Massachusetts

23 Courtesy of Historic Deerfield, Deerfield, Massachusetts

24 Collection of the New-York Historical Society

25–28 Author's collection

29 Courtesy of Pocumtuck Valley Memorial Association's Memorial Hall Museum, Deerfield, Massachusetts

30 Courtesy of Pocumtuck Valley Memorial Association's Memorial Hall Museum, Deerfield, Massachusetts

31 Author's collection

32 Courtesy of Pocumtuck Valley Memorial Association's Memorial Hall Museum, Deerfield, Massachusetts

33–51 Author's collection

52 Courtesy of Historic Deerfield, Deerfield, Massachusetts

53–54 Courtesy of Pocumtuck Valley Memorial Association's Memorial Hall Museum, Deerfield, Massachusetts

55–57 Author's collection

58 Courtesy of Historic Deerfield, Deerfield, Massachusetts

59–60 Author's collection

INDEX

||||||||||||||||

Page numbers in *italics* refer to maps and illustrations.

ABOUT THE AUTHOR

James L. Swanson is the Edgar Award–winning author of the *New York Times* bestseller *Manhunt: The 12-Day Chase for Lincoln's Killer*, and an executive producer of the 2024 Apple TV+ *Manhunt* series. *Bloody Crimes: The Funeral for Abraham Lincoln and the Chase for Jefferson Davis* is the *New York Times* bestselling sequel to *Manhunt*. *Chasing Lincoln's Killer* is the bestselling, young-adult adaptation of *Manhunt*, and *Chasing King's Killer: The Hunt for Martin Luther King, Jr.'s Assassin* was a finalist for an NAACP Image Award. James has held several think-tank and government posts in Washington, D.C., including at the U.S. Department of Justice and the National Endowment for the Humanities. He is a Senate appointee to the U.S. Semiquincentennial Commission created by Congress to plan the celebration in 2026 of the 250th anniversary of the founding of the United States. He has a law degree from UCLA and studied history at the University of Chicago. Swanson received a Historic Deerfield Fellowship in early American history in Deerfield, Massachusetts, where he lived in the Allen House, a pre–Revolutionary War home up the street from the site of the massacre.